FEEDING
THE BEAST

FEEDING THE BEAST

HOW WEDTECH BECAME THE MOST CORRUPT LITTLE COMPANY IN AMERICA

MARILYN W. THOMPSON

CHARLES SCRIBNER'S SONS

New York

Charles Scribner's Sons
Macmillan Publishing Company
866 Third Avenue, New York, N.Y. 10022
Collier Macmillan Canada, Inc.

Library of Congress Cataloging-in-Publication Data

Thompson, Marilyn W.
    Feeding the beast : how Wedtech became the most corrupt little company in
America / Marilyn W. Thompson.
        p. cm.
    ISBN 0-684-19020-6
    1. Wedtech (Firm) 2. Defense contracts—United States—Corrupt
practices. 3. Government purchasing—United States—Corrupt
practices. I. Title.
    HD9743.U8W438 1989
    364.1'323—dc20   89-70073
                                                                 CIP

Macmillan books are available at special discounts for bulk purchases for
sales promotions, premiums, fund-raising, or educational use. For details,
contact:

Special Sales Director
Macmillan Publishing Company
866 Third Avenue
New York, N.Y. 10022

10 9 8 7 6 5 4 3 2 1

PRINTED IN THE UNITED STATES OF AMERICA

To Patrick Cory,
who made it all worth it

CONTENTS

ACKNOWLEDGMENTS

THIS BOOK COULD NOT have been written without the help of my husband, Robert Wood Thompson, Jr., whose name deserves to appear with mine as a coauthor. A veteran Associated Press newsman who now works as Washington correspondent for the *Greenville News* (South Carolina), Bob became intrigued by the Wedtech story and helped me in every stage of the production of this manuscript. He sat through long hours of the Wedtech trials and meticulously transcribed notes from the testimony. He provided major assistance in writing, rewriting, and copy editing, bringing a fresh eye and clean style to a subject that had consumed me for three years. He helped me with research, interviews, and computer problems, and even pulled together photos. Most important, he encouraged and supported me during an extremely difficult year.

I also owe a tremendous debt to Kevin McCoy, my colleague at the *Daily News* in New York, who helped not only in development of the Wedtech story but also in the production of this book. Kevin, who knows this story as well as anyone and reported many of the major developments in the case, served as a fountain of practical advice and a daily sounding board for ideas and frustrations.

It would be impossible to name everyone who offered help and encouragement, but a few from the *Daily News* deserve special mention: former editor Gil Spencer and current editor Jim Willse, who allowed me the time to write this book; columnist Jack Newfield, who introduced me to my editor at Scribner's, Ned Chase; librarian Faigi Rosenthal; Washington office manager Kay Lewis; photographers Mike Lippack, Harry Hamburg, and others whose work is reproduced here.

I am especially grateful to Mary Shannon, Ed Little, Steve Cossu and Donna Merris of the Wedtech prosecution team in New York for their extraordinary assistance. Federal prosecutor Gary P. Jordan in Baltimore also was very helpful.

Finally, I thank my family and friends for enduring me through this frightening but exciting event, my first book.

FEEDING
THE BEAST

THE GANG
THAT COULDN'T
SHOOT STRAIGHT

THEY WERE SIPPING DRINKS at poolside in the warm Florida sunshine—trying to forget the bribes, the eighty-hour work-weeks, and the mounting troubles they had left behind at Wedtech Corporation headquarters in the bleak South Bronx—when Fred Neuberger calmly posed the final solution. "I'm going to shoot the son of a bitch," he snarled. John Mariotta, Neuberger's partner and the front man for one of the most successful minority business scams in American history, had to be eliminated. Murder seemed the only answer.

As Neuberger posed the idea to his loyal lieutenant, Mario Moreno, behind his eyes was the steely resolve of a veteran gunslinger. The cold-blooded Neuberger liked to boast around the plant of his underground connections, of the violence committed during his stint in the 1940s as an Israeli freedom fighter. For a few thousand dollars, he told Moreno, he could hire an Israeli hit team to assassinate Mariotta. They could fly in, do the job, and be gone in a day—and no one could ever trace it back to Wedtech.

Moreno, the company's easygoing executive vice president, listened with trepidation. There was a strong chance that Neuberger was bluffing, but no one who knew him doubted his capacity for violence. Around Wedtech, Neuberger had a reputation as a corporate Jesse James, who carried an unregistered handgun in the pocket of his $900 suits and sometimes whiled away his lunch breaks by shooting rats for target practice. His second wife, Helen, had died in a suspicious suicide at their Long Island home, and Neuberger, who thrived on creating fear, had callously told his associates she used his gun to shoot herself. No one was surprised a few years later when Neuberger's third wife, Eileen, a sad-eyed, brunette schoolteacher, mysteriously disappeared. Within days after filing a missing person's report with police, Neuberger—a squat, homely man so vain he sometimes paid beautiful women to pose for photographs sitting on his lap—was cruising Manhattan's glitzy discos and had his name on the roster of a high-rollers dating service. Around the Wedtech plant, workers speculated that one day they would discover Eileen's body entombed in one of the 100-ton pontoon boats Wedtech was building for the U.S. Navy.

But Moreno was cut from a different cloth. The gregarious businessman, who emigrated from his native Colombia when he was nineteen years old, had started as a messenger at Bache & Company on Wall Street, then climbed to management slots at several companies and was teaching seminars for small businesses at New York University when he was lured from academia into Wedtech's unseemly web. He met Mariotta while helping the befuddled businessman get a bank loan he needed to secure a defense contract. From the start, Moreno was amused that Mariotta, certified by the government as a Hispanic businessman, could speak virtually no Spanish.

Moreno first joined the firm in 1978 as a $150-a-day consultant, while on the side he ran a catering business with his longtime companion, Caridad Vazquez. By 1979, he had learned of Wedtech's secrets. He discovered a secret slush fund Mariotta and Neuberger were using to dole out small payoffs and hide money skimmed from the corporation for personal extravagances. Two years later, Moreno was part of the conspiracy. He had advanced to a full-time $80,000-a-year job that by 1984 had grown to $262,500 in cash and bonuses, plus a secret gift of 9 percent of the company's stock.

Moreno was the suave mingler—a Hispanic completely at ease in the Anglo's world—who brought polish to Wedtech, an ability to schmooze with bankers, politicians, and bureaucrats. But although he had longed to be rich, Moreno had never expected to be a criminal. Slowly and insidiously, Wedtech had eaten away his moral fiber to the point where many considered him the prime architect of Wedtech's venal ways. His own values had become so skewered, his life-style so secretly ostentatious that he and Vazquez bought an $80,000 home in a modest Bronx neighborhood and spent $800,000 in stolen Wedtech money on remodeling, which included installation of a palatial pool and a lavish tropical greenhouse. He put Vazquez on the Wedtech payroll, paying her $35,000 a year, and brought his family into the conspiracy, persuading his sisters and their husbands to set up companies they could use to bilk the Wedtech treasury. A gambling addict, he spent more than $1 million playing the tables in Atlantic City.

But murder was another matter. "Fred, I'm not sure I could go along with that," he objected.

Neuberger eyed him with a sneer. "That's the trouble with dealing with Boy Scouts."

It was around Christmas in 1985, the end of a meteoric year in Wedtech's short history as a Department of Defense contractor, and pressure to eliminate Mariotta was building from all sides. The top two leaders of the Teamsters local wanted him out, afraid he would squeal to authorities about the payoffs they had been receiving for years. Other recipients of Wedtech's bribes feared that Mariotta was a dangerous loose cannon, capable of blurting out the company's many unsavory secrets. Mariotta was one of the few officers fully aware of

Wedtech's tangle of influence—a network that enmeshed the feet of several sitting congressmen and some of the most powerful officials in the Reagan administration.

With the Mariotta problem evolving into a crisis, there was little cause for Neuberger or Moreno to celebrate the holiday. As they settled in at their posh vacation homes in the Tampa suburb of Apollo Beach, they could think of little else. Murder seemed almost the inevitable next step, for they were already at the helm of what was arguably the most corrupt company in the country, a greedy machine that had steamrolled its way to $494 million in federal contracts through payoffs and palm greasing at every level of government. Before another Christmas rolled around, "Wedtech" would evolve into a national buzz word for corruption and bribery.

The day after his poolside talk with Neuberger, Moreno found himself in another discussion of the murder plot with Anthony Guariglia, who had just taken over as president. Guariglia also wanted Mariotta out, seeing an ouster as a way to further his own growing influence in the company. Guariglia lived most of the year in a $2 million Long Island mansion, but he had joined the others on the Christmas holiday in Apollo Beach, with his wife, Cynthia.

An Italian-American street kid who had watched many of his childhood friends fall under the influence of the Mafia, Guariglia had grown up instead to become a respected senior accountant for the prestigious KMG Main Hurdman firm in Manhattan. By most accounts, he was straight until he became involved in an audit of the Wedtech account that uncovered years of massive fraud and chicanery. Obligated under the law to expose his findings, Guariglia opted instead to conceal the company's fraud and strike a handsome deal to go to work for Wedtech. Guariglia was installed as an $80,000-a-year senior officer and received a large block of company stock. By 1984, his salary with bonuses was $155,769 and growing. Guariglia also had developed a huge gambling habit, squandering thousands of stolen company dollars in Atlantic City's glittering casinos.

"I understand Fred talked to you about having John eliminated?" Guariglia asked Moreno.

"I can't get involved in that thing at all," Moreno said.

Guariglia agreed. He, too, was not ready to cross the line into murder, no matter how easy a solution it seemed.

Neuberger was not about to let the subject drop. A few days later, on New Year's Eve, Neuberger and Guariglia took their wives to celebrate at a festive Spanish restaurant in Tampa, and there Neuberger called the senior officers aside and suggested they reconsider the murder scheme. Again Moreno and Guariglia backed off. Murder was too rash.

Back at Wedtech in January, things deteriorated rapidly. At first, Mariotta seemed under control, living up to his stock agreement. But he went wild when the executives offered him an honorary job title as chairman emeritus in the hope of getting him out of the way. Indignant, he threatened again to block the public stock sale.

Watching Mariotta's behavior, both Moreno and Guariglia came to agree with Neuberger that something must be done. Moreno found himself the target of a humiliating Mariotta tirade when he tried to promote his secretary, Deborah Scott, to administrative assistant. Mariotta, as Moreno recalled the scene, had been disturbed by Scott's meticulous record keeping of company campaign contributions. He began screaming at Moreno, demanding that he fire Scott.

"She's no more than a fucking secretary!" he bellowed.

Moreno shot back, "If she goes out of this company, I go, too."

"If you really have a pair of balls between your legs, you will resign immediately," Mariotta replied.

Moreno told Neuberger he would quit unless something were done to bring Mariotta in line. Finally, Neuberger recalled the two executives telling him, "We have no choice. We'll really have to kill him. Get rid of him."

Neuberger set up a meeting with their Teamsters connection, Frank Casalino, who, along with the union's president, Richard Stolfi, had been shaking down Wedtech since at least 1980. The Wedtech officials assumed that their payoffs to the union had also bought sufficient entrée to the local Mafia to enable them to negotiate a contract for a simple execution.

They scheduled a January meeting at the United Airlines

Terminal at JFK Airport. On this particular day, Neuberger, Guariglia, Moreno, and Wedtech treasurer Larry Shorten were scheduled to leave for California to promote the new stock issue. They took their seats around a table in an airport bar with Casalino, and Neuberger came right to the point. Mariotta, he said, was "getting impossible. . . . We have to do something about it." He asked Casalino how much it would cost to have Mariotta taken care of. Casalino stalled, but listened with intense interest. The union, he said, was very worried about Mariotta. "It's very dangerous to have him running around with that kind of information," he said.

The Wedtech officers left for California with uplifted spirits. They were convinced that as long as they protected their Washington allies, as long as they maintained the payoffs and kept mavericks like Mariotta under firm control, they could proceed with impunity. In fact, they were convinced that if their criminal trail finally caught up with them, they had bought the power to squelch any investigation and walk away free men. After all, they had in their corner, they would later claim, none other than the first lawman of the land: Edwin Meese III, Attorney General of the United States.

2

ROUGH BEGINNINGS

IT WAS A QUESTION they would often ask themselves: How did it all come apart? After all, for years they had been respected businessmen—street fighters who had worked their way up from the gutter. It was difficult in retrospect to say just when the line was crossed—when aggressive actions taken in the normal course of business became coarse, calculated, and corrupt.

There were early signs, of course. Mariotta, the dreamer, and Neuberger, the pragmatist, seemed destined somewhere down the line to come to blows. Their personalities mixed like oil and putrid water. Mariotta, whose staccato voice could climb to the highest octave in the human range, was the type to cajole bureaucrats with crying fits and hysterics. Neuberger negotiated with grunts, cold stares, and fumes from a foot-long cigar. Once, a company official watched in disbelief as Neuberger talked turkey with a high-ranking bank official, anxious about Wedtech's delinquency on a loan. "You want your money?" he said, sticking his cigar inches from the banker's face. "We already spent it, you schmuck."

An uneducated tool and die maker, Mariotta was a masterful manipulator who could convince a host of government agencies that his two-bit machine shop deserved better than the small contracts on which it had subsisted for years. He grew so used to being on stage that, even on the witness stand in his 1988 federal racketeering trial, he appealed to the jury with a well-rehearsed sob story embellished with free-flowing tears and frequent glances at his loyal wife, Jennie.

Neuberger was his polar opposite. A mechanical engineer, he was an expert metal fabricator who could quickly decipher complex government blueprints. His gruff exterior and boastful ways masked a flamboyant personal life, populated by a stream of troubled women. Neuberger was so convinced of his latent sex appeal that, even after he gave himself up in the Wedtech scandal, his coconspirators reported to investigators that he had bet them $10,000 that he would be the first to bed a tough female prosecutor handling the case.

From the outset, their visions of the company were light years apart. Mariotta dreamed of snaring enough huge defense contracts to turn Wedtech into a Fortune 500 rival of General Electric or Grumman Corporation. Neuberger—a member of Mensa with a 145 IQ—wanted to build a respectable business from modest jobs that the company did best, like Army personnel-carrier cooling kits and missile-fin assemblies. Their views on this—as well as every other issue of importance—were so disparate that Neuberger finally moved his office to a company outpost on East 149th Street, where he did little but watch his stocks and chase women. He told his associates he could not bear to watch Mariotta drive the company along a path that he knew was destined for disaster.

Neuberger was stingy to an extreme. Mariotta, on the other hand, liked to make a grand show of his generosity. He would walk onto the factory floor and pass out hundred dollar bills like penny candy to favored employees. When their political allies began asking for Wedtech stock, Mariotta handed it over so lavishly that Neuberger often complained he soon would give away the company.

Despite their differences, however, both Mariotta and Neuberger were smart enough to see the genius in each other. When Mariotta began looking for a new partner for his small South Bronx enterprise in 1970, he saw Neuberger's business savvy as a way to make up for his own weaknesses. The two became partners in a firm then known as the Welbilt Electronic Die Corporation.

They won their first government contract after Neuberger set about combing through blueprints at the Defense Department procurement office on Hudson Street. He found one so illegible that he knew no one else could intelligently bid on it. He took home the blueprints, worked out a bid, and soon Welbilt had its first job working for the federal government.

A few years later, he had another brainstorm. He had heard about a government program that enabled companies to win federal contracts without subjecting themselves to competitive bidding. A company could literally ask for a job and receive it at the whim of an obscure but powerful federal agency that headed the program. There were only a few minor requirements. A company had to be "small," a definition that regularly changed but usually meant no more than 500 employees, and at least half-owned by a black, Hispanic, Eskimo, or American Indian. Once those essentials were met, it was only a matter of submitting voluminous paperwork to win federal certification as a minority-owned firm and to become eligible for no-bid work.

The program, known as Section 8(a), was Congress's response to the insistent demands of civil rights leaders, who had seized upon the glaring lack of opportunities for minorities in government contract awards. It was run by the U.S. Small Business Administration, an Eisenhower-era agency set up to promote American entrepreneurship and protect small firms forced to compete against the Goliaths of the marketplace. The SBA was the place to turn for government-backed and guaranteed loans, business development grants to buy equipment and set up new businesses, and bailouts in times of natural disaster.

As part of President Lyndon Johnson's Great Society endeavor, the 8(a) program was set up in 1967 as an incubator for minority businesses. They would be nursed along with government backing until they were large enough to "graduate" into the competitive marketplace. The SBA would act as an agent for 8(a)-certified companies, searching out available contracts and persuading other agencies to set aside work specifically for minority businesses.

A major target of the SBA's efforts was the Department of Defense, because of the massive amount of work it doled out to private contractors for ships, aircraft, munitions, and other supplies. The SBA engaged in a constant battle to convince the Pentagon that minority-owned businesses could not only do the work capably and quickly, but also that helping such fledgling businesses could prove politically wise—whenever the President and Congress got around to writing the budget.

When it made its debut, the 8(a) program quickly proved to be a godsend for small, struggling companies whose minority owners were fighting for work. But, like most other SBA programs, it also opened up fertile territory for cheating. By the early 1970s, opportunists had begun setting up black and Hispanic front companies, which raked in contracts without detection by the myopic SBA. The program was so laxly managed that mobsters, celebrities, and millionaires alike slipped through the SBA's net, snaring contracts intended for the economically disadvantaged. Despite years of blustery condemnations of abuses, Congress seemed incapable of cleaning up the program. Every year, it seemed, there was a new, innovative legislative proposal to rewrite the SBA rules: to keep millionaires out of the program, to limit it to certified minorities, to create new incentives to wean the bottle-fed 8(a) firms from government dependence. But most of the proposals vanished as quickly as they appeared.

One day, Neuberger posed the idea to Mariotta: "Do you mind being a minority?" he asked.

Mariotta, puzzled, replied, "What do you mean, minority?" Neuberger said, "Puerto Rican."

Mariotta, still befuddled, responded, "I am Puerto Rican. What are you talking about?"

With that, the two embarked on a plan to milk Mariotta's Hispanic heritage for all it was worth. There was one major problem with trying to qualify their company as minority-owned. It wasn't. They each owned 50 percent of the firm. To them, the solution seemed simple. Under a handshake agreement, they drew up a document to submit to the SBA, showing Mariotta holding two-thirds of the company's common stock. But privately, they knew they were equal partners and would split their profits fifty-fifty.

The SBA bought their presentation without question. On September 25, 1975, a letter went out to Welbilt from acting district director Walter Leavitt, notifying Mariotta that "ownership of your company meets our eligibility criteria." The letter spelled out the requirements for remaining in the 8(a) program, including the submission of quarterly financial statements, disclosure of fees paid to consultants, and reporting of any changes in company ownership. Failure to comply, the agency warned, "will be cause to . . . terminate your company's participation in the 8(a) program."

The prospect of untold riches was an appealing one for Mariotta, who had watched three businesses go belly up before his fortunate pairing with Neuberger. As a child growing up in the slums of New York City, the son of Puerto Rican immigrants, Mariotta liked to say that he had been educated in the school of hard knocks, always struggling to get ahead, to ward off the next inevitable setback.

Before John was born, his mother moved the family to the Bronx to get his alcoholic father out of the harmful clutches of his drinking buddies in Puerto Rico. As an infant, John lived with his parents on 112th Street in Manhattan's Spanish Harlem before the Mariottas moved to the Prospect Park neighborhood of Brooklyn in the waning years of the Great Depression.

Growing up among youth gangs, the young Mariotta attended elementary school, first at P.S. 57 in Manhattan and later at P.S. 39. He spoke both English and Spanish so poorly that his teachers put marbles in his mouth and paraded him in front of his classmates to try to shame him. To escape the torment of the constant fights between his parents, Mariotta spent many childhood weekends sleeping on subway trains snaking through New York. At age seventeen the oldest student at his junior high school, P.S. 52, Mariotta was "pushed" into Morris High School, where most of his classmates were three years younger than he was. He still couldn't read.

Mariotta had wanted to become a chemist, but because of poor grades he was unable to get into the prestigious Bronx High School of Science. He soon decided that he would become a tool and die maker, the line of work that his father, originally a cabinetmaker, had adopted. He enrolled at Bronx Vocational High School.

Often, John stayed home from Bronx Vocational High to referee his parents' fights. As Mariotta told the story at his federal trial, one day an unsympathetic truant officer learned that John wasn't really ill and had him suspended from the school. He never went back.

Mariotta's training, however, continued at home. His father set up a milling machine, a drill press, and a lathe in the family's small apartment, and Mariotta boasted that he got a "damn good education" there despite his father's drinking.

Too young to serve in the armed forces during World War II, Mariotta worked as a kick-press operator at a company called Duke & Duchess. After six months, he moved on to a firm called S&S, where he polished and removed imperfections from dies, which are tools used to shape sheet metal. Soon, Mariotta was setting up grinders and milling machines and was teaching older employees as they returned from the war. Leaving his dead-end job at S&S, Mariotta went to Cameo Novelty, an electronics shop, where he grew accustomed to the occupational hazard of having to shout over the din of huge power presses weighing as much as forty tons.

His father, who besides his alcoholism was also a diabetic, used his milling machine and lathe to found a shop called Mariotta Mechanical Display, which made animated displays for department stores. But after John Mariotta was drafted by the Army in 1951, his father was forced to close the shop. Mariotta served two years in the Army, where, because of a bad left eye, he was given a menial job cleaning drums of petroleum.

Mariotta's illiteracy haunted him even during his military service. Unable to write to his girlfriend, he had other soldiers pen letters for him, but she soon tired of that. "All I know is, when I came back, since I did not write enough, I lost my girlfriend," Mariotta recalled.

The Army sent Mariotta to Yokohama, Japan, where he worked in a motorcycle transmission repair shop. Ironically, although he had always been too poor to own an automobile, Mariotta soon learned how to repair one. When he came home, his father wanted him to invest in a car, but he balked, preferring instead to invest in another family machine shop. Father and son went to a private lender on Canal Street in Manhattan's grungy Lower East Side; they got a loan and set up a shop that made handles for jewelry boxes. John worked long hours in the shop with his father and younger brother, sometimes staying until midnight.

In 1957, three years after the shop opened, Mariotta's father died, and Mariotta moved the shop to a two-car garage. Times were hard. His younger brother died eight months later of pneumonia, and Mariotta closed the shop and took the first in a series of short-term jobs.

After several business failures, he joined a former customer, Irving Lonstein, in setting up a business that they called J&L. Lonstein had just sold his own profitable die shop. He admired Mariotta's industriousness and thought he was worth a shot as a business partner.

J&L set up shop on 148th Street in the notorious Bronx neighborhood known as Fort Apache, a pocket of burned-out buildings with a long history of crime and violence. Lonstein soon decided he wanted to change the name to Welbilt Electronic Die—a tribute to his wartime success rebuilding Welbilt-brand batteries. They split the company fifty-fifty, and Lonstein, who was semiretired, would commute up from

Florida with his wife, Gerrie, to handle the bookkeeping. Soon, Welbilt had five employees, including Mariotta, working out of a 25-by-100-foot shop.

Even then, Mariotta realized that he needed a business partner with savvy and style to offset his lack of polish and education—as well as what he perceived to be a racial stigma. As he put it, "I needed Irving Lonstein, someone that can speak English okay, someone that would not look like a Puerto Rican."

Without Lonstein constantly around to drum up customers, Welbilt plodded along. When Lonstein's wife became ill, he told Mariotta to find another partner who could devote more time to the business. By that time, the Welbilt work force was down to two full-time employees—Mariotta and Lou Chico—plus a youngster who worked part-time in the evenings.

Chico exemplified the type of person Mariotta liked to employ—someone who makes up for a lack of education and opportunity by working hard, and being eager to listen and learn. Chico was a Mexican mechanic who couldn't find a job in the United States because of his poor English; he was washing dishes at a hotel when he applied to Mariotta for work.

Mariotta was working himself to exhaustion, arriving at the shop about 7 A.M. and often working until one o'clock in the morning, seven days a week. He married his wife, Jennie, in 1965, and the couple moved into a four-room Bronx apartment. From 1965 until 1970, Mariotta paid himself only $100 to $150 a week, an attempt to show his partner he believed in the business.

During that period, one of Welbilt's customers was a sheet metal company called Fleetwood, owned jointly by Fred Neuberger and Murray Brown. Mariotta was especially proud of an intricate job he did for Fleetwood, and Neuberger began channeling more work to the company. Mariotta by that time was looking for a new partner, and he was impressed with Neuberger's shrewd business sense. He offered him half-interest in Welbilt if Neuberger would handle the company's marketing, a task at which Mariotta was woefully inept.

Neuberger accepted the offer, and the two became equal partners in June 1970. Neuberger used his old Buick as collateral for a loan, and he and Mariotta each chipped in $2,000 to get the business rolling. They used $1,200 to buy out Lonstein and put the rest into working capital.

A stubborn willingness to tackle adversity was perhaps the only thing the partners had in common. Neuberger, born in Romania in 1930, spent his childhood living in cellars and hiding in the streets to avoid detection by the Nazis. He watched helplessly as family members were carted off. At age twelve, he was rounded up in a street raid and taken to a commercial rail yard to await transport to a labor camp. As he later described the incident, "Hundreds of people were milling around trying to find a way to go home, to no avail. We were all put into a cattle car. The sliding doors were chained and locked, leaving only a narrow space for air. Being so small from my sickly childhood turned out to be a mixed blessing. I was able to squeeze through the slats and escape. Miraculously, I found my way home."

In 1943, German soldiers shot and killed about forty children who were traveling with Neuberger, under Red Cross supervision, on a five-week journey on foot and by train through Bulgaria to Palestine. "The route was supposed to be over land by train. . . ." he once explained. "A few hours out of Bucharest, we had to disembark and travel on foot. . . . I was 14 years old when I left Europe walking at night, hiding by day, eating raw potatoes off the fields. We were always afraid of German patrols or being denounced by the local farmers. . . . It lasted for weeks."

At fifteen, Neuberger lied about his age to join the British Army, with which he fought in the African and Italian campaigns. But plagued by the memory of thousands of Jews turned away from Palestine by the British, he then joined the infamous Stern Gang, was arrested and thrown into prison for some time. The British government finally "suggested" that he leave the country.

Neuberger emigrated to the United States in 1947 with only the shirt on his back and found employment as a laborer in metalworking companies. He passed admissions tests and enrolled at a small college in Chicago after telling admissions officials that his records from high school—which in truth he never attended—had been lost. He then got a mechanical engineering degree from New York University before he and Murray Brown founded Fleetwood Metal Products in 1954. After Brown died in 1970, Neuberger borrowed enough money from Mariotta to buy out the remainder of Fleetwood from Brown's widow.

Even after he and Mariotta became business partners, Neuberger initially devoted most of his time to Fleetwood, leaving Mariotta to run Welbilt. Attempting to carve out a business in the depressed South Bronx was a challenge, to say the least. Mariotta would look out his factory door and see that "the dope pusher was on one side and the car thief was in the next door, and I was in the middle." Fortunately, the Welbilt plant looked so run-down that vandals and thieves left it alone.

In the beginning, Welbilt avidly sought nongovernment contracts but, as Mariotta said, "as soon as you mention the South Bronx, forget it. . . ." Once, when an officer from Britain's Royal Air Force came to the Welbilt plant, he jokingly told Mariotta that he didn't realize that the RAF had made bombing raids that far south during World War II. But the attempt at humor did not go over well with Mariotta. The South Bronx was grim reality to him.

Mariotta, however, was the eternal optimist. In 1971, with a $25,000 loan from the SBA, the company was able to move to a slightly larger, 3,000-square-foot building at 164th Street and Washington Avenue. Soon, using Neuberger's expertise, Welbilt snared its first defense contract, a $500,000 Army job to make an aluminum air-filter assembly for the Bell UH-1 helicopter.

Mariotta liked to brag about how he kept down overhead costs by hiring minorities—black, Hispanic, Russian—who would otherwise be on the unemployment lines. He would pay them about $4 per hour, rather than the $10 that experienced sheet-metal workers could command. In return, the Welbilt workers got job training and a helping hand from Mariotta whenever they were beset by hard times.

But his public displays of charity concealed a much less generous spirit. In conversations with his confidantes, Mariotta was shockingly racist, belittling the Hispanics who comprised the bulk of his work force and entertaining government contracting officers with crude ethnic jokes.

In the early years, Neuberger showed up at Welbilt only about once a week to look over the books. Mariotta was disturbed by Neuberger's many distractions, including his obligations to Fleetwood and his emotionally troubled second wife, Helen. He had married his first wife, Gertrude, an older woman, while he was still in college, but they drifted apart. Helen was a refugee with a serious drug problem. She worked briefly as a secretary at the Welbilt plant and showed up once "wigged out of her mind," as Mariotta recalled. Helen's drug dependency deepened when the couple moved to Long Beach. She found the town's free medical clinics to be a ready source of methadone, one of the many drugs to which Neuberger saw her turn with alarming frequency.

In late 1973, with Fleetwood on the brink of collapse, Neuberger finally began working full-time at Welbilt in hopes of building up the company's financial base. At Neuberger's prodding, Mariotta applied to the SBA to have Welbilt certified as a minority-owned 8(a) contractor.

Mariotta, however, clearly did not own 51 percent of the stock as required under SBA rules. So on April 18, 1975, Mariotta and Neuberger, the firm's sole stockholders and board members, sat down for a joint meeting of the board of directors and stockholders of Welbilt and rearranged their stock distribution so that Mariotta could qualify as primary owner of the firm. The minutes show the transfer of stock was made "by reason of the fact that John Mariotta is devoting all his time and labor in the interests of the corporation, and Fred Neuberger, by reason of personal problems," was unable to devote "his full time and energy as outside salesman and promotion man of the corporation."

The agreement looked good on paper and was convincing enough to pass muster at the unquestioning SBA. But by gentleman's agreement between the Welbilt officers, it was well understood that Neuberger would continue as an equal partner in the venture. The fraud was the first in a series of such scams that Neuberger and Mariotta would pull on the SBA.

While their business prospects brightened, Neuberger's home life continued to deteriorate. On September 26, 1974, Long Beach police were called to Neuberger's home to investigate a report that Fred's wife, Helen, had killed herself. There had been two witnesses to the event—Neuberger and Carlos Rivera, Mariotta's brother-in-law.

Neuberger and Rivera told police that they were downstairs when a despondent Helen shot herself while sitting in a half-filled bathtub. After lengthy interviews with Neuberger, the detectives investigating the case concluded that the massive chest wound was self-inflicted, and an autopsy report concurred. Years later, after Neuberger's third wife mysteriously disappeared, Manhattan prosecutor John Moscow resurrected this case as questionable.

Neuberger said no prayers and conducted no wake for his dead spouse, but those who knew him believed Helen was the real love of his life. The only tangible legacy of Helen Neuberger, however, was that, when he opened a corporate account at a Bronx bank, Neuberger used his late wife's initial in the account name—FHJ Associates, short for Fred, Helen, and John.

Ironically, the FHJ account would soon become a slush fund for under-the-counter payoffs—a memorial that had the ring of a morbid joke.

3

A THUG IN A CONGRESSMAN'S SUIT

THE WELBILT COMPANY'S second step into venality began with a colorful bon vivant named Bob Strahle, who was in business with former Yankees pitcher Whitey Ford; they represented other companies as business agents, and Welbilt was one of their clients. Welbilt owed Strahle and Ford a considerable sum of money.

Nevertheless, Strahle told me, he and Ford were thoroughly impressed with Welbilt's untapped potential. They knew about the SBA set-aside program, and one day Strahle had a brainstorm. Both he and Ford were good friends with Mario Biaggi, an influential Bronx congressman. Strahle reasoned: Why not set up the financially strapped Bronx businessmen with a politician who had the clout to help them?

Biaggi was no stranger to Welbilt. He had been the first in

19

line to congratulate the company in 1978 when it received a glowing newspaper write-up. Under the letterhead of the Congress of the United States, a hand-signed letter arrived in early February from Biaggi's office, congratulating Welbilt on "Your successfulness in overcoming the surrounding devastation. . . ." It concluded with the standard politician's offer. "If I may be of any assistance to you in your future endeavors, please feel free to contact me."

A phone call from Strahle came shortly afterward: "How would you like to meet Congressman Biaggi?"

The miserly Neuberger listened suspiciously. He wanted to know only one thing: How much would it cost? Biaggi was an ex-street cop turned lawyer whose former firm in lower Manhattan had earned a reputation as an able "fixer" for business people facing problems with government agencies, and in the South Bronx, no official favors came without a price.

Biaggi was a kingpin in a notoriously corrupt Democratic Party machine. His power and popularity were so entrenched—and his suspected underworld ties so well advertised—that other local politicians were loath to cross him. Since his 1968 election to Congress, he had established himself as a force to be reckoned with by anyone seeking to do business in the city's most depressed and desperate borough.

Neuberger had dealt with Biaggi once before at Fleetwood Metals, which was having delivery problems on a contract it had with the Navy. He had been disappointed by the congressman's efforts. By 1978, Welbilt had grown through its own initiative into a firm with fifty employees and $1.5 million in sales, virtually all of it in contracts awarded under the SBA's 8(a) program. Despite its constant cash-flow problems, things were looking good for Welbilt. If Welbilt had made it this far without Biaggi, who needed him? Or so Neuberger reasoned.

Within limits, Neuberger had nothing against lining the pockets of people who mattered. Already, the Welbilt executives were dipping into the FHJ account to pay modest "Christmas gifts" of about $1,000 to Stolfi and Casalino from Teamsters Local 875, which had signed on a year earlier as the sole bargaining agent for Welbilt's small work force. (The Teamsters' price for union peace would soon rise astronomically.) Neuberger saw the payment of gratuities as a fact of life in doing business in New York, but it had to be kept within reason.

Mariotta, however, thirsted for the chance to show off to someone who mattered. He and Neuberger agreed to have lunch with the congressman. A few days later Biaggi, carrying a cane and walking with a pronounced limp from an old police injury, toured the factory site at 1049 Washington Avenue. The visit was courteous and gentlemanly, and there was no talk of money. Biaggi left after suggesting that if the Welbilt officials ever needed help, they should not hesitate to call.

It did not take long for Neuberger, as pragmatic as he was stingy, to come around. As usual, Welbilt needed money, and both he and Mariotta—still earning only $20,800 a year for their dawn-to-dusk workdays—were exasperated by the constant battle to keep the company afloat. They had applied to a federal agency, the Commerce Department's Economic Development Administration, for a $2 million loan and another $2.7 million in loan guarantees. The EDA made loans and gave loan guarantees for companies in poverty-stricken areas. With this money, the firm could buy machinery and purchase a new building. The company had been assured that the loans were coming, but a stubborn EDA loan officer in Philadelphia bluntly said Welbilt would have to wait in line behind all the other loans due to be processed. With bankruptcy looming, the Welbilt executives needed special treatment, and they needed it fast.

The firm also had several contract applications pending with the regional office of the SBA, an agency in which Biaggi was known to exercise influence. Welbilt was seeking a lucrative 8(a) contract with the Army to overhaul the refrigeration and air conditioning systems of armored personnel carriers. After a meeting with Mariotta, Neuberger agreed that Biaggi could do "a lot of good for us politically."

The Welbilt executives set up a meeting at Biaggi's district office. In his ever-busy waiting room, lines of worried shopkeepers and immigrants from the nearby ethnic neighborhoods waited patiently for an audience with the great man, hoping Biaggi would help them cut through confusing gov-

ernment red tape. Biaggi was a master at nuts-and-bolts constituent service, and this had won him the fierce loyalty of his
electorate. But Biaggi's real work was done behind the closed
doors of his inner office, a frequent conference center for
Bronx Democrats who had seized every opportunity to feed
themselves on the infusion of federal and state dollars to an
area that desperately needed them. Biaggi held a recognized
claim on companies doing business with the Defense Department. Party boss Stanley Friedman helped concoct an elaborate $22 million scam to raid the coffers of the city's Parking
Violations Bureau, which would eventually send him to jail on
state and federal charges. Even the borough's newly elected
puppet president, lawyer Stanley Simon, could expect to be
taken care of in exchange for his crucial votes on the city's
powerful Board of Estimate.

The Welbilt executives were as generous as they could afford to be, given the company's precarious finances. In 1979,
they agreed to pay Biaggi's law firm a $20,000 retainer, which
even Neuberger agreed was not excessive in light of Biaggi's
vast influence. In return, Biaggi promised to use "his influence
or whatever to help us," Neuberger recalled. Little did they
know that the $20,000 was only a meager down payment.
Word soon spread through the Democratic machine that Welbilt was Biaggi's company. He had staked his claim on it, and
others could come near only with his approval.

Biaggi was not about to sell his power for a pittance. Once the
most decorated cop in America, an ambitious fighter who
worked his way through night law school at New York University while supporting a wife and four children, he had been
transformed during his tenure in public life into what federal
prosecutor Ed Little would later describe as a "thug in a congressman's suit." Greed consumed him. Early in his career he
was suspected to be a congressman on the take, but it would
take years for investigators to learn the extent and audacity of
his shakedowns. It was as if Biaggi saw dollar signs in every
phone call, every letter, every routine congressional duty.

Possessed of mesmerizing charm and good looks, Biaggi
was a fresh, promising face when he retired from the police

force and breezed onto the city's political scene in the late 1960s. Born October 26, 1917, the son of Italian immigrants, he had never outgrown his humble Bronx roots, proudly raising his strapping young family in a modest apartment on Mosholu Parkway. The limping gait of this self-proclaimed law-and-order candidate was an effective reminder that Biaggi had been injured ten times in the line of police duty. The city's newspapers regularly featured his photograph under the heading, "Hero Cop," as he received twenty-eight commendations for heroism in twenty-three years; he was the only New York cop inducted in the National Police Hall of Fame.

He was forty-six when he graduated from law school in 1963. Two years later, he retired from the police department with a handsome pension and set up a small private law practice. He made his first political foray in 1968, when Republican Paul Fino retired from the House of Representatives after sixteen years in office. Biaggi easily won election to Congress, representing the eastern Bronx and part of northern Queens. In 1973, he ran for mayor on a law-and-order platform. But by then he was beginning to get a less favorable press.

In 1971, Biaggi had been called before a grand jury investigating whether he had collected fees for sponsoring private immigration bills. The probe brought his finances under close scrutiny and included an allegation that Biaggi had secured a no-show job for his daughter at an advertising agency connected to the president of the Yonkers Raceway. Although no indictment resulted, federal agents questioned whether the job was a payoff to Biaggi for his backing of a controversial proposal to build the race track.

The grand jury investigation was mostly forgotten until the press began to disclose that he had repeatedly taken the Fifth Amendment when questioned about his personal finances. This was hardly in keeping with his tough law-and-order campaign. With dramatic indignation, Biaggi flatly denied the reports and challenged the news media to prove them. He even went to court and asked a judge to release the transcripts of the secret grand jury proceedings. Perhaps he banked on the assumption that no judge would grant such an unorthodox request. But the judge complied, and the delighted press discovered that Biaggi invoked his rights against self-incrimination sixteen times. Biaggi's mayoral campaign quickly self-destructed.

The press revelations also resurrected larger, lingering questions about his character. He seemed forever under the scrutiny of one investigative agency or another. Federal investigators examined whether his law firm had bribed a judge in a bankruptcy case. In the early 1980s, his name surfaced again in FBI surveillance tapes from its investigation of former U.S. Labor Secretary Raymond Donovan. In the tapes, a reputed mobster boasted that he had paid off Biaggi to win a dirt-hauling contract on Rikers Island, site of a city prison. No formal charges resulted. And in the Bronx, the district attorney's office reopened a probe into one of Biaggi's most celebrated acts of police heroism, the shooting of a paroled convict who had climbed into a car driven by the off-duty Biaggi. Biaggi blew away the intruder and was honored with a police department Medal of Honor for Valor. In hindsight, investigators found it intriguing that Biaggi's passenger was a Bronx businessman long suspected of ties to organized crime. Again, no charges resulted.

Biaggi spent years portraying himself as the devoted family man; he was even named Father of the Year in 1959 by a Long Island civic group. But his honesty came under attack in 1974 when a young woman who had worked as a volunteer in his mayoral campaign filed a paternity suit against him. A judge cleared him of the charge, but the widely publicized case eroded his family-man image.

Biaggi retreated to the safety of Washington after the mayoral debacle and left his business dealings in the hands of others. He was well-liked in Washington, where he was committed to an eclectic mix of causes that won him some national attention. He became the chief congressional advocate of the Irish Republican Army. As chairman of a Merchant Marine subcommittee, which writes maritime legislation, Biaggi became a chief backer of maritime interests and an influential force on the New York waterfront. His cozy dealings with one financially strapped company led to his 1987 federal conviction on a charge of accepting free Florida vacations from the firm while pushing its cause in Congress. Biaggi had taken a Christmas junket with his striking redheaded mistress, Barbara Barlow, who unknowingly befriended FBI undercover agents at poolside. While Biaggi cavorted, his wife stayed at home, battling Hodgkins disease.

Publicly, he claimed by 1979 to have removed himself from the affairs of the law firm he founded, Biaggi & Ehrlich. On paper, he concocted an elaborate buyout plan to divest himself of his interest in the firm, and henceforth the firm's stationery described him as "of counsel" to his partner, Bernard Ehrlich. But Biaggi was never more than a phone call away from the law office. His access was made abundantly clear to the firm's high-paying clients by Ehrlich, his loyal soldier and partner.

When I first met Mario Biaggi in the fall of 1986, I had written a story exposing how he had become a millionaire while earning a modest congressional salary. The story was based on an analysis of five years of financial disclosure reports filed by the congressman, which showed him receiving substantial consulting fees from his former law firm. He had also reported—in the barest details—a bulging portfolio of investments, including several real estate transactions, each of which had earned him at least $250,000 in profits. Biaggi refused requests for an interview, and after the story was published, he held a press conference to lambast the irresponsible reporting and groundless accusations. From the front row, I could see him glaring at me.

A few months later, I expected to encounter hostility when I called his media consultant, Mortimer Matz, to request an interview on Biaggi's involvement with Wedtech. Surprisingly, I was told that Biaggi would see me.

The Biaggi who welcomed me at his office door a few days later had undergone a total transformation. The attentive gentleman, he shook my hand, led me to my seat, and spoke in dulcet tones. For more than an hour, he explained that his interest in Wedtech was purely that of a dedicated congressman. He urged me to call federal agencies who were doing business with Wedtech. Nowhere would I find his fingerprints. Sure, his son held stock in Wedtech, he explained, but that had nothing to do with him.

As I was leaving, he shook my hand like an old friend and added in a conspiratorial whisper that I should look into New York Congressman Joseph Addabbo, the former chairman of the House Armed Services Committee. Addabbo repeatedly had gone to bat for Wedtech, Biaggi said.

There was only one problem with Joe Addabbo. He had died a few months earlier. Biaggi had been one of the first to mourn Addabbo's death in public.

Bernard Ehrlich struck a strong contrast to the smooth, dapper Biaggi. A Republican with considerable sway in his own state party, Ehrlich handled the congressman's day-to-day dirty work. Invoking Biaggi's name, Ehrlich was the point of contact for Bronx businesses seeking government work, subtly informing them of the help Biaggi could provide if given proper allegiance. As his friend Bob Strahle recalled, the Bermuda-born Ehrlich was Biaggi's "good soldier who always did what he was told."

Ehrlich boasted of his own ties to Department of Defense decision makers. A short, bespectacled man with a firm stomach suggesting years of sit-ups, he had developed a certain cachet through his long years of service in the National Guard. Ehrlich had enlisted in 1955 as a 101st Calvary platoon leader, climbed to company commander, and in 1958 was transferred to the Sixth Battalion as an intelligence officer. By 1985, he had risen to commander of the 42nd Infantry Rainbow Division of the New York State National Guard. The honor, he believed, was not undeserved.

This opinion was not shared by the Guard's rank and file. When I first began writing about Ehrlich's Wedtech involvement, the *Daily News* was besieged by phone calls and letters from Guard members offended by the commander's arrogance, mean-spiritedness, and self-promotion. His subordinates charged that Ehrlich was using the Guard for his personal financial benefit, an allegation which touched off an investigation by Manhattan District Attorney Robert Morgenthau into fraud, sweetheart contracts, and self-dealing by Ehrlich and other members of the state's volunteer army. Ehrlich had also used his Wedtech contact to secure cushy consulting jobs for a number of his Guard buddies, including his boss, Gen. Vito J. Castellano. Castellano, who was fired by Gov. Mario Cuomo after he refused to return from an Italian vacation to help manage a disastrous hurricane, was a bigamist, loan shark, and shameless self-dealer parading in uniform. He once cut a deal with *Penthouse* magazine publisher Bob Guccione, in which he had free use of a luxury car in return for allowing *Penthouse* to be sold in armory PXs.

Ehrlich often alluded to a Korean War record, but his military credentials gave no evidence of active combat. He sometimes found his military career in conflict with his legal duties; once, by day, he was representing a striking city mail carrier's union while at night activating his Guard troops to deliver the stalled mail.

Around the time of Wedtech's first public stock offering, he met a fellow reservist, White House counselor Edwin Meese, who was in New York for a speaking engagement. Meese had just been cleared by the Army inspector general of irregularities in his promotion to National Guard colonel. Ehrlich took Meese along to an uproarious, drunken dinner with his Guard buddies at Umberto's Clam House, a mob-controlled Little Italy restaurant. Two years later, when Ehrlich was seeking a promotion to commander, he put aside a long-brewing feud with Meese's friend, Bob Wallach, and asked him to seek Meese's help in his own successful promotion.

Ehrlich's credentials were similarly enhanced by his close ties to Sen. Alfonse D'Amato, whom he had met when D'Amato was a town supervisor on Long Island. Ehrlich committed himself to D'Amato's Senate campaign, and when D'Amato was elected, he named Ehrlich his military adviser and gave Ehrlich's daughter a press aide position on his staff. Ehrlich's title was largely ceremonial, but he used it to impress uncooperative bureaucrats and anxious businessmen. When he ran into one unhelpful officer at the Defense Contract Administration Services office, Col. Don Hein, Ehrlich informed him of the strong possibility that Hein's supervisors would learn about his troublesome behavior. Later, when Hein still wouldn't budge, he was promptly replaced by an officer more to Wedtech's liking.

Ehrlich strutted into meetings with government officials, often dressed in uniform. At their New York regional offices, he was held in such regard that he could order them to vacate their offices while he made telephone calls. He liked to be called "General Ehrlich," a gesture of respect he expected even from the Bronx businessmen he was shaking down. He once showed up at a South Bronx plant site in a car chauffeured by a Bronx borough employee, who often served as his driver while reaping a handsome city salary. The plant's owner says he always felt he was expected to salute "the General" before writing out the check for the law firm's monthly retainer.

Ehrlich used his National Guard position to advance highly profitable schemes. Jerry Brown, an Albany businessman who runs a computer design firm, told me that Ehrlich promised to accommodate Brown's company, General Cad-Cam, with a National Guard deal that would likely evolve into future Army work—provided he would pay hefty commissions to unnamed politicians who put the deal in place. Brown refused to play along. Ehrlich was charged, along with Bronx Democratic boss Stanley Friedman, in a plot to sell a bogus hand-held computer that Friedman was marketing for a company called Citisource Inc., for use in taking National Guard inventory. When he took Wedtech on as a client, Ehrlich began pushing the use of Wedtech products to the National Guard. He even persuaded the company to hire his Guard boss, Castellano, as a $58,000 consultant.

When the Wedtech and National Guard scandals began closing in on him simultaneously, Castellano was the first in the state prosecutor's door, offering to plead guilty to bribery and give up his close friend Bernie in exchange for a light sentence. But this treachery backfired. When prosecutors put Castellano on the stand, they heard him admit under cross-examination that he had been lured to Wedtech for money to finance a secret bigamist life-style. The jury, shocked by details of Castellano's escapades, came to regard the chief government witness as a lower variety of criminal than the accused felon. Ehrlich was acquitted on a state bribery charge. (He was later convicted in the federal Wedtech racketeering case.) But Castellano's betrayal was one Ehrlich would not soon forget.

No one suffered a more devastating fall from grace as a result of the Wedtech scandal than did Bernie Ehrlich. When I first called him at his Bedford Hills home in October 1986, his stiff military facade quickly disappeared. Sensing disaster, he begged desperately that his name be kept out of the newspapers. He said he could not bear to think of the humiliation that it would bring to his children. Months later, when he showed up at court in uniform, his spirit broke completely after an angry prosecutor dramatically stripped the decorations from his uniform. He attempted suicide several times before his federal trial, once by hurling himself in front of a bus. In court appearances, he stared blankly at the floor. He would tell reporters later that, much as he regretted his improprieties as a lawyer, what devastated him was the thought that he had disgraced the military. He left for prison in the summer of 1989 still holding the hope that he could be buried in uniform.

Although Ehrlich ostensibly ran the show at Biaggi & Ehrlich, by his own admission, his legal talents were minimal. The firm's prestige was hardly enhanced when Ehrlich was joined by Biaggi's son, Richard. Born in 1949, Richard, a bespectacled younger version of his father, had jumped to three different law schools and dropped out for a time to serve active duty in the U.S. Army Reserves. It took several tries before he finally passed the New York bar examination.

At the law firm, Richard performed mostly administrative tasks and helped clients deal with the federal Department of Housing and Urban Development. He seldom worked later than 6:30 P.M. before retreating to his home in Fort Lee, New Jersey, and his young wife, Toni. Although no one would attest to his legal brilliance, Richard's friends considered him an extraordinarily nice guy whose tragic flaw was his inability to stand up to his father. In time they would see the elder Biaggi—who had implicated his own son in a web of corruption—weeping before a federal judge and begging for a light sentence for Richard.

The Biaggi & Ehrlich firm was known to have a solid hold over several major city and federal agencies, where Biaggi loyalists were installed in key posts. Among the agencies was the New York regional office of the SBA. Until the Reagan administration took over in 1981, the agency's regional director had been Ivan Irizarry, who left the agency to serve as an officer for the New York National Bank, a new Bronx bank that he formed with several other businessmen. Welbilt officers quickly became major stockholders, and the company was the bank's most important client. The Wedtech officers would later testify that they paid consultant fees totaling $130,000 to Irizarry and his bank president, in return for a range of highly irregular banking services.

Irizarry's replacement at the SBA was a matter of some concern for Biaggi & Ehrlich and for Welbilt, which needed someone in place to protect its interests. But with a Republican administration taking over, a new man had already been recommended: Peter Neglia, the son of longtime Brooklyn Republican leader Joseph Neglia. The younger Neglia, who had put himself through night law school at Fordham University, had gotten a job as clerk to a state judge through his father's political connections. His nomination to the SBA also was a tribute to his dad's sway.

Ehrlich was troubled at first, since the younger Neglia was an unknown quantity. But soon afterward, Ehrlich began ardently courting him with expensive lunches and dinners. After one such session with Neglia, Ehrlich confided to Neuberger that he had found ways to "make him inclined to help" Welbilt. Before long, the Biaggi & Ehrlich firm could promise its clients that any matter before the regional SBA would reach satisfactory resolution.

Soon after they retained Biaggi & Ehrlich, Welbilt started getting results. The stalled EDA loans were approved like lightning. Biaggi also intervened to help Welbilt seal the $5.5 million Army contract for armored personnel-carrier cooling kits. Flushed with success, the Welbilt officers took out additional insurance by striking up a friendly relationship with an Army contracting officer in Michigan named Gordon Osgood, who was assigned to monitor the firm's performance. They treated him to dinners and shows, and soon agreed to pour money into a private company that Osgood owned. Over the next four years, they would later testify, their relationship with Osgood cost the company nearly half a million dollars.

In the beginning, Biaggi helped the company openly, writing letters to federal agencies and pressuring city officials to bend to the company's wishes. But in 1978, Congress passed an ethics law which made it illegal for congressmen to intervene on behalf of companies in which they had a direct or indirect financial interest. Careful to protect himself, Biaggi began calling on his two closest allies in Congress, Addabbo and D'Amato, when Welbilt needed phone calls made and letters written on its behalf.

Addabbo, a husky, round-faced machine Democrat, was particularly well-positioned to take up Welbilt's cause. Elected in 1960 from a southern Queens district encompassing Ozone Park and Jamaica, he served in Congress for a quarter of a century and rose to the chairmanship of the powerful defense subcommittee of the House Appropriations Committee. He also remained a member of the House Small Business Committee. His committee jobs gave him a platform from which he fiercely protected New York interests, pushing for contracts to bolster Long Island's aircraft industry and Staten Island's navy yard. He boasted clout with both the SBA and the military establishment, which feared his reputation as a cost-cutter who had opposed funding for the B-1 bomber and MX missile systems.

D'Amato was a local pol who came out of nowhere in 1980 to defeat veteran Sen. Jacob Javits for the GOP nomination. The Catholic grandson of Italian immigrants, a graduate of Syracuse Law School, D'Amato encountered prejudice when he began knocking on the doors of Wall Street law firms. Turned away, he returned to Long Island and, at age twenty-eight, became the youngest public administrator ever to serve Nassau County.

D'Amato owed his later advancement to the boss of one of the last old-time GOP machines in New York, Joseph Margiotta, the authoritarian chief of the Nassau County Republican organization. The party rose to prominence with the postwar white flight to the suburbs, and by the 1970s, the Margiotta machine controlled nearly 300,000 Republican votes and a powerful bloc of thirteen Republican seats in the state legislature. D'Amato's allegiance to Margiotta was so extreme that the weekly newspaper *The Village Voice* dubbed him the "Devil's Disciple—the most ambitious apprentice of suburban bossism." With D'Amato's help, Margiotta turned his county into a patronage fiefdom financed largely through coercive fund-raising. County employees who wanted their jobs protected were expected to pay 1 percent of their salaries to the GOP organization.

In 1980, D'Amato decided to mount a challenge against the liberal Javits, sensing that the elder statesman was out of touch with the state's growing conservative element. After a campaign in which he savagely attacked Javits' age and health, the brash D'Amato won the primary by a landslide. He went on to throttle his Democratic opponent, Liz Holtzman, but not without a new infusion of support from an important Democratic backer, Rep. Mario Biaggi.

The favor was one D'Amato would not forget. Soon, with a seat on the important Senate Appropriations Committee, D'Amato was in a position to help Biaggi on important funding requests. When the Welbilt executives came to call on Biaggi, the congressman could assure them with certainty that with a telephone call, Al D'Amato also would take up their cause.

By 1980, Welbilt needed all the congressional muscle it could summon, for Mariotta had pinned his hopes on winning a huge Army contract—potentially worth $200 million—through the 8(a) program. He had heard about the contract through the Latin American Manufacturers Association, a Washington-based lobbying group for Hispanic businessmen, which he joined in the mid-1970s. LAMA campaigned actively to force government agencies to set aside more large contracts for minorities. Then, it rode herd on the SBA to make sure its Hispanic members got a fair shot.

The leader of the group was José Aceves, a Mexican-American businessman. Aceves first met Mariotta when he came to

New York to recruit new members for LAMA. Mariotta was enamored with Aceves, believing he could do great good for Welbilt in Washington, where the company had few contacts. He hired Aceves to work on the side as a Welbilt marketing consultant. Aceves told me he received payments from Welbilt for about a year while still working for LAMA and later, between 1978 and 1980, drew about $21,000 in fees for pushing the company to federal agencies in Washington.

But Mariotta's enthusiasm was not shared by Neuberger. Once, when Mariotta discovered that Neuberger had failed to return a phone call to Aceves, Mariotta became incensed, and the argument erupted into a fistfight, with chairs and picture frames flying.

In 1978, word spread within the 8(a) community of a new, potentially lucrative contract that was to be made available under the set-aside program. Maj. Gen. Richard Thompson, the commander of the Army's St. Louis-based Troop Support and Aviation Material Readiness Command (known in Army parlance as TSARCOM), decided under pressure to seek a minority firm to help build a production run of 13,100 six-horsepower, air-cooled gasoline engines—devices roughly similar to a lawnmower engine. The Army used the engines to power portable field generators, heaters, pumps, and service units. It was important that the engines be built to exacting standards, with interchangeable parts that could be easily repaired in the field.

The procurement was fraught with problems. First, the Army proposed teaming a minority firm with an established engine-building company to provide technical support and oversee the contract. But after a wide solicitation, only one company—the Avco Corporation—agreed to sponsor an 8(a) company to build the engines.

There also was only one 8(a) company waiting in the wings—a firm called Hartec. It was owned by none other than Aceves, who went after the contract at full steam. Aceves persuaded the SBA to stake its claim on the contract, then he persuaded the SBA to choose his firm. The Army, however, had a rather serious objection to the selection. When it performed a preliminary assessment in May 1980, it found that Hartec was a paper company with no facilities, no employees, and no plans for how it would build the engines.

Aceves scrambled for a way to save the project. He remembered his friend Mariotta, whose Welbilt corporation had at least some of the needed facilities. He asked Mariotta if he would like to team up with him. Welbilt would build the engines; Aceves would get a 20 percent subcontract for bringing the work to the firm.

The SBA regional office okayed the idea, but the agency's designation was only the first step in a long, rocky road to winning the contract. The procurement director at TSAR-COM, Dr. Thomas Keenan, had been a formidable obstacle since the first day the contract was set aside for a minority company. He had tangled viciously with Aceves, who walked away convinced that Keenan was prejudiced against minority companies in general. After Keenan's staff went to the South Bronx to look over Welbilt's production facilities, they returned to describe a largely empty, two-story building equipped only with two sophisticated metal-cutting machines, which Welbilt had just bought using its EDA loans.

There also was a wide discrepancy between what Welbilt wanted to charge and what the Army was willing to pay. Welbilt submitted a proposal, which had been prepared in consultation with Avco, to build the engines for $99.9 million—or $7,672 for each engine. But the Army's pricing analyst had calculated a fair-market price of $19 million—roughly $1,485 per engine. The Welbilt proposal provoked "hysterical laughter" among officials at TSARCOM.

The Welbilt officers began to smell a rat. They suspected they were being set up by Avco to submit a bid that was totally unacceptable, so that the Army would then give the entire contract to Avco. They believed Keenan favored Avco and was giving the company favorable treatment in negotiating TSARCOM contracts.

Ehrlich went with the officers to a precontract conference at TSARCOM headquarters. They returned to present Biaggi with a dismal report: Keenan was determined not to bend to the company; something had to be done to force his hand. Biaggi promised to talk to Addabbo about the worrisome

Army official. If anyone could apply pressure, Addabbo, with his Defense Department influence, was the one.

In April 1981, they went to Washington with Ehrlich in tow to meet again with Biaggi. Things were looking grim. They had submitted a new proposal—again rejected—to build the engines for $38 million, an amount that would hardly cover their start-up and equipment costs, but they had presented it without any supporting documentation, and Keenan had again dismissed it.

Biaggi, whose appeal to Addabbo had yielded few results, listened to the latest woes and promised to set up a meeting with D'Amato. He got the senator on the phone: "Al, I have the Welbilt people here, and they would like to talk to you on this problem that we have." A few minutes later, they were in D'Amato's office meeting with the senator and a senior aide, Mike Hathaway. D'Amato told them Hathaway would develop an information paper on the contract talks, which he could use to write a letter to Army Secretary John Marsh.

By then, the Welbilt officials had embarked on a smooth public relations campaign handled by David Epstein, an erudite Harvard graduate who had been hired to serve as Mariotta's special assistant. Epstein became Mariotta's speech writer and coach. He authored a speech that became the standard twenty-minute Mariotta spiel, blessed with such musical prose that even Mariotta's fractured pronunciation could not ruin it. Epstein coached Mariotta day and night until he could present the speech verbatim, then went with him to Washington to testify before a congressional hearing on the 8(a) program. Soon, with Epstein's smooth contacts, the Welbilt engine saga attracted writers from *Forbes* and *Inc.* magazines and a flurry of New York media interest.

A letter sent to Marsh on April 14, 1981, over Mariotta's signature outlined what came to be known as the Welbilt philosophy. Epstein even coined a phrase for it: "Off Welfare, On Welbilt." Welbilt's argument was that the engine contract would create 300 new jobs in the South Bronx and save the government $24 million by taking the company's new workers off the welfare rolls.

"[The] South Bronx [is an] enclave of high unemployment

and low expectations. . . . Eighty percent of our people have
been and otherwise still would be on welfare. They have been
stigmatized as 'obviously unemployable,' as 'machete swing-
ers,' as 'spear chuckers.' We work metal here," the letter
concluded ringingly. "We also erase stigmata."

Biaggi and Ehrlich were aware that Welbilt's fortunes were
closely tied to their own, for the company had become the law
firm's single most important client. As Welbilt prospered, so
did its legal counsel. In 1980, Biaggi & Ehrlich had increased
its yearly retainer to $40,000 and, soon afterward, to $50,-
000. With each new success for the company, the retainer
rose, jumping to $125,000, then $200,000 by 1985.

Ehrlich handled most of the routine contacts with the company, but Biaggi stepped in frequently. The Welbilt officers
began to refer to the silver-haired congressman as the Chairman of the Board. But he was also the law firm's bill collector
when the company fell behind in its payments. Biaggi quickly
let Mariotta know his displeasure, blaming the "cheap Jew"—
his standard slur for Neuberger—for much of the tardiness.
This constant dunning made Neuberger livid. At one point,
he angrily accused Biaggi of operating "like the cop on the
beat, putting the arm on the corner bookie."

But the pressure was getting to Mariotta, who was alarmed
by Biaggi's threats to turn his back on the company. He was
convinced that without Biaggi's help they would lose the engine contract. In a panic, he met with Biaggi to plead for
patience and made a promise the company executives would
soon regret: He would make Biaggi a millionaire by giving
him part equity in the company. One night, as he drove Ehrlich home, he made the figure specific. "This thing is going to
be good," he boasted. "I feel you can make $5 million."
Ehrlich sealed the figure in his memory.

Neuberger became livid when Mariotta told him of his
promise. "What are you giving such crazy promises for?" he
shouted. He was convinced Mariotta was going to give away
the company before either of them had a chance to cash in.

Over the next months, the Welbilt officials came to realize
the seriousness of Mariotta's boastful promise to Biaggi. One
day, visiting Biaggi's district congressional office, Moreno no-

ticed a fleet of limousines parked outside and saw Biaggi holding court with a gang of suspicious-looking men, all of them chattering in Sicilian.

"Who are they?" he asked Ehrlich.

Ehrlich pointed his finger to his head—as if imitating a gun—and fired it.

"That's the reason," he said, "people take the congressman seriously."

4

PRIVATE EYES

HAROLD "HAL" LIPSET liked to think of himself as Paul Drake, Perry Mason's soft-spoken private eye. From his San Francisco headquarters, he ran a private detective agency that handled 500 cases a year. In the spring of 1981, Lipset received a cross-country call from an old friend, David Epstein. Epstein wanted to know if Lipset would consider doing a job for his new employer, Welbilt Electronic Die Corporation, which was having trouble getting an Army engine contract.

Welbilt's problems seemed to go beyond the Pentagon's natural reluctance to deal with an obscure firm located in one of America's worst urban ghettos. The Welbilt crew suspected that somewhere in the procurement system money was changing hands. They had already used payoffs themselves to put one Army officer in Welbilt's pocket; they could not bear the thought of a competitor using bribery to beat them at their own game.

Their suspicions centered on Dr. Keenan, the recalcitrant Army officer at TSARCOM headquarters in St. Louis. Keenan not only had rejected summarily Welbilt's qualifications, he had stymied their request that the Army audit their inflated cost projections. Without the audit, they argued, they had no chance of justifying their revised $38 million proposal.

They suspected—without foundation—that Keenan was rigging the bidding to ensure that the engine contract would eventually go to a Houston firm, a small, recently formed minority company known as Garcia Ordnance Corporation. They speculated that Keenan was in collusion with Ronald J. Bolden, who had gone into business in 1980 with Armando A. Garcia, a Mexican-American former milkman who owned a tiny Houston company that distributed fast-food products to schools. Their new defense firm operated out of a filing cabinet in a corner of Garcia's office. But the Welbilt officials confided to Lipset that they believed Bolden had an "in" with Keenan.

The Welbilt officers proposed that, for a modest retainer, Lipset could rummage around in Keenan's background in search of skeletons in his closet. Lipset agreed to help Welbilt, but his cursory investigation of the ties between Keenan and Bolden bore no fruit. This was only the first step in a prolonged effort by Welbilt to ruin Ron Bolden and drive his company out of business. Information which Welbilt gathered on him was channeled through Bernie Ehrlich to the Army and sent up to the Justice Department. Two years after Garcia Ordnance won a contract away from Wedtech, the U.S. attorney in Brownsville indicted Bolden, Garcia, and other company officials for allegedly substituting iron for steel in its crankshafts. Although Bolden was convicted, the other officers were cleared and the investigation was condemned by a federal judge as a waste of government effort. It succeeded, however, in driving Garcia Ordnance out of business and eliminating one of Wedtech's most threatening competitors.

Lipset told the Welbilt officers straightaway that he didn't think an investigation of Keenan and Bolden was the way to solve their frustrations. What Welbilt needed was representation in Washington, where the logjam was. Political clout, he suggested, might succeed where espionage failed.

Lipset offered them a connection—a friend in San Francisco, a liberal personal-injury lawyer with a background in advocacy who would identify with their minority cause. The friend had acquired a certain Washington cachet with the new Reagan administration. His name was E. Robert Wallach, a fellow with a peculiar habit of spelling his name in lower-case letters, like the poet e. e. cummings. He happened to be the best friend of one of the president's most trusted advisers, Edwin Meese III.

Bob Wallach and Ed Meese, by all accounts, were a political odd couple, a peculiar marriage of arch-conservative philosophy and bleeding-heart liberalism. Yet they were linked by a bond of friendship that defied party labels and mystified virtually all who knew them. The two met in 1958, their final year at Boalt Hall law school of the University of California. Meese came from a devout German-American family with strong California roots. The Bronx-born Wallach was Meese's polar opposite. His middle-class Jewish parents divorced when he was young, and he moved to Los Angeles with his mother.

Wallach worked to earn money for college, holding a series of jobs while attending high school in Los Angeles. There, debating and liberal causes became his early passions. His debating skill won him a scholarship to the University of Colorado, but he left after six months when the money ran out. Another scholarship brought him to the University of Southern California. In college, he worked in canneries to earn spending money, was elected sophomore class president, and, as a class project, adopted a Los Angeles boys' club dominated by Hispanics and blacks.

He graduated in 1955 and left for Berkeley, where Meese came after graduating from Yale. In their senior year, they were partners on the debate team. After they graduated, both settled in Oakland with their families, living within a mile of each other. Even after Wallach's marriage dissolved in 1974, the families spent weekends together. And when the Meeses left for Washington in 1980, Wallach scheduled visits with the Meeses to coincide with his East Coast trips.

Wallach set up practice with a partner and established himself as one of the city's leading civil advocates. But after the breakup of his nineteen-year marriage, his personal image changed dramatically. He was seen around town, flamboyantly dressed and often in the company of women half his age. He traded in his battered Rambler for a Jaguar and was trailed everywhere by his expensive dog, a golden Saluki.

The next year, he served as president of the San Francisco Bar Association, where he took credit for opening the doors of the organization to minorities and forcing the city to increase funding for the public defender's office. The position gave him a base from which he could flirt with politics. In 1976, at age forty-two, Wallach ran a disastrous campaign for the seat of popular U.S. Sen. John Tunney, dropping out of the race a month before the Democratic primary.

Meese's career took a different path. He went to work in the Alameda County district attorney's office, a straitlaced defender of law and order who made a name for himself by initiating more than 100 prosecutions to quash the Berkeley Free Speech Movement. His performance also attracted the notice of California's new conservative governor, Ronald Reagan, who recruited Meese to head his Office of Legal Affairs in Sacramento. Meese was one of a handful of California loyalists who would follow Reagan to Washington and enjoy the President's utmost confidence.

From the beginning, Meese was dogged by controversy. He served as chief of staff of the 1980 Reagan–Bush campaign, a position that eventually brought him under fire when it was discovered that the campaign had mysteriously secured secret debate briefing books from the Jimmy Carter campaign. Soon after Reagan's November victory, Meese helped set up a presidential trust funded by private contributions, an arrangement that brought him under investigation when it was discovered that he had received $10,000 from the trust, ostensibly for moving expenses. He was criticized by the press for everything from failing to report free trips and lodging to accepting jade and gold cufflinks from the government of South Korea.

But his closeness to Reagan was never questioned, nor was his absolute loyalty to old friends. Since the election, Meese had known that he would move into the White House to serve as counselor to the President, Reagan's right-hand man. He was formally named to the post the day after Reagan's inauguration on January 21, 1981.

He shared a bit of his new glory with Wallach by promptly naming him to the Presidential Task Force on the Administration of Justice. Wallach's head swelled. Later, he put his San Francisco friends on notice that he could serve as a link to the White House through his close friendship with Meese. He invited a group of fifty civic and legal leaders to a luncheon at Jack's Restaurant in San Francisco, where he earnestly touted himself as a conduit to the White House and urged his listeners to bring their problems and ideas for the Reagan administration to him. Some who attended were offended by Wallach's shameless self-marketing. Others, like Lipset, remember the occasion as an obvious sign of Wallach's political naiveté, not realizing that his Democratic history would preclude him from the ranks of the Reagan era's great movers and shakers.

Over the next few years, as Wallach sought to build a new Washington-based legal practice, he came to define himself almost solely in terms of his relationship with Meese. While working with Bechtel Corporation on a 1985 project to build a controversial oil pipeline in Iraq, he drafted a résumé for presentation to foreign leaders which listed as his professional qualifications:

Graduate of University of California School of Law, Berkeley, 1958-Valedictorian.

Classmate of Edwin Meese III; and Moot-Court Partner team of Meese/Wallach were States Champions. This was the beginning of a 27 year friendship involving regular close family and professional contact, from Mr. Meese's marriage, birth and raising of his children, his career as Governor Ronald Reagan's Chief aide to present.

Wallach, however, did not overstate his clout. From the day Meese moved into the White House to serve as one of Reagan's most influential advisers, his office door was open to Wallach. Proudly, Wallach penned a memo to his friend on his first day in office, suggesting candidates for positions in the new administration. Meese and Wallach had plans as early as 1980 of Wallach assuming some role in the new administration. Later that year, he defined a possible role for himself more clearly. He wanted a job that would be

. . . low-profile but significant, drawing upon my talents of organization and leadership to accomplish tasks, and my rather extensive, if sometimes superficial, range of knowledge, particularly in the world of foreign affairs . . .

Meese responded by helping his friend win a nonsalaried presidential appointment in November 1982 to the U.S. Advisory Commission of Public Diplomacy, a bipartisan group that oversees the programs of the U.S. Information Agency. From that point, Meese juggled his official calendar to meet with Wallach over an endless stream of meals, bought with public funds, during which Wallach shared his views on affairs of state and bantered with his oldest friend about his latest business propositions. They scheduled cross-country trips so they could fly together, often on government aircraft. Their contacts were so frequent between 1981 and 1987 that a list of them compiled by the Justice Department consumed forty-five typewritten pages.

When the two were apart, Wallach developed a habit of sharing his thoughts with Meese in detailed memos, written as letters to a friend. The correspondence, sometimes as frequent as two or three times a day, was dictated, typed onto Wallach's characteristic pale-blue or peach-colored stationery

and sent to Meese's White House office. The memos—
stamped "Personal and confidential"—served as both detailed
briefing papers on issues in the Soviet Union, Poland, and
Israel, and loving advice columns, touching on subjects like
Meese's vacation plans and his struggles to stay on the Pritikin
diet.

Virtually everything about Wallach rubbed Meese's conservative friends the wrong way. He and Meese were not only
philosophical opposites, but physically resembled the comedy
team of Laurel and Hardy. A jogger and fitness enthusiast who
tried unsuccessfully to coax his corpulent friend into an exercise regimen, Wallach was an intense man with a lean, narrow
face dominated by oversized ears and a carpet of thick, dark
eyebrows. Meese was round-faced, crimson-cheeked, and
roly-poly, a pleasant, lumbering fellow who would have
seemed at home running the lawnmower in a suburban backyard. In public, his voice boomed, and his eyes shifted nervously; it took only the slightest annoyance to send the blood
rushing to his cheeks.

The contrast in the two men was not only striking but unset-
tling to those who knew Meese. Former Meese associate Terry
Eastland recalled: "I couldn't understand what an ostensibly
conservative attorney general was doing with a palpably liberal San Francisco Democrat." Yet Wallach was so frequently
closeted with Meese—consuming so much of his official
time—that Eastland and other senior officials came to see him
principally as a "drain on executive branch energy."

Wallach's family bond with the Meeses, always close, was
cemented forever in 1982. The Meeses were out of town
when their oldest son, Scott, was killed in a car crash on a
winding road near their McLean, Virginia, home. Wallach
went to the morgue to identify the body and handled many
intimate details of the funeral. Wallach and his mother, Eva,
who worked part-time for the Jewish National Fund in Los
Angeles, later donated $5,000 to have a grove of trees planted
in Israel in Scott's memory.

In May 1986, they flew with Meese, his wife, Ursula, and
daughter, Dana, to Tel Aviv for the memorial service Wallach
arranged. It was a deeply emotional moment for Meese, and

Wallach made certain his important friend did not have to worry about the unpleasant details of overseas travel. He arranged for the New York-based Friends of Tel Aviv University to pick up the $4,000 tab for Meese's travel in exchange for his brief remarks to a university gathering. During the week-long trip, Wallach hovered over Meese, anticipating his every need as the group traveled to Jerusalem for a series of state events, including a dinner with President Herzog and Prime Minister Shimon Peres. Wallach's unflagging support during the Meese family's darkest days left Meese with "an emotional tie to that person . . . that probably could excuse anything," Eastland theorized.

But the Israel trip also demonstrated the disturbing flip side of the Meese–Wallach relationship—the frequent intersection of Wallach's private business interests with Meese's influential position. During the trip, on a stopover at the King David Hotel in Jerusalem, Wallach placed a call to Fred Neuberger, who happened to be in Israel checking on Carmo Industries, Wedtech's Israeli plant. Wallach told Neuberger that Meese wanted to meet him, and that he should stop by the hotel for an introduction. Neuberger arrived as Meese and his entourage were arriving in three chauffeured limousines, and went upstairs to have a drink with them.

Wallach's introduction of Meese almost immediately worked to the benefit of Wedtech. Neuberger and several Carmo officials used Meese's name to induce an Israeli bank to grant extensions on the repayment of a delinquent $2.5 million debt.

In 1985, when Wallach expressed an interest in a job as delegate to the United Nations Human Rights Commission, Meese went to bat for him, helping him secure an alternate position. Shortly afterward, Meese began making phone calls to the State Department and Office of Presidential Personnel pushing Wallach for a more prestigious slot as representative to the commission, with the rank of ambassador. Reagan approved the job on December 4, 1986, but by that time, the news media and federal investigators were closing in on the Meese–Wallach relationship. It was delayed at the Department of State and eventually withdrawn.

*   *   *

The Welbilt factory stood only a few blocks from the Grand Concourse neighborhood where Wallach had grown up. So in late April of 1981, as he met the company's officials to discuss a consulting job suggested by his friend Hal Lipset, Wallach was intrigued by the prospect of working with the Hispanic company; it appealed to his liberal sensibilities.

Like Mario Biaggi, Wallach was given the grand tour of the Welbilt plant. In an interview with Senate investigators years later, Wallach gave this version of his first meeting with John Mariotta and Mario Moreno:

> The plant outside was in a disheveled area of the Bronx. But inside was remarkable. They had all this fantastic computerized equipment. . . . It was a Saturday and they had a working shift going.
>
> And John and Mario walked through there and John knew everybody by their first name. There were maybe seventy-five to one hundred employees and they were all minority. . . . [T]here were some whites there, but they were all minority in the sense that they were all underpriveleged [sic]. It obviously was a South Bronx composite. . . .
>
> Then he took me upstairs and he showed me a chapel and they had Pentecostals and Seventh Day Adventists, Catholics and Jehovah's Witnesses and they would rotate for chapel worship, which I have only seen on military bases.

The Welbilt officials were equally taken with Wallach. He was not only sympathetic to their plight, he also held out real hope of helping them through his connection with Meese. Wallach told them he felt that the Reagan administration would have a vested interest in helping Welbilt, since its success would reflect positively on the White House.

Although Welbilt was too financially strapped to compensate Wallach adequately at the time, company officials agreed to pay him handsomely somewhere down the line if he could intervene on their behalf with his White House connections. Wallach agreed to assist them on one condition—the name of his "good friend" in the White House must never surface. In fact, after his initial conference with the eager Welbilt executives, Wallach would rarely mention Meese by name again.

He had hardly left the factory before he dashed off a long letter to Mariotta, marked "Personal and confidential," in which he spelled out what he needed to take Welbilt's case to Meese. He wanted an "Evaluation Brochure" to submit to the "appropriate person . . . on or about May 6, 1981." Wallach warned that the brochure "should be professional in appearance but need not be a work of art." He suggested that it include sections on the background of the contract talks, a general description of Welbilt, biographies of the officers "with emphasis on John," photographs and a statement of "Corporate philosophy." Wallach also asked that Lipset be provided with "information, if any, relating to the possible vulnerabilities in our position. The proposition of complete disclosure to those who seek to assist you must be followed completely. In this way, as I am sure you understand, we can both anticipate and evaluate the significance of any problem. . . . I believe that I have sufficient current information to hold meaningful discussions with appropriate persons on your behalf. . . ."

As promised, Wallach lost no time going to work on Welbilt's behalf. He had planned to accompany the Meeses to West Point during the weekend of May 6, to celebrate the birthday of Meese's son, Michael. As Wallach had requested, he was able to take along Welbilt's hurriedly prepared "Evaluation Brochure," which he left with his "good friend." Before leaving for San Francisco, he also had lunch with Meese and Meese's deputy, Herbert Ellingwood, and briefly discussed Welbilt's contract problems as well as the possibility that Mariotta be brought to the White House for an appearance that would mutually benefit the President and Mariotta.

Wallach followed up the meeting with a May 11, 1981, memo to Ellingwood referring to Mariotta as "an absolute perfect candidate for a breakfast, luncheon, or dinner speaker for a group which has a Christian orientation. . . . I sincerely believe that this is the kind of individual which the administration will want to feature as an absolute confirmation of the desire of Americans of minority background to 'make it on their own' and share in the great American dream. . . ."

He also went to work on the issue at hand—the stalled engine contract. He sent an Express Mail memo to Meese at the White House, warning him that Senator D'Amato was getting involved in the contract matter and might try to steal credit that could more appropriately go to the White House. He wrote that "a direct interview with Secretary Marsh or the intervention of Secretary Weinberger might be all that is necessary to accomplish the task." He also called Mariotta "a real find."

Two days later, with an even greater sense of urgency, he sent another Express Mail letter to Meese to warn him that the SBA might open the contract for competitive bidding. Over the next few months, Wallach wrote Meese about every turn and twist in the convoluted and prolonged contract dispute. If Meese considered the memos trivial, his actions did not show it. He assigned his staff to "look into" Welbilt's contract problems to see if the firm was getting a fair shake from the Army.

The task fell first to Edwin Thomas, who held the title of assistant counselor to the President. On May 19, Wallach dictated a lengthy telephone message to Thomas, alerting him that the SBA administrator, Michael Cardenas, was planning to testify before Congress on possible changes in the 8(a) pilot program. Wallach feared that Cardenas was about to cancel Welbilt's special designation for the Army contract.

Shortly after receiving the letter, Thomas dashed off a memo to Craig Fuller, a Meese aide who was director of the Office of Cabinet Affairs, asking Fuller to "look into" the Welbilt matter and report back to him or to Wallach. As if to signal the urgency, he wrote, "Bob Wallach . . . is an extremely close friend of Ed Meese."

Fuller asked his assistant director, T. Kenneth Cribb, to get a report from the SBA. Cribb placed a call to SBA Associate Deputy Administrator Robert Turnbull to advise him of the White House concerns.

The flurry of activity by Meese's aides on behalf of the small company would prove to be instrumental in helping Welbilt win the contract. But Meese, when asked in sworn testimony months later about the activities of his staff, claimed to have only a vague memory of the Welbilt saga.

He testified that he had only a "general recollection of . . . being asked by [Mr. Wallach] to see if we could be sure that . . . Welbilt was treated properly or fairly by the Army. . . ."

Meese would tell investigators many of the excruciatingly detailed memos from Wallach were never even opened.

5

THE NOFZIGER CONNECTION

THE WEDTECH GANG had a simple philosophy when lobbying the Reagan administration. They believed there was safety in numbers. While Wallach was working his promised magic with Meese, they began reaching out for other connections.

David Epstein persuaded the Welbilt executives to hire an old Harvard buddy named Dickey Dyer. A prominent Republican and civic leader, Dyer had built a respectable business as a consultant to hard-goods distributors. Even more appealing to the Welbilt executives, Dyer's kid sister, Margie, was married to James Pierce, the older brother of Barbara Bush, the wife of the Vice President. When Bush announced he would seek the 1980 Republican presidential nomination, he had called on Dyer for fund-raising help.

The connection was enough to convince the officials at Welbilt that Dyer was a man of considerable sway with the Vice President. When he got the call from Epstein, Dyer listened with interest to Welbilt's federal procurement saga and agreed to meet with Mariotta and Neuberger at the South Bronx plant. He suggested two New Jersey Congressmen who could help the company—Rep. James Courter, who sat on the House Armed Services Committee, and Rep. Christopher Smith, who held a post on the House Small Business Committee. Bush's name didn't come up, Dyer later told me.

Dyer was moved by the company's plight. "I thought it was as good as the Second Coming," he recalled. "It looked like they had a simple problem of cracking the bureaucracy." He agreed to work with Welbilt for a reduced fee of around $18,000 and to lobby his friends in Congress, who promptly wrote letters to Secretary of the Army John Marsh on Welbilt's behalf. Dyer himself wrote in August 1981. In a veiled reference to Dr. Keenan, Dyer noted that someone in Marsh's bureaucracy was "misbehaving" and explained that a speedy review of the contract by Marsh "will redound spectacularly to the credit of the Reagan–Bush administration."

Dyer also sent two letters to Bush. The first was an introductory note to alert Bush that the Welbilt officers were to attend a reception sponsored by LAMA at the Old Executive Office Building. Bush was to speak at the event, and Dyer suggested that he seek out the Welbilt officers. Bush did exactly that, shaking hands with the Welbilt executives.

A few weeks later, when it appeared the company might cut through the Army red tape and snare the engine contract, the officers asked Dyer to write Bush and invite him to the South Bronx to present the contract. Dyer did so, suggesting that the image of Bush standing in the rubble of Jimmy Carter's failed promises would be "good for America."

Dyer says he never got a response to the letter, for by that time Welbilt had hit another snag in the contract negotiations. Dyer personally became so discouraged by Marsh's response that he gave up on the company and terminated his consulting relationship. "I said to them, 'This thing is crooked. . . . Don't get involved in it. Look for something else,'" he recalled.

Soon afterward, Dyer also began pushing his friend Epstein

to speed up payment of his long-overdue consulting fees. Welbilt stretched out the payments so long that it took him until 1984 to collect.

Years later, when the FBI came to interview Dyer about his Welbilt work—by then a source of great embarrassment—he told the agents he could not fathom what had gone wrong with the noble Mariotta and his well-intentioned plan to save the South Bronx: " 'Mr. Dyer,' they told me, 'you obviously don't understand greed.' "

Buoyed by the signs of activity in Meese's office, the Welbilt executives were convinced that the White House was the key to winning the contract. What they sorely needed was exactly what Wallach was trying to deliver to them—a White House ally to take hold of the contract negotiations and ramrod them through a reluctant bureaucracy. They began seeking help from the White House office of Franklyn Curran "Lyn" Nofziger, the assistant to the President for political affairs.

Nofziger was a blunt, outspoken former California newspaperman who, along with Ed Meese, his friend of many years, was one of the old Reagan hands who followed him to Washington. Nofziger had worked for Reagan for the better part of twenty years. He was a reporter for the Copley News Service in Washington, covering the Barry Goldwater campaign, when Reagan's brother Neil recruited him in 1964 to go to work for the aspiring California governor. Nofziger at first did not know what to make of the idea; he had had newspaper ink in his blood since high school. At San José State College, he became the editor of the college newspaper, and after graduating, he was snapped up by the *Glendale News.* He spent eight years shuttling between the *News* and the *Burbank Press,* where he eventually rose to become managing editor.

Conservative politics was also in his nature. When he interviewed with Ronald Reagan, the two felt an instant chemistry. Nofziger believed from the start that this man could be President if he put his mind to it. He worked as Reagan's press secretary for three years, resigning amid charges that he had leaked unfavorable news to the press. Nofziger denied it, but his loose lip, combined with a permanently disheveled appearance, offended some loyal Reaganites, including the governor's wife, Nancy.

After persuading Reagan to challenge Richard Nixon for the Republican nomination in 1968, unsuccessfully, Nofziger went to work for eighteen months at the Nixon White House, where, among other distinctions, he helped draw up the notorious White House enemies list. He left the job to work for a spell as deputy chairman of the Republican National Committee. He managed Nixon's reelection campaign in California in 1972, then opened a political consulting firm in Los Angeles. Among his clients was 1976 presidential hopeful Ronald Reagan.

Reagan lost the GOP nomination to President Gerald Ford, who in turn suffered an embarrassing defeat at the hands of political neophyte Jimmy Carter. In 1977, Nofziger was again looking for work, and he found it—again with Reagan—as chairman of the Citizens for the Republic, a group set up by Reagan with $1 million in leftover campaign funds to keep his political organization intact for another try in 1980. The group offered campaign assistance to select conservative Republicans and worked amazingly well in building support for a Reagan nomination. When the Reagan campaign officially got off the ground, Nofziger, then fifty-six, emerged as the most visible and controversial member of his staff. With his beer belly and rumpled shirts, he squared off to protect Reagan against an often-hostile press and frequently found himself in hot water. Once, when a newspaper erroneously reported that Reagan had had a heart attack the previous year, Nofziger retaliated. "Write this down," he quipped. "Jimmy Carter has the clap." His irreverent sense of humor and his politics did not sit well with Reagan's campaign manager, John Sears, who pushed Nofziger farther and farther aside until he finally resigned from the campaign. After Sears himself was ousted, Nofziger was lured back by his old friend, the campaign's chief of staff, Ed Meese.

It was in his role as campaign press secretary that Nofziger accompanied Reagan on a fateful August 1980 campaign appearance in the South Bronx. Reagan already was leading Carter in New York State, but political analysts speculated that he needed to build support among working-class Democrats. Nofziger and other Reagan advisers were trying to wipe out what they insisted was a false perception that Reagan had no social conscience or understanding of the problems of minorities. The decaying South Bronx seemed the perfect place to prove it.

Although Carter had visited the South Bronx in 1977, promising $55.6 million for rehabilitation of the ravaged Charlotte Street neighborhood, the federal government had effected little change during the Carter years, largely because of its perpetual head-butting with the administration of Mayor Ed Koch. Reagan's appearance on the same vacant lot where Carter had stood three years earlier was a carefully calculated one-day visual, and Nofziger stood at his side while television cameras duly recorded the event. In the background stood a graffiti-strewn building spray-painted in bright orange with the word "Decay." Across the street was another boarded-up shell scrawled with the message, "Broken promises." Surveying the devastation, which he compared to "London after the Blitz," Reagan promised to rebuild the neighborhood through a new Republican approach hinged on tax incentives and the involvement of private industry.

But in a deviation from the script, about seventy demonstrators planted behind police barricades across the street began heckling Reagan, chanting "You ain't going to do nothing," and "Go back to California." Upset by the intrusion, Reagan crossed the street to confront them. "Look, if you will listen—I can't do a damned thing for you if I don't get elected!" But the chanting grew louder, especially when Reagan, angry and flustered, was whisked away to his waiting limousine.

In early 1981 Nofziger was installed by the newly elected President to run a new arm of the White House, the Office of Political Affairs. He took on the job as a temporary mission, telling the President and staff that he would stay only one year before leaving government. To remind himself of his vow, Nofziger grew back the beard he sported in World War II. He said he would not shave again until he left the White House.

The $60,663-a-year job—an outgrowth of Nofziger's work for Citizens for the Republic—was the first of its kind in the White House. Never before had an administration concentrated so much effort on ensuring its own survival. The office was designed, quite simply, to get Reagan reelected. It also served a certain public relations function since Nofziger, the first with a quick quote or witty one-liner, was a favorite source for many in the national news media.

At Nancy Reagan's insistence, Nofziger had been passed over as Reagan's first-term White House press secretary in favor of James Brady, who presented a more polished image. But it was Nofziger who calmed the nation when Reagan and Brady were felled in an assassination attempt. As soon as he heard the news, Nofziger took charge, rushing to Reagan's bedside, then going before the cameras to report on Reagan's condition. His easy manner had such a soothing effect that, for months afterward, he received fan mail from all over the nation. His performance also improved his relationship with Nancy Reagan. In characteristic fashion, Nofziger wrote her a note after the incident: "The President was not the only one. You done good, too."

He set up his shop in a spacious suite in the Old Executive Office Building, located 50 feet from the West Wing of the White House. The political shop soon emerged as the administration's real personnel office with input on thousands of federal appointments. When a name was recommended, it went through what was known as the "Nofziger clearance," a forty-eight-hour period in which his office could raise political objections to new appointees.

Nofziger ran his office casually, puttering around the office in his stocking feet and an oversized cardigan sweater, but behind the easygoing image was a ruthless political infighter. In 1981, when a group of Southern Democrats refused to go along with Reagan budget proposals, Nofziger hit them where it hurt with a negative publicity campaign in their districts. He also believed in amply rewarding Reagan's friends, assuring Republican state chairmen that they could each be assured of four patronage appointments in the new administration. Nofziger was a walking library of campaign promises and back-room deals—commitments he considered sacrosanct.

The memory of the South Bronx visit was still vivid in the fall of 1981 when an unpaid assistant to Nofziger, Pier Talenti, had an audience with the director of LAMA, Stephen Denlinger. Denlinger had replaced Mariotta's friend, José Aceves, who left LAMA in 1979. Denlinger was more than familiar with Welbilt's problems. He had recruited Mariotta to join his organization while conducting a membership drive in the New York area, and by 1981, out of a membership of more than 100 Hispanic-owned or operated businesses, Welbilt had come to preoccupy much of LAMA's energy. Unbeknownst to the LAMA board, Welbilt had struck a deal with Denlinger to supplement his modest association salary by $2,000 a month in return for his concentrated efforts to help the company win the engine contract. They considered him such a team player that, at one point, they asked him to pass along a $10,000 bribe to a friendly SBA official in Washington. When the official turned down the money, Denlinger pocketed it himself. In all, he received between $175,000 and $200,000 from Welbilt in return for his free-lance consulting work. He pleaded guilty to conspiracy to bribe a public official.

Denlinger began knocking on White House doors in August 1981, making visits to the Office of Public Liaison and to Nofziger's office. The public liaison office was headed by Elizabeth Dole, a charming Southerner whose own Republican Party credentials were enhanced by her marriage to the powerful Kansas senator, Robert Dole.

At Dole's office, Denlinger gained an audience with aide Henry Zuniga, an assistant to the president on Hispanic issues, and Wayne Valis, a minority affairs adviser. Again, he went through the saga of Welbilt's frustrating contract negotiations, emphasizing the political ramifications for Reagan if the deal fell through. Zuniga agreed to contact the SBA, and Valis agreed to put the White House imprint on a letter drafted by Denlinger to Army Secretary Marsh.

Valis made no attempt to check out Denlinger's assertions;

he merely sent the September 4 letter to Marsh, noting that "a matter affecting an important constituency group has come to my attention. . . . This is of interest to us, since the President made a campaign appearance in the Bronx a year ago (Aug. 5, 1980). . . ."

Down the hall at Nofziger's office, Denlinger met with Talenti, a multilingual, Italian-born engineer who was one of several volunteers working in Nofziger's office. In the Nofziger shop, Talenti was generally viewed as a nuisance who was always buttonholing the busy staff to push his projects.

Because of his engineering background, Talenti listened to the Welbilt story with particular interest and accepted Denlinger's invitation to see the South Bronx miracle for himself. On August 17, he toured the Welbilt factory and met with Mariotta, Neuberger, and Moreno. The message he got from the principals, he later recalled, was "audit, audit, audit."

Talenti's visit gave the Welbilt officers new hope. For the first time, as Moreno described it later, they believed they had a real chance of thwarting the Army's opposition.

On August 28, Talenti placed two phone calls to the Army, first to Army General Counsel Delbert Spurlock, who had won appointment to the office with Nofziger's help. He also summoned three Army officials—Juanita Watts, the director of the Office of Small and Disadvantaged Business, Robert Stohlman, an aide to Assistant Army Secretary Jay Raymond Sculley, and Watts's aide, Col. Albert Spaulding—to the White House to discuss the audit. He told them, "These people are waiting for an audit. Give them an audit. Tell them if they are no good."

Somewhere around that time, Talenti brought up the subject of Welbilt during one of the daily 8 A.M. staff meetings conducted by Nofziger. Nofziger, as his assistant Ed Rollins later recalled, was at least aware of Welbilt in "broad detail" since the company "was discussed enough that I can remember it after five years."

Welbilt also solicited Nofziger's aid from another angle. In October, a package of memos arrived on Nofziger's desk from Phillip Sanchez, who worked as a special consultant to LAMA on Hispanic business concerns and had been hired by Welbilt to put in an extra pitch for the company. The Welbilt executives were attracted to Sanchez for two reasons. Besides his contacts with Nofziger, his résumé also included a stint as an aide to Frank Carlucci, who was then serving as deputy secretary of defense. Welbilt had been led to believe Carlucci might be the one to make the final decision on the Army contract, and Sanchez's advocacy might thus be especially important.

Sanchez hand-delivered an "Action Memo" to Nofziger entitled "Hispanic Political Opportunity in New York." He described Mariotta as "a modest, soft-spoken Hispanic manufacturing genius who has built a multi-million dollar empire in the ghetto, employing over 250 people, most of them former welfare recipients." He went on, "John Mariotta, president of Welbilt Electronic Die Corporation, should be invited to the White House for a picture with President Reagan. I believe that this 15-minute session in the Oval Office would yield significant political pluses for our Administration. That photo on the walls of corporate headquarters of Welbilt in the Bronx will be a constant link with us."

The concept of using Welbilt to promote White House interests appealed to Nofziger. Sanchez visited him in October and repeated the idea. "I hope we can get some things moving here. I will try," Nofziger promised in a letter. He also sent copies of the package of Sanchez memos to Dole with the notation: "His ideas, I think, are great." Nofziger said it would be a good idea for his shop and Dole's to work together on the project.

On September 8, Welbilt won its first victory. The Army, pressured from all sides, agreed to conduct an audit, a decision handed down by Assistant Secretary Sculley's office over the strong objections of Keenan and his men in St. Louis. The decision was made purely because high-ranking Army brass were "getting hit over the head" by the White House, one official later explained. Keenan, however, was unintimidated. In an angry conversation with the persistent Denlinger, Keenan reportedly told him, "I've had experience countering White House pressure before. You're not getting the contract." His obstinacy was promptly communicated to the highest levels of government. Sanchez wrote Nofziger: "Pier Talenti has been helpful, but he needs your added clout. . . . If Dr. Keenan continues his apparent predisposition against Welbilt he should, at best, be removed from this case and replaced with someone more in tune with the stated objectives of this Administration."

The Army audit proved to be a mixed blessing. It concluded that Welbilt's $38 million price, which included the cost of tooling a new factory, contained about $6 million in questionable costs but at least could be used as a basis for negotiating a price. Keenan, however, would not give up. He sent in his own team of auditors from St. Louis who brought back an unfavorable report and concluded that Welbilt's price was still $10 million more than the Army could possibly accept. The impasse continued as the year drew to a close.

The month of January 1982 was an important one for Welbilt and for Nofziger, who, as promised, was preparing to leave the administration to start a private consulting firm. He had spent most of his life earning modest government salaries or scraping by on newspaper pay. His goal, he told his associate Ed Rollins, was to "put away one or two million dollars in a couple of years," then retire.

With the Reagan–Bush team in place for an indefinite stay, Nofziger had two highly marketable assets—his closeness to the President and wealth of White House connections. After several discussions with prospective partners, he decided to set up shop in Washington with Mark Bragg, a former Navy officer and California radio newsman who had worked in Reagan's 1980 California campaign. Bragg was a recent convert to Republican ideas, having once supported the presidential campaign of liberal George McGovern. Bragg agreed to run the office and take care of mundane day-to-day business. Nofziger had to do little more than sign letters, make phone calls, and put his name on the stationery.

As Nofziger's departure neared, Talenti seemed determined to resolve the contract dispute. If anything, Welbilt seemed to be losing ground. Despite discreet warnings from

Talenti and Zuniga that the contract was important to the White House, the SBA's director, Michael Cardenas, was doing little to move the talks with the Army along. Cardenas had even hinted that he might be ready to open the contract to competitive bidding.

Cardenas, a California businessman approved by Nofziger for the SBA job largely because of his Hispanic credentials, had taken office early in March 1981, determined to clean up the agency. He quickly became a thorn in the side of the administration. Cardenas seemed to court controversy, showing up late or not at all for scheduled appointments and failing to return congressional phone calls. Internally, Cardenas almost touched off an insurrection with his crackdown on unnecessary spending and his disdain for the SBA's bloated ranks. Occasionally, he ordered his staff in from the suburbs for 7:30 A.M. weekend staff meetings that had no apparent purpose.

In early January 1982, with the Army still unwilling to sign the Welbilt contract, Cardenas and Donald Templeman, his deputy administrator, called a meeting at SBA headquarters of representatives from the Army, the SBA, and Welbilt. The purpose of the meeting was for the Army to explain its refusal to accept Welbilt pricing. The Army came into the meeting with a firm position—it was not budging one inch to accommodate Welbilt. But the participants at the meeting got a clear signal that their actions were being closely watched when Talenti and Zuniga signed in as representatives of the White House. The SBA officials "looked at each other and raised our eyebrows," Templeman recalled.

At one point in the meeting, Talenti rose to defend the company, telling the Army officers, "Give them a fair chance. Tell them that they are no good. Tell them the SBA can cover the difference in price. But tell them something. This thing is almost a year old." Talenti concluded his remarks by noting— as Wallach related it in a memo to Meese—that this was "Lyn's last week, and it would be nice if he could go out with a bang and get this contract."

But the day after the session, things took a turn for the worse. The Army officially requested that the SBA withdraw its designation of Welbilt so the contract could be put out for bids. This action put the matter squarely in the court of SBA administrator Cardenas.

Cardenas did not know what to make of the meeting and the unusual display of White House interest. Not long after taking office, he had been visited by Sanchez and warned that the contract was important because of a Reagan campaign promise. He also had been called to the White House by Vice President Bush in the fall of 1981 to explain, in a general way, how the pilot program worked.

But the Army had convinced Cardenas that Welbilt was perhaps an unwise choice for the plum. He was reluctant to move until their objections had been satisfied, so he decided not to push the Welbilt contract through. The decision may have been one of the most consequential he made during his one-year term in office. Scarcely a month after the unsuccessful meeting at the SBA, Cardenas was notified that he was being removed as administrator under the specific order of Meese, James Baker, and Michael Deaver.

Waiting in the wings to take Cardenas' place was one of his assistants, a low-key operator named James Sanders. Sanders, a California insurance agent, was a personal friend of White House aide Mike Deaver and had been recruited to serve as Cardenas' associate administrator for management. Cardenas had taken him on reluctantly after receiving his name on a "Must Hire" list from Nofziger's office. Sanders' performance as Cardenas' deputy was hardly distinguished, but he was capable of doing what he was told without attracting headlines.

While Sanders' confirmation was pending, Templeman was named acting SBA director. He had been in office only a few days when he received a letter from Wallach urging him to approve the Welbilt contract—a matter of "true urgency," which could not wait on Sanders' confirmation. Templeman says he never read the letter. Unaware of Wallach's White House connections, his secretary shipped the letter to a more appropriate destination, the SBA's minority small business office.

Nofziger was not able to leave office with the "big bang" his aide had hoped for, but in his last days, Welbilt was rewarded with a ringing endorsement from the Reagan White House. At the initiative of Dole's office, Mariotta had been included on a select list of presidential guests for a conference on an Urban Enterprise Zone bill backed by the administration. Years later, when federal investigators tried to piece together who was responsible for pushing Mariotta's name, no one would admit to it. But the list had to be cleared by both Dole's and Nofziger's offices.

Photos of the event, which were used in Welbilt's promotional efforts, show Mariotta seated at Reagan's side in the Oval Office, where he confidently lectured the President, Vice President Bush, and an assemblage of high-ranking dignitaries on the successes of his little company. In the background sat Democratic Rep. Robert Garcia, whose Bronx district encompassed Welbilt and who had coauthored the Reagan-backed Urban Enterprise Bill with Buffalo Republican Rep. Jack Kemp.

It was a proud moment. Reagan was so impressed with Mariotta that he asked that the seats for a luncheon be arranged so he could sit next to him. Mariotta's performance of the twenty-minute, Epstein-scripted lecture was so flawless that, after the event, Meese came up to shake his hand.

The next day, January 22, 1982, Lyn Nofziger resigned from office to go to work at his new company, Nofziger & Bragg Communications. One of the first clients in line to retain the high-powered new consulting firm was the Welbilt Electronic Die Corporation.

6

PRESSURE
FROM ABOVE

LYN NOFZIGER AND MARK BRAGG were retained by Steve
Denlinger as consultants to LAMA on March 8, 1982, primarily to represent Welbilt on the engine matter. In short order,
Nofziger—relying mostly on Bragg as his message bearer—
put the people that mattered on notice that the White House
had an interest in seeing the contract talks wrapped up and the
prize awarded to Welbilt. The message was quickly dissemi-
nated throughout the bureaucracy, for no one who owed his
job and allegiance to the Reagan administration doubted Nofziger's residual influence.

At the Pentagon, the warning went out to Army Secretary
John Marsh from his general counsel, Delbert Spurlock, on
March 29: "It is likely that you will be getting a call from Lyn
Nofziger on the Welbilt matter today. He will indicate the

presence of White House interest in contracting in the South Bronx where Welbilt is located. I have indicated to his associate (Mark Bragg) and to Mr. Talenti at the White House that $24 million is about as much as the Army technical people would justify in awarding the Welbilt contract. Even this amount is apparently very high. . . .''

When the expected call from Nofziger came that afternoon, Marsh returned it promptly. He later told a Senate subcommittee that Nofziger was just "letting us know he was interested" in the engine negotiations—nothing more. At Marsh's afternoon meeting, already scheduled to discuss the disagreeable Welbilt issue, he and his deputies decided that, despite the White House pressure, they could not reasonably change their position to accommodate Welbilt, whose price was deemed "too great for reasonable negotiations."

At the SBA, Administrator Jim Sanders had been in office only two weeks before he was summoned to a May 3 lunch at Nofziger & Bragg's townhouse offices to discuss their new South Bronx client. It never occurred to Sanders that there could be perception of a conflict of interests in his socializing with the lobbyists for his agency's most politically active 8(a) firm. As he described it to the Senate Subcommittee on Oversight of Government Management: "I think they invited me to come to lunch, and I considered because of the prominence of Nofziger that it would be useful to do that. . . ."

Nofziger also succeeded in doing something that Bob Wallach had been unable to achieve in more than a year of incessant efforts. Nofziger galvanized his old friend, Ed Meese, into action. Although forbidden by federal ethics rules from lobbying the White House until one year after leaving office, Nofziger met with Meese on the Welbilt contract in early April and followed up the session with this characteristically blunt April 8 memo written on Nofziger & Bragg stationery. He urged Meese to contact Marsh, adding that the Army chief also would "listen carefully to Carlucci or Weinberger . . . or even Reagan.

"Ed," he wrote, "I really think it would be a blunder not to award that contract to Welbilt. The symbolism either way is very great here."

The memo, written only a few months after Nofziger vacated his White House post, would prove to be a crucial miscalculation on Nofziger's part, once the Wedtech case caught up with him. It formed the basis of one of the counts of violations of the Ethics in Government Act of which Nofziger was convicted in February 1988, a judgment later overturned by a Court of Appeals panel. Meese, while not prosecuted for aiding and abetting Nofziger's lobbying, was roundly criticized by Justice Department ethics officials for not stopping Nofziger from lobbying him before the year's moratorium was over.

Wallach was still flooding Meese's office with information on Welbilt, including a detailed flow chart of Army personnel involved in the matter along with their telephone numbers and thumbnail descriptions on where they stood.

The memo, titled "Key Participants," gave Meese background on Marsh, Sculley, and George Dausman, the Acting Deputy Secretary for Acquisitions, whom Wallach called the "key obstacle at DOA." Dausman "has supported Dr. Keenan's hard line almost as vigorously as Keenan himself," Wallach wrote.

Much further down in the chain of command, Wallach's summaries also included an assessment of Dr. Keenan which read, "he is the key protagonist in the entire MSE project— professes to be for the project, yet has done everything conceivable to defeat it. . . ."

Except for tracking the matter, making a few phone calls, and keeping Meese informed, Meese's staff had taken little action on the Welbilt matter. Nofziger's April 1982 memo, however, set off a chain of events. Meese, who later claimed little memory of actions taken on his behalf, assigned his assistant Jim Jenkins to look into the matter and make sure Welbilt got a "fair hearing."

Meese's instructions were closely followed by a visit from Bragg and Denlinger, who called on Jenkins to brief him on the contract status. Jenkins, a rotund fellow with drooping jowls that gave his face a permanent look of displeasure, had a personal stake in seeing the contract successfully signed and

delivered. It would please his boss and also Nofziger, whom
Jenkins considered a close friend and longtime professional
ally. It would also pave the way for a lucrative deal for Jenkins
himself.

A little more than a year after he left the White House in
May 1984, Jenkins signed on as a Wedtech consultant, working at first out of Nofziger & Bragg's offices. Eventually, he
was named Wedtech's first full-time Washington marketing
director. Jenkins earned $169,055 from the company in
1985–86 and won options to purchase 30,000 shares of stock
at below-market rates.

At Welbilt, Wallach sent word to David Epstein that he had
spoken to "Ed" and learned that the matter would be handled
by Jenkins. The company executives did what they could to
highlight for Jenkins the importance of their cause. Denlinger
sent Jenkins a handwritten note extolling Mariotta's Republican connections and contributions.

The Army seemed unimpressed by Jenkins' entry into the
fray. Battered from all sides, Marsh and his lieutenants had
recently come under pressure from another contingent interested in the engine contract, this one led by Wisconsin Sen.
Robert Kasten on behalf of the Chrysler Motor Corporation.
Kasten had been informed of the unusual White House interest in the engine contract and dashed off a letter to Deputy
Defense Secretary Frank Carlucci, demanding to know what
was going on. Kasten sensed a "political decision" had been
made to award the contract to Welbilt.

On April 16, worn down by months of debate, Secretary
Marsh called together Spurlock, Jay Raymond Sculley, and
other top officials to settle the matter once and for all. They
decided to put their collective foot down. None of them
wanted Welbilt to have the contract. It was their unanimous
decision that awarding the contract to Welbilt was not in the
best interests of the government. Marsh said the decision was
final—the Army would commence a competitive solicitation
and award the contract to a deserving company.

Spurlock was placed in charge of informing the appropriate
parties and sent out letters to Sanders, Addabbo, and
D'Amato. He also notified Denlinger, who in turn called

Bragg to break the bad news. Bragg replied that, on the contrary, other things were happening that gave cause for optimism.

One optimistic sign was that Spurlock still seemed to be wavering. His office was required to give the go-ahead to TSARCOM to seek bids on the job, but Spurlock was sitting on the authorization letter.

At the White House, Jenkins was convinced that some way could be found to bridge the gap between Welbilt's offer and what the Army was willing to pay. He had contacted Templeman at the SBA; perhaps the SBA could kick in a few million dollars to make Welbilt's proposal more palatable.

The Army had asked the agency in March if it would provide additional funding to Welbilt through a Business Development Expense grant, an allocation generally made to a company for the purchase of new equipment. Templeman's assistant, Robert Turnbull, had written back that the SBA usually limited its BDE grants to $100,000. "For us to make a multi-million dollar BDE grant to a single firm would, we believe, raise questions about our management of the 8(a) program as a whole," he wrote.

Templeman also had not resolved his concerns about Welbilt's ability to do the work. The company was essentially a sheet metal fabricator, which had never before engaged in so complex a task as building an engine. He worried that the size of the contract—ten times the size of the company's previous largest project—would be too much for the company to handle and create severe management problems for Welbilt.

But under pressure from Jenkins, who called his office numerous times in the spring of 1982, Templeman had reevaluated the agency's position. First and foremost, he saw himself as a presidential appointee whose mission was to "do what we could do" to carry out the wishes of the White House. He looked at the money available under BDE grants—approximately $6 million that year for the entire nation—and decided it was not unreasonable for the SBA to allocate $3 million to Welbilt. He testified later, however, that he never would have gone along with the allocation without the White House interest.

Jenkins also brought pressure to bear on Templeman's boss, Jim Sanders. On April 22, Jenkins wrote him:

> Ed Meese has asked me to look into the Welbilt problem . . . which has been too long on the back burner.
>
> I expect that a meeting here between the Army, Welbilt, SBA plus others possibly, will be necessary in order to resolve the issue. However, before I call such a meeting, I would like to meet privately to be briefed on the SBA's role, its actions to date, commitment if any, etc., and to get SBA's recommendations.

On May 7, Sanders trooped over to the White House for a private talk with Jenkins. As Sanders later explained it to the Senate, Jenkins called him over for one purpose—so he "understood the importance of a contract like this to the administration."

Finally, Jenkins told Templeman he intended to call a meeting at the White House to bring together the Army and SBA. Welbilt, he explained, had been working with various federal, state and city agencies to try to generate additional funding and support. But the financing package was extremely fragile. Welbilt had gotten a commitment from HUD for a grant to help it buy an abandoned building near the company's headquarters, which would be used to set up the engine assembly line. But HUD had imposed a June 21 deadline for Welbilt to provide the contract documents. Time was of the essence or the entire funding package could collapse.

Jenkins also briefed another interested party on his plans for this unprecedented meeting. When Wallach dropped by to see Meese in early May, Jenkins told him about it, and Wallach passed word to the Welbilt executives. Things were definitely looking up.

No one at the federal agencies involved in the dispute had ever seen such a display of White House interest in a procurement matter—for understandable reasons. White House counsel Fred Fielding had bluntly warned White House staffers in 1981 to steer clear of involvement in procurement matters. He had circulated a lengthy memo, which was later incorporated into an official policy statement, warning that "no member of the White House staff should contact any procurement officer about a contract in which he has a personal financial interest or in which a relative, friend or business associate has a financial interest. This is true not only as to calls or contacts in which influence is directly exerted, but also as to so-called 'status' calls or other communications. . . .''

The warning should have prevented Meese's office from ever intervening in the Welbilt contract dispute. Meese knew his friend Wallach had been retained by the company, and Nofziger certainly made no secret of the fact that he had taken on Welbilt as a client. Meese passed the matter on to Jenkins, but Jenkins also considered Nofziger a close friend, which should have triggered special precautions.

As he began preparing for the White House meeting, Jenkins was concerned enough by the ethical questions to run it by Cabinet Secretary Craig Fuller. As Jenkins described the situation in a memo to Fuller:

> Lyn Nofsiger [*sic*] has asked Ed Meese to urge the Army to award this contract to Welbilt instead of to Chrysler. The Bronx needs the jobs.
>
> I think that instead, Ed (by memo) or you directly should simply ask for a status report, or for a copy of the response to this LAMA letter to Spurlock. Quite possibly, we should do nothing at all. Do you have existing guidance on this type of thing?

Fuller needed only to recall the cautionary Fielding memos to send off a handwritten response. "Strongly recommend that no White House action be taken," it said. Jenkins, however, was undeterred by Fuller's pointed advice. He later told Senate investigators that "he [Fuller] wasn't my boss, so he couldn't tell me not to."

He summoned Army and SBA procurement officials to the White House for a meeting on the Welbilt contract. He testified later he was certain Meese would have been told about the meeting. Meese said he could not remember.

*   *   *

The meeting, which took place on May 19, was attended by Sculley and Spurlock from the Army and Templeman from the SBA, as well as a Welbilt delegation that included Mariotta, Moreno, Ehrlich, and lobbyists Denlinger and Bragg, and three representatives from the City of New York's Urban Development Action Grant office. They met in the Ward Room, a basement pub adjacent to the White House mess which had been reserved at noon for a luncheon. In the background, the sound of clattering dishes reminded them that they had only minutes to work out a two-year-old dispute.

Jenkins, in a calm, reasonable voice, took command at the head table, with Templeman at his side. Templeman had come prepared to announce the SBA's willingness to forward the $3 million BDE grant and an additional $2 million in advance payments to Welbilt. The two faced the Army delegation head-on. But the confrontational spirit had mysteriously evaporated by then. Sculley came in "like he had been dragged in like a little dog on a leash," Moreno later recalled. He said little, deferring to Jenkins.

Jenkins quickly laid the ground rules. He wanted to find a way to narrow the $1.75 million price difference that remained between Welbilt and the Army's acceptable price. He reminded the participants of the President's campaign promise to deliver jobs to the South Bronx. With the award of the contract, Welbilt had promised to hire 300 new employees, making it one of the South Bronx's largest employers. The argument was suddenly persuasive to the Army—which had decided a month earlier to deny the contract to Welbilt and seek competitive bids. Apparently Sculley at last had realized what a good idea it would be to pump money into the South Bronx firm.

The bureaucrats exited the meeting like shamed schoolboys slinking out of the woodshed, leaving Moreno and the Welbilt team confident they would get the contract. As Moreno later testified, "We realized the White House was involved now, all the way."

After the meeting, a week passed with no response, and the Welbilt officials began to get nervous again. The HUD deadline was nearing, and they were in danger of losing their claim on the dilapidated building at 350 Gerard Avenue, which they planned to use as their factory site. With the entire engine contract contingent on their having the actual facilities to do the work, they approached their representatives with a sense of urgency. They had to have the contract soon, they claimed, or their factory site would be lost.

Denlinger called Bragg, who called Jenkins and Spurlock. Jenkins advised them to ask the Army and the SBA for "letters of intent," assuring Welbilt that the contract was on the way. The Army was not in the practice of issuing letters of intent, but in this case, perhaps an exception could be made to buy additional time.

There were some practical problems in carrying out the advice. Nofziger had suffered a mild stroke and was at home recuperating. Bragg was preparing to fly to the West Coast for his wedding and a honeymoon in the Bahamas. On his wedding day, Bragg and Denlinger kept the cross-country phone lines hot with calls back and forth about the Welbilt problem. Denlinger drafted a letter requesting a "letter of intent" and addressed it to Sanders, signed by a secretary at the lobbying firm with Bragg's name.

Jenkins mounted pressure from his end. He called Templeman demanding to know why the SBA hadn't formally committed the $3 million business development grant. One problem, Templeman explained, was that Welbilt had not yet submitted a formal letter requesting the assistance.

But the SBA officials were so rattled by Jenkins' phone call that Sanders signed a formal commitment letter on June 18, 1982. Later, they would describe it as a mere technicality that they approved the grant ten days before the company submitted its letter asking for money.

Sculley followed suit by directing TSARCOM to make "all possible efforts" to award the Welbilt contract by September 30, 1982. No one seemed to care that most of the Army's original concerns about the company had not been addressed. In addition, new doubts had surfaced, raising questions about Welbilt's financial capability. An Army audit had shown that Welbilt was likely to overrun the contract by $200,000.

But the White House clearly had spoken, and the Army, like the SBA, was left with little choice but to carry out the wishes of the President. The Army juggled its figures, added a few million dollars to cover revised contract language and raised its Fair Market Price from $23.6 million to $27.8 million, a price Welbilt deemed acceptable. On September 13, 1982, Welbilt and the Army finally came to agreement on the proposed price.

Sanders' office trumpeted the deal in a press release headlined "$28 Million SBA Award to South Bronx Firm Boosts Economy—Creates Jobs." Sanders went on to say that Welbilt is "one of our America's best investments," a company that by then had amassed $48 million in federal contracts and planned to double its work force.

The October 4 signing ceremony was a joyous victory celebration for Welbilt. Although Wallach failed to bring President Reagan out for the signing, politicians from every level of government turned out to take their share of the credit: Biaggi; D'Amato, who called Welbilt's success a "remarkable effort" by all levels of government to revitalize the South Bronx; Neglia; and Sanders, who flew in from Washington along with HUD Secretary Pierce.

In a press conference, Mariotta graciously thanked the hateful Army officials at TSARCOM, saying, "They really put us through the paces, and we are going to give them the best engine ever, on time and at cost."

The promise proved to be little more than hot air. For, as the Army's auditors had discerned, Welbilt was in the throes of a serious financial crisis. Within three months, Welbilt could not pay its vendors, who were demanding cash in advance of delivery. The company soon fell behind on its deliveries. The first engines were a year late, and its final deliveries were two years behind schedule. Although it collected $22 million of the promised $27.7 million, Welbilt in the end delivered only 4,892 of the 13,100 engines it had contracted to build.

But that distressing ending couldn't have mattered less to Meese's office in the fall of 1982. Bragg called Jenkins to congratulate him on his skilled delivery of what had seemed like an impossible task a few months earlier. Jenkins sent Meese a copy of Sanders' press release, with a telling note. "Though you cannot tell from reading any of this, your personal go-ahead to me saved this project," it said.

Mariotta penned a grateful letter to President Reagan—with copies to White House aides Elizabeth Dole and Henry Zuniga—inviting him to drop by the Welbilt plant on a scheduled trip through the New York area. He attributed his victory to a joint venture between "our silent partner, God" and Ronald Reagan.

The next day, the Welbilt crew and their White House allies felt another rush when CBS anchorman Dan Rather did a late afternoon radio report. He told about Welbilt's engine contract victory, which, he said, was due largely to John Mariotta, an American success story. In graphic detail, Rather reported Mariotta's rags-to-riches story and his "Buy One, Get One Free" philosophy that jobs at Welbilt meant reduction in the federal welfare rolls.

"In his office there is a memento that suggests he is succeeding: a picture of Mariotta talking to a man with a well-known face," Rather said. "They are talking about urban enterprise zones. The well-known face is that of the President of the United States. He is listening most intently."

CORPORATE
CRAZINESS

WITHIN WEEKS AFTER the engine contract was signed, Mariotta and Moreno found themselves in another meeting a world away from the White House. This one was in a cheap cafeteria in the Hunts Point section of the Bronx, just around the corner from the friendly New York National Bank.

The Welbilt executives had just deposited their $3 million SBA business development grant in the bank. But the SBA funds, earmarked specifically to help Welbilt buy new equipment to build the Army engines, offered no way out of a financial crisis in which the company found itself.

Despite the glowing picture its executives had tried to portray to federal officials, Welbilt was going broke at record speed. Like a ravenous monster, the company was growing too rapidly, greedily acquiring contract after contract before it had the capital or resources to support them. Moreno had coined a phrase for the company's unsound business philosophy. He called it "feeding the beast."

Welbilt was keeping its head above water only by winning new federal contracts and surviving for a time on the advance payments and government grants that came with them. Soon after the engine contract was approved, the Welbilt executives realized their first payments could not realistically be expected until June 1983. Unless some new source of funding were found, the overextended company would be bankrupt within a matter of weeks.

Mariotta and Moreno had grown accustomed to turning for help to New York National, where both of them were major stockholders. Founded in February 1982 with $6 million in assets, the bank had amassed $40 million in assets and ranked as one of the nation's largest Hispanic-owned banks. It, too, had benefited from glowing national publicity and from deposits from federal, state, and city agencies. It also boasted a special relationship with members of the Bronx political machine; relatives of both Biaggi and Simon held bank stock and Representative Garcia had used the bank as a source of personal loans.

The bank also had been approved by the Small Business Administration to disburse SBA monies, a designation it won shortly after Irizarry left the agency to become New York National's vice president. Welbilt had quickly emerged as the bank's single most important client. As a gesture of gratitude, Welbilt's officers came to expect a range of highly unusual services. To prevent Welbilt from overdrawing its account, the bank frequently held Welbilt's checks in limbo until enough money had been deposited to cover them. Welbilt also was one of the first to line up for a $150,000 loan from New York National when it opened its doors, an amount that then was the bank's lending limit under federal regulations.

Though they had already borrowed as much money as legally allowed, Mariotta and Moreno held out hope that their friends at New York National could once again come to Welbilt's rescue. In the Hunts Point cafeteria, Moreno laid out the facts to Irizarry and Serafin Mariel, the bank's president: They needed $500,000 as soon as possible, or Welbilt would no longer exist.

According to Moreno, Mariel listened but responded with bad news. "The bank is restricted with loans it can give to a single company, but there is a person who would be willing to consider a request for financing. The interest will be very high . . . and the amount will have to be given in cash," Moreno recalled him saying.

Moreno testified that Mariel would not identify the potential financier, but that he defined the terms of the loan: The officers were expected to repay within three months; the money would be lent at a 100 percent interest rate—which would translate into $150,000 on a $500,000 loan; and they could not deposit the money at New York National. (Under federal banking law, cash transactions over $10,000 have to be reported to the Treasury Department.)

The arrangements gave the Welbilt officers pause. The loan smelled bad to them. But Moreno told Mariotta, "John, the situation is so bad that . . . I don't see any other solution. . . ." The two of them talked with Neuberger and agreed there was no other alternative but to go ahead with the suspicious and possibly dangerous deal. At a second meeting with the bank officers a short time later, they gave Mariel the go-ahead. Mariel said he would let them know when the money was available.

A few weeks later, Moreno said he got a call from Mariel, who told him to bring Mariotta and Neuberger to the bank offices at noon on a Friday to pick up the money. They arrived on time and waited an hour and a half before Mariel rushed in, carrying a black briefcase. He closed the door and opened the satchel. Inside were neatly arranged stacks of $50 and $100 bills.

Neuberger gasped. He had never seen so much money crammed into a single briefcase, and the sight of it was awesome. Mariel wanted to run the money through the bank's counting machine, but when he found out the machine was broken, he and Irizarry poured out the stacks of cash and began counting it by hand. Finally, the officers testified, Mariel turned over the money, instructing a bank guard to accompany the three Welbilt officers to Mariotta's car as a safety precaution.

They did not discuss the source of the money. But when the briefcase was emptied, Neuberger spotted a white business card in the briefcase bearing the name of Pat Simone. The very mention of the name gave the Welbilt officers pause, for unlike the easily bamboozled federal funding agencies, they felt they could not trifle with Pat Simone. Simone was a well-known figure in the Bronx, a major owner of commercial real estate whose principal business was a huge auto parts salvage yard on Sheridan Avenue—a sophisticated, highly computerized operation that dealt in huge sums of cash. Bronx authorities had been intrigued with Simone's operation since his son, Donne, was shot gangland-style outside the auto yard on March 11, 1981. Donne died the next day. Police finally attributed it to an act of vengeance by a disgruntled former employee.

Simone was known to exert strong control over the operations of New York National through another son, Joseph, a bank officer and director. The presence of Joseph Simone's name on the bank's licensing application to the Comptroller of the Currency had prompted concern. Federal investigators had checked out the Donne Simone murder for links to organized crime, but approval of the bank's license was granted after they could prove no solid underworld links. In private conversation, Pat Simone frequently referred to New York National as "his" bank—a prospect the Welbilt officials suddenly found sobering. They knew that, despite their dire financial status, they had better find some way to repay the loan promptly.

With their briefcase full of cash, they headed for a midtown Manhattan bank. They decided to deposit $80,000 in the name of a Neuberger relative whose business customarily required large cash transactions. They stashed the rest in a safe deposit box while they pondered a way to launder it. Over the next few days, they doled out large sums of cash to relatives and friends who, in turn, wrote checks which could be deposited without detection in their corporate or personal accounts.

Another crisis had been averted, but by January 1983 the

Welbilt officers were extremely worried again. They did not have the money to repay the $650,000 they owed. According to Moreno, they scheduled another meeting with Mariel to plead for an extension. Mariel was not optimistic but promised he would try.

The next day, Moreno said, Mariel called Welbilt to let them know the extension had been approved. Again, he did not disclose the name of the lender, but he solemnly warned them this could be the last extension. They also would owe another $150,000 when the loan came due in three months.

By April, their debt had grown to $800,000 and once again they could not come up with the money. They called Mariel in a panic, seeking another extension. As Moreno recalled, Mariel summoned Mariotta and Moreno to a Jehovah's Witness church he was helping build in the South Bronx. Over the din of hammers and shouting voices, Mariel walked with them to a quiet place and told them in somber tones that he was very worried. Their mystery lender was not willing to grant another extension. They would have to find the money somewhere to repay their debt.

The atmosphere was thick with panic as the officers drove back to the Welbilt plant, weighing their options. "John, I am really very worried," Moreno said. "These people may be very dangerous individuals. We don't know what may happen to us."

But the next day, Moreno had a brainstorm when General Ehrlich dropped by corporate headquarters. He explained that he, Mariotta, and Neuberger had taken out a loan from a man named Pat Simone and were worried they could not repay it.

"Simone? If it's Simone, my partner knows him very well," Ehrlich said, referring to Congressman Biaggi. "Let's see if he can do something for you there."

Ehrlich called Moreno later that day and told him to show up at a Bronx banquet hall, where Biaggi was scheduled to appear at a fund-raiser. Moreno and Ehrlich were there when the congressman entered, followed by an aide carrying his black tuxedo.

Ehrlich buttonholed the congressman: "Mario needs to talk to you about what we discussed this morning."

At Biaggi's signal, Moreno followed him into a bathroom. While the congressman changed into his tux, Moreno explained the Welbilt predicament with the overdue loan. Adjusting his tie, Biaggi dismissed Moreno with a wave of the hand, promising to make a phone call to see what he could do.

A few days later, Ehrlich called with good news, Moreno testified. The congressman had spoken to Pat Simone, who agreed to an extension. But Simone was making a new demand. He wanted the loan guaranteed with something besides the good faith of Welbilt officials, Moreno later testified. Simone had instructed his lawyer, John Tartaglia, to work out new arrangements with the Welbilt officers to satisfy the debt.

With Ehrlich monitoring the proceedings, the Welbilt officials testified, they met with Tartaglia in May 1983 and offered Simone the only real asset they had—stock in the company. Attorneys were preparing the paperwork for Welbilt's first public stock offering. They could give Simone $500,000 worth of Welbilt stock with a promise that they would purchase it back from him the day after the public offering at a considerably higher price.

At Tartaglia's instruction, the Welbilt officers said, they placed the stock in the name of the Belenguer Corporation, an offshore account maintained by Tartaglia in the Netherlands Antilles. The transaction raised eyebrows as soon as it was reported to the lawyers preparing Welbilt's initial prospectus, which was the document required for its first public stock sale. The attorneys at the prestigious firm of Squadron, Ellenoff, Plesent and Lehrer—who testified that they worried among themselves that the Simone deal was not kosher—made unsuccessful efforts to find out the principals involved in the mysterious Belenguer Corporation. Tartaglia refused to disclose the names, and the Squadron firm did not pursue it.

Immediately after the closing on the public offering, Moreno said, he, Mariotta and Neuberger met with Tartaglia, Pat Simone, and Joseph Simone to buy back their stock. Each of them had sold a substantial part of their shares in order to come up with the money. They also dipped into the sizable FHJ account to pay the interest on the loan.

The officers claimed that, at Mariotta's insistence, the next year they channeled $180,000 to their friends Mariel and Irizarry for their help in arranging the Simone loan. But this generous gift angered Simone, who by that time had dropped his anonymity and was meeting frequently with Welbilt officers at his auto junkyard. After all, they said, Simone told them, it was he—not the bankers—who had put up the $500,000. He also had protected the company, posting a $1 million certificate of deposit at New York National to cover the company's bounced checks, according to the officers.

The Simone stock deal was reported matter-of-factly in the initial prospectus the Squadron firm filed with the Securities and Exchange Commission—a document in which the company was required under law to air all its dirty laundry to potential investors. It reported that on May 13, 1983, Mariotta, Neuberger, and Moreno sold Tartaglia stock for an aggregate purchase price of $500,000 or $12.50 per share. During August 1983, they bought the stock back, the document read.

None of the investors who snapped up Wedtech stock when it came on the market would have had any way of knowing what the company officials by then truly believed—that in their desperation to keep their sinking company afloat, they had sold their souls for a suitcase of cash.

The Simone deal was only the most dramatic in a series of corporate shenanigans at Welbilt. By 1982, the Welbilt officers were defrauding every government agency within their reach. They also had discovered that, even though their company was forever teetering on the brink of financial collapse, it still afforded them ample ways to line both their own pockets and those of their growing ranks of coconspirators.

In their quest to stay out of trouble, they adopted an incredibly successful policy. When they encountered a potential troublemaker who could blow the whistle on them, they hired him. One by one, they co-opted their enemies with high salaries, stock, and options until, finally, they moved in a sphere of friendly, unquestioning faces.

Moreno was the first example of the strategy. In August 1981, Moreno had threatened to quit unless he were given an equity position in the company. He had literally laid his life on the line for Welbilt and felt his loyalty should be rewarded. Once, when the firm faced a 5 P.M. deadline for making an $80,000 overdue payment on its EDA loans, he boarded a helicopter in a raging thunderstorm with General Ehrlich to deliver the money to the agency's Philadelphia regional headquarters. As they stood at the helipad watching the thunder and lightning illuminating a black sky, Ehrlich, the decorated guardsman, thought Moreno was insane.

"Surely, you're not going to go in this helicopter today!" he exclaimed. But Moreno gathered his courage. "General," he said, "you're a general in the army. I am a little soldier. We got to get into this thing." They climbed aboard for a rocky ride punctuated by precipitous dips and lightning bolts. But they made it, planting their shaky feet on ground in Philadelphia for a hurried ride to EDA headquarters.

Of more importance than his loyalty, Moreno was perhaps the only man who knew all Welbilt's skeletons. Mariotta and Neuberger could not afford to part company with him on bad terms. So the partners decided to give Mariotta and Neuberger 45.5 percent of the company stock and Moreno 9 percent plus a 9 percent share of the secret FHJ account. Their only concern was that Biaggi would find out about it, for despite Mariotta's premature promise, they had not yet executed the papers turning over 5 percent of the firm to the helpful congressman. They also decided to keep the arrangement secret from the SBA, which still was under the assumption that Mariotta owned more than half of the firm.

Although the officers had agreed to limit their income on paper to $50,000—a condition of their federal financing from the EDA—they had found ways to supplement their income off the books. Moreno had his longtime companion, Caridad Vazquez, placed on the payroll in a $35,000 no-show job and returned the favor by giving Mariotta's wife Jennie a job at

Bronx Borough Security, a company he owned that provided Welbilt's security services. The officers also were dipping lavishly into the secret FHJ account, which they maintained at Banco Popular. Unlike Welbilt's other finances, the FHJ account was prospering from kickbacks that the officers arranged to get from subcontractors and suppliers.

All told, in 1981, Mariotta and Neuberger took home about $100,000, and Moreno reaped $20,000 from the FHJ account, none of which they reported to the IRS. Only one other person in the company knew about the account—Ceil Lewis, Mariotta's longtime secretary and the office busybody. Nothing happened at the Welbilt plant without Lewis' knowledge, and she served as Mariotta's dependable gossip pipeline. The officers trusted Lewis enough to place her in charge of disbursements from the FHJ account. She kept the account ledgers stashed in her desk, and when the officers needed cash, she wrote a check on the FHJ account, then returned to distribute the money.

While the White House was doing back flips to deliver Welbilt the engine contract, the company's officers also were engaging in a plot to defraud the SBA and the Defense Department by submitting phony invoices to generate much-needed cash. The illegal scheme—in which they concocted paperwork to justify early payments under their contracts—worked so well that they used it with regularity from 1980 until 1983 when it was discovered by their independent auditors as preparations began for the public stock offering. They brought in $4.7 million in cash through the fraudulent invoices and earned $1 million in interest at the government's expense.

Like the Simone loan, the invoice scheme was hatched out of desperation in the summer of 1980 as Moreno, Mariotta and Neuberger conferred on ways to get the company out of another of its never-ending financial crises. Again, the company was on the verge of bankruptcy, with no funds to buy materials or even to pay employees.

Although Welbilt held a number of moderately profitable defense contracts, it could collect money under them only through what is known as a percentage-of-completion method of accounting. Instead of receiving their money in a lump sum, the contract amount was doled out incrementally as the company moved toward completion of the work in so-called progress payments. The company had to submit documentation showing that it was steadily progressing toward completion of the contract. It filled out an application showing payments made to vendors and labor costs, then used a formula to calculate the percentage of the contract it had finished.

The forms were signed by Mariotta and submitted to the regional office of the Defense Contract Administration Services Management Area (DCASMA). Normally, it took several weeks for DCASMA to process the applications. However, over the years Welbilt developed such cozy relationships with DCASMA officials that its progress payment applications were processed and in the company's bank account within a matter of several days.

They knew some of their claims included honest accounting errors which had never been detected by the Defense Department.

The Welbilt officers seized on the idea. If the controls were this lax, then why not submit intentional "mistakes" that would enable Welbilt to receive monies prematurely? Submission of false statements to the government is a federal crime, but to them, the scheme almost seemed legal. Welbilt was due to receive the funds eventually; all they were doing was speeding up the process. Or so they told themselves.

With a Xerox machine and a bottle of correction fluid, they began cutting and pasting invoices to duplicate the authentic bills they had received from vendors. Once they had a phony form, the process was simple. They would fill in new amounts, run the phony bills through the Xerox machine, and staple copies to a Defense Department progress-payment form. Eventually, they contracted with an outside printing firm to give their fake invoices a more professional appearance.

The scheme worked without a hitch until January 1983. The phony invoices sailed past the unscrutinizing eyes of the Defense Contract Audit Agency, the branch responsible for monitoring the progress-payment applications. Welbilt, as usual, had taken out extra insurance by shamelessly courting DCAA auditors. In March 1982, the company hired Alfred Rivera, a DCAA auditor, to serve as senior vice president for finance and awarded him stock options for 13,500 shares. It courted other auditors with free meals and job offers when they began to catch on to the scheme. Mariotta even picked up another auditor's contributions to Jewish charities because so many of the DCAA auditors were Jews.

But the scam came back to haunt them in January 1983, as they began putting their books in order for the public stock offering. In late 1982, with the engine deal greatly enhancing the company's prospects, the officers had gone to Wall Street and recruited Moseley, Hallgarten, Estabrook and Weeden Inc. as underwriters for a $29 million stock offering, which they planned for the following year. But they also needed a certified public accounting firm recognized by the Securities and Exchange Commission to audit the company's financial statements for the previous two years. The audit was crucial, for without a clean bill of financial health the company could not proceed with the filings at the SEC.

In November 1982, Welbilt hired the respected KMG Main Hurdman accounting firm, one with the cachet that Welbilt needed to be taken seriously on Wall Street. In its agreement with Welbilt, Main Hurdman promised to conduct an examination in "accordance with generally accepted auditing standards," to submit a written report on the company's 1981 and 1982 financial statements and to provide advice to correct "any material weaknesses in internal accounting control that come to our attention." The Main Hurdman audit manager assigned to the Welbilt account was Tony Guariglia, a CPA with twelve years' experience. The audit was supervised by a Main Hurdman senior partner, Richard Bluestine.

Although Welbilt was required under law to air all its dirty linen, opening the company's books to an outside accountant was like taking the lid off a rank can of aged sardines. Ten years of corporate monkey business were, for the first time, laid bare before professionals with a sworn duty to expose their findings. With only a cursory review, the auditors began to raise eyebrows as they discovered political contributions and unsupported expense payments. Auditor Frank Musso also came across $400,000 in Welbilt checks and strange cash transactions credited to something called the "FHJ account." When Guariglia brought up the matter with the Welbilt officers, he was told that their salaries were limited to $50,000 under the terms of their EDA loans and that the account was being used to circumvent the restriction.

Soon, Musso began unearthing gross discrepancies in the company's progress-payment records. He went to Welbilt for an explanation. Why, he asked, were invoices which had been submitted to the government not reflected in the actual accounting records of the company? Moreno quickly called a meeting with Mariotta and Neuberger.

They were at a loss for how to proceed. Mariotta grew angry. He had long since lost his early admiration for Moreno, and now it was easy to place the blame squarely on him. Moreno had come to him in the first place with the phony invoice idea. "Every job that I give you, you always fuck it up," he snarled.

In January, as promised under the Main Hurdman agreement, Bluestine began meeting with the Welbilt executives about the questionable audit findings. Main Hurdman, he told them, would have an ethical obligation to disengage from the audit now that fraud had been discovered. The company's long-awaited public offering would be nixed, and everyone involved in the fraud could be prosecuted for serious federal crimes.

The Welbilt officers, however, were not about to let this minor obstacle foil their plans. They testified later that they began a costly, elaborate effort to lure Bluestine to their side. Mariotta began talking with Bluestine about the company's need for new, high-level management, men with connections in the New York financial community and with technical experience as CPAs. Bluestine seemed eminently qualified. He told Moreno he planned to offer Bluestine a job with a high salary and a stock package attractive enough to lure him away from Main Hurdman.

Mariotta broke the news to Neuberger as the two, along with Moreno, left for a long lunch on the Upper West Side of Manhattan. Mariotta was driving and briefing his two companions on the progress of his job negotiations with Bluestine. With his usual generosity, he had decided to give Bluestine between 7.5 and 9 percent of the company's stock.

Neuberger turned livid: "You continue to give stock away like this stock was limitless, like a bottomless pit." Pretty soon, he said, Mariotta would have given the company away and left them with nothing.

Mariotta was fed up with Neuberger's stinginess. Calling Neuberger a cheapskate, he angrily jammed down the accelerator and sped through upper Manhattan, running red lights and swerving off the road. Neuberger thought Mariotta was going to ram the car into a wall, but eventually they pulled up in front of the restaurant and piled out. Then the agitated Mariotta suddenly disappeared, leaving his companions stranded.

Eventually, the partners came to agreement on the issue and offered Bluestine 3 percent of the company's stock if he would come to work for Welbilt. Bluestine was receptive, but he also wanted Welbilt to hire his friend Tony Guariglia and give him a similar stock deal, the officers testified. At Bluestine's insistence, they also agreed to hire Larry Shorten, who was still working as a consultant.

First, however, they had to deal with the problem at hand—how to cover up their fraud successfully enough to proceed with the stock offering. In meetings with Bluestine, they hatched a plan acceptable to all parties, they later testified. The audit would be stopped in its tracks, and the other partners at Main Hurdman would be informed of the discovery of the progress-payment fraud. Moreno would take the fall for submitting the false paperwork to government agencies, and the company would solemnly swear to Main Hurdman that Moreno would be stripped of all accounting responsibilities. Welbilt also would come up with proof that it had informed the government of its fraud, evidence that Bluestine would submit to the Main Hurdman ethics committee. Bluestine would then push for Main Hurdman to reengage or continue the Welbilt audit and to issue the essential report showing the company in sound financial standing. The FHJ account, through some creative bookkeeping, would be disguised as a loan to Neuberger and reflected as such in the audit.

The plan moved ahead perfectly. For their proof that government agencies had been informed, the executives turned to their attorney, Bernie Ehrlich. They called the General to a Saturday meeting with Bluestine, in which the grave situation was described. Bluestine asked Ehrlich to accompany him as Welbilt's lawyer to a meeting between the Welbilt officers and the ethics committee at Main Hurdman. Bluestine also told him they would have to provide proof that the government had been informed of the fraud.

If there was one thing Welbilt did not need, it was another problem with the SBA, for around the same time, the agency had notified the company it had improperly received $112,-000 in advances to which it was not entitled. Ehrlich and Moreno went to the SBA to discuss the situation, promising several junior officers at the agency that the advance payments were an honest mistake that the company would repay.

But the progress-payment fraud was too serious a situation to discuss with unfriendly, low-level SBA officials. Instead, Ehrlich scheduled a meeting with his frequent and congenial dinner partner, Peter Neglia, the regional administrator. Ehrlich told him there was a "major problem" with the Defense Department, which was being investigated by Main Hurdman. Few details were discussed.

Ehrlich assigned a junior lawyer in his firm to write an "opinion letter" required by Main Hurdman, outlining the status of Welbilt's pending legal problems. The letter contained a pithy reference to the firm's conversations with the government regarding the invoice fraud. It said, "Mr. Ehrlich has discussed the matter extensively with the SBA and the matter has been resolved. . . . Accordingly, it is our understanding based on these discussions with the SBA that they will not proceed in any way against Welbilt."

Ehrlich's assurances that the government had been fully informed were enough to satisfy Main Hurdman. After the officers appeared before the ethics committee, portraying Moreno as an Attila the Hun who would be duly punished, Main Hurdman proceeded with the audit and rendered its written opinion that Welbilt's financial statements were fairly presented.

The report, which was submitted to the SEC, gave Main Hurdman's stamp of approval to the public offering. Nowhere in it was the invoice fraud mentioned or the fact that the Defense Department, after discovering some of the phony bills, had decided it must audit every Welbilt progress payment in the future as a safeguard against fraud.

As promised, Guariglia, who was earning between $60,000 and $65,000 a year at Main Hurdman, went to work as Welbilt's treasurer in mid-May of 1983. His starting salary was $80,000, but it would be supplemented by annual bonuses. He also had gone in with Mariotta's promise of stock valued at $1.5 million.

Bluestine, however, did not come on board until October 1983, after the company's stock offering had been completed. Strategically, Welbilt decided it was better for Bluestine to remain at Main Hurdman until any possible complications with the audit and the public stock offering were out of the way, the officers testified.

For his kind assistance, the Welbilt executives promised Bluestine 3.5 percent or 153,350 shares of stock, with a value of $16 per share when the company went public. With a new title as Welbilt's senior vice president, he earned a 1984 salary of $125,000 with a $25,000 bonus. When the IRS hit him with a $900,000 tax liability on his Welbilt stock, Mariotta, Neuberger, and Moreno met with their new senior executives, Guariglia and Larry Shorten, and decided to lend Bluestine the money. Eventually, Neuberger would plead guilty in state Supreme Court to participating in a scheme to bribe Bluestine to the tune of $2.5 million.

In between the pressing demands of his bicoastal life-style, E. Robert Wallach was keeping a close watch on Welbilt as the company prepared to go public. He had good reason to do so. He had acquired a substantial financial stake in the company. In December 1982, he and Moreno had worked out an agreement—which was drawn up but never signed—for him to serve as "legal and policy advisor" at a cost to the company of $200,000 over a fifteen-month period. He was to be given a $50,000 retainer, $10,000 a month during 1983, and $30,000 for his 1982 services between October and December.

But the company was too poor in 1982 to begin making the promised payments. Mariotta tried to make it up to Wallach in January 1983 by promising that at the time of the company's public offering he would get 1 percent of the company's stock, with an estimated value of around $1 million.

The offer suddenly gave Wallach a vested interest in the success of Welbilt's public offering. He knew that the company was on the verge of bankruptcy, desperately seeking a $3 million bridge loan to get it through the crisis until its payments under the engine contract began coming in. Worse yet, there were strange rumblings from St. Louis that the Army might renege on the engine contract. Wallach promptly notified Meese and Jenkins of the problem in a lengthy memorandum, in which he once again suggested that the Army was trying to throw the contract to the Garcia Ordnance Corporation, Welbilt's chief rival. Even though Keenan had been removed from his post at TSARCOM, Wallach wrote that Welbilt was convinced that Keenan was " 'running' the St. Louis operation through his old contacts."

Wallach also began appealing for more presidential recognition for Welbilt. Reagan's trip to the Welbilt factory, scheduled for the fall of 1982, had been canceled at the last minute because of scheduling conflicts. Wallach wrote Meese in March suggesting a presidential visit to Welbilt and, at the very least, a letter of commendation for Neuberger and Mariotta, who were scheduled to receive a humanitarian award from the Save Russian Jewry Educational Institute. Meese arranged for the presidential letters to be written and mailed to the Welbilt officers on May 12, 1983.

In early 1983, Wallach took it upon himself to address what he considered one of the company's most pressing needs—upgrading the quality of the firm's legal representation. Welbilt needed to portray itself as a class act, he argued, and although General Ehrlich definitely served a certain purpose, the company had outgrown the small, poorly regarded Biaggi

& Ehrlich. It needed a firm with corporate experience and Wall Street connections that could guide it through the complicated red tape of the SEC. Wallach, in fact, had the perfect candidate—the firm of Squadron, Ellenoff, Plesent and Lehrer.

Wallach had met Howard M. Squadron, the firm's senior partner, in 1981 while Squadron, the longtime president of the American Jewish Congress, was giving a speech in San Francisco. The two struck up a fast friendship, at one point traveling to Israel together with their families. He introduced Squadron to his friends at Welbilt, and in late 1982, he put the desperate officers in touch with Squadron, suggesting that the lawyer could use his connections at Bank Leumi to help them get a bridge loan. The bank agreed in September to give Welbilt a loan, but only if the bank could have first claim on the company's money in the event of bankruptcy.

In Wallach's eyes, Squadron—whose most lucrative client was Rupert Murdoch's New York *Post*—was the perfect lawyer to represent Welbilt. As he recalled in 1987, the Squadron firm, he felt, could lend "an atmosphere of professionalism" to the company, and the relationship would prove to be mutually beneficial. "This struggling South Bronx company ended up being their second largest client," Wallach recalled in the 1987 interview. "The first was Murdoch and then was Wedtech. And [Squadron, Ellenoff] ultimately earned somewhere in the vicinity of $4–5 million in fees over the period of representing Wedtech."

While on one of his numerous visits to New York, Wallach asked the Welbilt officers to introduce him to Ehrlich. Ehrlich and Biaggi had known that Welbilt would need a corporate law firm to help prepare for the public offering, but they had been pushing the politically well-connected Shea, Gould firm. The Welbilt officials had been agreeable up to a point, retaining Shea, Gould for help on an infringement lawsuit filed by the Welbilt Stove Corporation, which was demanding that the South Bronx firm change its name prior to the public offering.

Mariotta and Moreno accompanied Wallach to the Biaggi & Ehrlich offices, but they had no idea what was awaiting them. Wallach had hardly taken his seat before he began talking very fast, delivering the harsh news to Ehrlich like a thunderbolt out of the blue.

"This firm has done a lot for this company up to this stage," Moreno remembered Wallach saying. "But the company is going to a new national stage, and therefore needs new representation. I don't believe that you can provide the services that are necessary for the company to go public."

The General's face turned a blustery red. He said little, but Moreno and Mariotta could see that he was extremely upset. Welbilt had become not only the General's most important client but his fiefdom, his entree to the Pentagon, his personal obsession.

The officers piled into a car for the ride back to the Welbilt headquarters, and as they dropped off Wallach in midtown Manhattan, he told them he would move ahead with arrangements for Welbilt to retain Squadron, Ellenoff. Wallach had additional reasons for pushing the firm. He had a deal with Squadron to collect a substantial finder's fee for hooking the firm up with Welbilt, an arrangement which would net him at least $227,000. Squadron would contend the fees were legitimate payment for outside counsel. Welbilt, however, was so pleased to have Squadron's counsel that the officers arranged to reward the firm with a stock gift of 45,000 shares.

Back at 595 Gerard Avenue, Mariotta and Moreno were met by a panicked secretary.

"Congressman Biaggi's trying to reach you," she said.

Moreno did not even have time to return Biaggi's call before the phone rang. As he described it, an incensed Biaggi attacked him from the other end of the line:

"Why did you take that fucking Jew bastard over there? Why did you let him do that to poor Bernie? If I had been there, I would have knocked him flat on the floor."

Moreno weighed his words carefully. "Congressman, we didn't know that Wallach was going to be saying those things over there. . . . Don't be concerned with the situation. We will not let it happen anymore."

Biaggi's message was clear: *He* controlled Welbilt, not E. Robert Wallach. And they had better not forget it.

Welbilt's relationship with Wallach, however, continued to

blossom. In May, after Neuberger and Mariotta received their presidential commendations, Wallach wrote them and Moreno a long letter chock full of caring advice as he made his way back to Washington on a 6 A.M. Metroliner. Wallach was in a contemplative mood, noting that although he suddenly found himself "privileged to move in circles of great prominence and affluence, I fully recognize the transient and unsatisfying nature of this lifestyle.

"Once again," he wrote, "I leave each of you with a sense of the inadequacy of my presence because of the infrequencies of my time spent with you. Each of you is understanding of the rather unique and unusual set of responsibilities which have befallen me in other arenas. . . .

"The financial rewards, if any, are a far more speculative motivation for me than the accomplishment of the concepts which you have so effectively intertwined to produce not only a successful financial venture but a meaningful social contribution."

In the eight-page letter, Wallach went on to compliment the officers for turning to seasoned professionals like Squadron, Ellenoff and Richard Bluestine for help. And he offered advice on their strained relationship with Ehrlich.

"You can accomplish more by including the General in a synergy with Squadron, Bluestein [sic], et. al. [sic] than by trying to satisfy each one in separate spheres of your personal attention. . . .

"Don't underestimate the ability of your other 'resources' to deal with these problems and to work in harmony. You need a variety of resources to assist you and all of us must learn to work together effectively—including the General."

8

THE FIVE PERCENT
SOLUTION

THE CONGRESSMAN and the General did not like what they were seeing as Welbilt turned itself over to the Wall Street underwriters, the uptown lawyers, and the slick, self-serving accountants who planned to take the company public by the end of 1983. Where, they wondered, was simple gratitude? Ehrlich had served at Welbilt's beck and call, winning the ear of the Pentagon or whatever agency was involved in Welbilt's ever-changing crisis of the week. Ehrlich had co-opted Peter Neglia with such speed and efficiency that Welbilt never had to worry about the SBA. He had strutted into defense agencies to demand that they speed up Welbilt's payments, and marched out with a salute and a signed check in hand. And when the Welbilt officers foolishly ventured out of their league and began playing footsie with a reputed loan shark, all he had to do was call, and the congressman came to their rescue.

Yet by early 1983, Welbilt still had not made good on Mariotta's vow to give Biaggi and Ehrlich 5 percent of the company's stock. Instead, Mariotta now was promising stock right and left to Welbilt's new "allies"—to Bob Wallach, Lyn Nofziger, Howard Squadron, Richard Bluestine, and others—while doing nothing to deliver the stock he had set aside for Biaggi and his partner.

The problem was complicated by Biaggi and Ehrlich's dismal failure to bail Welbilt out of its latest financial jam. With the help of Squadron, Welbilt had won a commitment from Bank Leumi for a $5.7 million loan package desperately needed to keep the firm out of bankruptcy. The deal called for the bank to give the company $3 million in desperately needed working capital and to assume a $2.2 million Citibank loan, which had been guaranteed by both the EDA and the SBA.

There was one hitch to winning final approval for the loan. Bank Leumi insisted that Welbilt get both the EDA and SBA to subordinate their interests in the company. In the event of a default, the so-called subordination agreement would give Bank Leumi first claim on Welbilt's assets.

Ehrlich was confident that with his connections to Neglia he could induce the SBA to sign the papers. But the Commerce Department's EDA was another matter. Welbilt already was more than $350,000 behind in repaying its $4 million direct and guaranteed EDA loans. The company had been under increasing pressure from EDA officials in Philadelphia to make good on its debt.

In May, with the Bank Leumi negotiations near completion, Ed Morris, the EDA chief in Philadelphia, wrote Mariotta to tell him that the regional office would not approve the subordination agreement. It was not that Morris himself was unsympathetic to the company. He had been blocked from signing the papers by his higher-ups in Washington, particularly by the tough assistant secretary for economic development, Carlos Campbell. Campbell, one of the highest ranking blacks in the Reagan administration, had taken office in 1981 with a mandate from President Reagan to prepare the EDA for eventual shutdown. Vowing to clean up waste and fraud, Campbell had zeroed in on the EDA's astronomical 40 percent loan delinquency rate and made it known he was determined to collect on the bad debts.

With no loan in sight and the company's prospects dimming, Mariotta had soured on Biaggi and Ehrlich. If they could not deliver the EDA, clearly they were not worth their high-priced retainer. Ehrlich and Biaggi began to fear that Mariotta would renege on his 5 percent promise. They wanted the agreement in writing, and they wanted it quickly.

Biaggi and Ehrlich had waited patiently at first, but in the summer of 1981, they saw that they might have to use a get-tough approach. One day, while Ehrlich was driving across town with Moreno, Moreno let slip that he had been given 9 percent of the company, an action the officers had hidden from Ehrlich. Ehrlich listened with interest and, a few days later, shoved a proposed stock agreement across Moreno's desk.

Ehrlich wanted to present the papers to Mariotta, but Moreno urged caution. Mariotta, he said, was frustrated over the stalled engine contract. The timing was not right. Ehrlich, knowing Mariotta's unpredictable temperament, shrugged and took the advice. All of them knew better than to provoke one of Mariotta's rages.

A few months later, Biaggi himself renewed the request. He paid a visit to Mariotta at his backyard swimming pool in his new home in Scarsdale. He made it clear he expected Mariotta to live up to his promise, and he wanted a meeting with Neuberger and Moreno to seal the deal.

When the congressman called 595 Gerard Avenue the next day to follow up, Mariotta arranged a dinner meeting at Joe Nina's, one of their favorite restaurants. But Neuberger flatly refused to go. By then he had had his fill of Mario Biaggi, the persistent bill collector. The animosity was returned by the congressman. He was convinced Neuberger was his enemy.

As expected, Biaggi scowled when he saw Neuberger's empty place at the Joe Nina's table: "Where is Fred Neuberger? Where is that cheap bastard Jew?" Moreno remembered him asking.

Moreno tried to appease him. Neuberger, he said, had a previous engagement and couldn't make it. He suggested they have a preliminary talk and schedule a later meeting with Neuberger.

Biaggi was skeptical, but Mariotta soothed him. He had promised Biaggi the stock, and he would deliver it.

Biaggi wasted no time getting to the point. Everything was set for Welbilt to get the engine contract, he said. The company also would be receiving the $3 million SBA grant as well as other government assistance. "Bernie," he said, "has spent a lot of time with you on this engine contract. You are going to get that contract because of us."

Five percent of Welbilt's stock, he suggested, was hardly fair compensation for all they had done for the company. He told them that in addition to the stock, he also wanted 5 percent of every contract he helped bring into the company.

"Congressman," Moreno stammered, "we cannot give you 5 percent of any contracts that we get from the federal government. The profit in them is only 10 percent, at the most 12 or 13 percent. If we give you 5 percent of the profits, the company would be left with only 5 percent to pay interest and a lot of expenses."

But Biaggi would not back down. Rummaging for a solution, Moreno proposed an alternative. Although they could not give him 5 percent on so-called prime government contracts—those that came directly from the government to Welbilt—they perhaps could provide a cut on subcontracts he helped them arrange with other companies. Subcontracts were not so closely monitored by the government and provided some leeway for extra "expenses."

With the subcontract issue resolved, the meeting ended with another assurance that the remaining part of the package—the 5 percent stock deal—would be delivered. But all of them knew it meant nothing without Neuberger's approval.

The day after the Joe Nina's dinner, Mariotta consulted Neuberger on the 5 percent solution, and the grumpy Neuberger delivered the speech that had begun to sound like a broken record: "You're crazy! One of these days, you and I are going to end up without anything."

He had not budged in his opposition to the plan a few days later when Biaggi and Ehrlich showed up at 595 Gerard, planted themselves in chairs in front of Mariotta's desk, and demanded once again to see Neuberger and get the stock matter settled.

Neuberger came in shortly afterward and made his position clear. The 5 percent offered by Mariotta in a rash moment was "totally outrageous," he said. Any reasonable person could see that. He was willing to give 2 percent—which would be worth something like $2 million—and not a penny more.

That's more money than you've ever seen in one place, he told Biaggi. "You should be happy with that."

Biaggi glared at Neuberger, with tension palpable in the closed office. "We have done a lot for this company. . . . You could not have gotten the engine contract if it had not been for our help and the time that Bernie is spending with you!"

"That's all you're going to get," Neuberger retorted.

When a vicious argument broke out, Mariotta pulled Neuberger aside and led him through a bathroom into Neuberger's adjoining office: "Fred, I already gave him my word. I gave my promise to the congressman. . . . We absolutely need them to remain with the company at this time."

When they reappeared, Neuberger had grudgingly acceded. "John has convinced me," he told the triumphant Biaggi and his sidekick. "Just because he gave his word, I will go along with the agreement."

Despite their oral commitment, the Welbilt officers did nothing to put the deal in writing until the spring of 1983 when the Squadron, Ellenoff firm was in the middle of preparations for the public offering. By April, Mariotta, Neuberger, and Moreno had handed out large stock gifts to all their new-found allies.

Ehrlich heard about these lavish gifts of stock, and he and Biaggi were concerned that their promised 5 percent share was going to be diluted. Ehrlich scheduled another meeting at Welbilt, this time in Neuberger's office, and Guariglia and Shorten also sat in.

The meeting promptly turned ugly. Biaggi and Ehrlich were adamant that Mariotta cough up the promised 5 percent.

Guariglia explained that they would hold title to 225,000 shares, evenly split between them, which would have an approximate value of $4 million.

"What else do you want?" Neuberger screamed.

Biaggi left them with a parting warning: "I have made this company what it is. I can also destroy it."

By the time the meeting broke up, Mariotta was nearly hysterical. "Look what these people are doing to us," he shouted at a Welbilt lawyer, throwing down the proposed stock agreements. "It's blackmail!"

Mariotta was insistent that they could tolerate no more demands from Biaggi and Ehrlich. Although the General had also been anxiously awaiting a promised seat on the Welbilt board of directors—which the officers had assured him would take place immediately following the public offering—Mariotta vowed to Guariglia that there was "no way would he have that stupid lawyer sitting on the board of directors."

Ehrlich took the opportunity to pursue the stock deal when he met the officers the next month at a $1,000-a-table Biaggi fund-raiser at the Sheraton Hotel. In a new attempt to demonstrate his prowess, he brought the EDA's Morris with him as a dinner guest. The occasion gave them a chance to consult Morris about their EDA problem, but Morris assured them their problem was with Carlos Campbell, not with him.

At the end of the event, Biaggi brought over Senator D'Amato, telling the Welbilt officers the senator could give them assistance with Campbell. Then, as icing on the cake, Ehrlich drew out drafts of the stock agreements that had been drawn up after several conferences at Squadron, Ellenoff.

After all his arm-twisting, Biaggi's name was noticeably absent from the stock documents. Instead, they showed 112,- 500 shares going to his son Richard in consideration of his past services to the company. The wording was an inside joke, for except for some minor legal work he did on a real estate closing, Richard Biaggi, just graduated from law school, had had virtually no dealings with Welbilt. In fact, he was a mere associate in his father's firm, not even a full-fledged partner.

Initially Biaggi had wanted the agreement drawn up to show stock held only in the name of the law firm. But he changed his mind after his longtime accountant, Irwin Wolf, warned him that a gift of stock to the law firm would have to be reported on his House financial disclosure forms and might put him over the congressional earnings cap on outside income. The only solution was to put the stock in Richard's name, with the clear understanding that it belonged to the congressman.

The long-awaited execution of the stock agreements gave the Welbilt officers a brief reprieve from the incessant dunning efforts of Biaggi and Ehrlich. But it only escalated the growing struggle between the lawyers for Welbilt's business.

Mariotta snubbed Ehrlich and turned to Squadron to make a presentation to the regional office of the SBA regarding the loan subordination. Squadron was eloquent, laying out a convincing case to Neglia and other SBA officials. But Ehrlich hit the roof over the latest attempt to undercut his proved hold on the SBA, and Neglia was similarly offended. After the meeting, the SBA chief called Moreno aside, demanding to know why Welbilt had brought in an outsider.

The Welbilt executives also placed less and less faith in Biaggi's ability to work out the EDA dilemma. They decided the only way they could get to the troublesome Carlos Campbell was through the White House, using their Washington connections, Wallach and Nofziger.

Campbell, the officers learned, was vulnerable in a number of areas. His get-tough approach to dispensing EDA favors had angered members of Congress, and pressure was building among Republican members for the White House to do something about the uncooperative assistant secretary. In addition, the Commerce Department was checking out charges that Campbell had shown a conflict of interest in his dealings with a computer firm owned by an acquaintance.

Wallach began the frontal attack with a series of phone calls in May and June to Meese's office, first talking with deputy Jim Jenkins. When Jenkins asked for more information, Wallach dashed off a letter, which he instructed Moreno's secretary to hand-deliver by messenger to the White House.

On June 1, after a meeting with Jenkins, Wallach ducked

into Meese's office to brief him on the EDA stalemate. He described an urgent situation, with the company in dire danger of not meeting its Friday payroll. A few days later, the matter was discussed in Meese's regular morning staff meeting. Jenkins announced that he wanted to expedite the loan discussions.

At least one White House staffer, Craig Fuller, Meese's liaison to the Cabinet, questioned the wisdom of White House involvement in the dispute between Welbilt and the EDA. He wrote White House counsel Fielding, seeking a legal opinion on what actions Meese's office could take.

Fielding's response was pointed. "Any communication from the White House could thus be misinterpreted by EDA and/or misperceived by the public as untoward and inappropriate interference. . . ."

But Fielding's warning did nothing to dampen Wallach's efforts. The Welbilt officers came to believe that Meese was the key to a solution on the EDA impasse and therefore that Wallach was clearly their most valuable friend. To them, he was justifiably miffed when word of the 5 percent Biaggi solution leaked out. Wallach's stock gift had been a meager 1 percent of the company, with a value of only $1 million.

But the stock gifts were set in stone and could not be changed. Guariglia tried to assure Wallach that, while his stock grant might have been disappointing, he would be amply rewarded with other treasures somewhere down the road.

9

CRISIS
IN WASHINGTON

WITH THEIR COMPANY rapidly sinking, no one was in a
festive mood on July 14, 1983, when the Welbilt officers
gathered to celebrate Fred Neuberger's birthday. As Moreno
put it, they had used "every Tom, Dick and Harry" to try to
get to Carlos Campbell. Nofziger and Bragg had barraged
Campbell's office with a series of increasingly hostile phone
calls. Someone even arranged for Clarence Pendleton, Reagan's director of the Civil Rights Commission, to telephone
the EDA chief and ask about the Welbilt loan. Yet, despite
their efforts, the loan subordination agreement was going nowhere. Just that day, the EDA's Philadelphia regional office
finally had forwarded its approved version of the agreement
to Campbell's office. But Campbell showed no willingness to
sign the documents.

The birthday party was interrupted by a phone call from Bragg, who told the Welbilt executives that Campbell had once again refused to play ball. Realizing they had to act fast, it was decided on the spot that Moreno would fly to Washington in a desperate plea for help from Ed Meese. Guariglia shelled out $500 for expenses, and Moreno sped to La Guardia for the next shuttle. He did not even have time to pack a change of clothes.

Moreno checked into a hotel and called Bob Wallach. They had to find some way to go around Carlos Campbell, Moreno told him, perhaps by putting pressure on Commerce Secretary Malcolm Baldrige. With Meese's intervention, could Baldrige be induced to sign the agreement?

Wallach, as it turned out, was scheduled to accompany Meese the next morning to a National Security Council meeting and a 7:15 A.M. breakfast. He promised to take up the matter with Meese but needed an update. He asked Moreno to meet him the next morning around 5:30 in Lafayette Park, directly across the street from the White House. Moreno placed a relieved call to Welbilt headquarters. Arrangements had been made to "get into the White House," he reported.

If anyone could identify with Welbilt's troubled finances, it was Edwin Meese, whose personal financial dealings provided fodder for two separate investigations during his eight years in the Reagan administration—a pattern of borrowing money from friends and agreeable bankers under favorable terms. Meese was one of the few homeowners in America allowed to fall a year behind on his mortgage payments—a delinquency which elicited nothing more from the bank than a few courteous phone calls and letters.

Meese regularly forgot to report the details of his finances in the annual financial disclosure reports required under the Ethics in Government Act. When confronted with his omissions, he would blame bad recordkeeping, misunderstanding of the requirements, and poor memory—even though his associates were constantly amazed by his uncanny ability to recall facts and obscure details, even though one veteran IRS investigator reported that he had never reviewed records so meticulously kept.

Curiously enough, a strange pattern developed over the years. Virtually anyone willing to bail Meese out of his latest money squeeze—predicaments which ranged from paying his overdue property taxes to bringing his California bar association dues up to date—ended up with a high-paying federal job.

Meese's friendship was quite helpful, to say the least, for anyone seeking a career. During his White House years, Meese sat with Mike Deaver and Jim Baker on the Senior Staff Personnel Committee, clearing all presidential appointments. From January 1981 to April 1984, he helped review more than 2,800 appointments.

One of Meese's most generous friends was Edwin Thomas, whom he had known since 1967 when Thomas left the Del Monte Corporation to come to work for then-Governor Reagan in Sacramento. He later worked for Meese at the Center for Criminal Justice Policy and Management, and while there, he and his wife made their first loan to the Meeses as the couple prepared for a European vacation. With nothing more formal than a handshake, the Thomases graciously lent the Meeses $8,000 so they could purchase a Volkswagen to use during their travels. The loan was repaid through a separate loan Meese took out with his most cooperative bank, the Great American Bank of San Diego, an institution that became a training ground for future federal appointees. In 1980, after Reagan won election to the presidency, Meese asked Thomas to come to work for him in the White House.

Around the same time, Thomas made a $15,000 interest-free loan to Ursula Meese, so she could buy some stock he had recommended. When the stock nosedived, Thomas was so embarrassed that he was reluctant to press for repayment. But in 1982, when he left Washington to take a new federal job in San Francisco, Thomas needed some ready cash to buy a house. The Meeses paid him back in two installments—one of $5,000 in November 1982, and another of $10,000 in June 1983.

Although he did not pressure the Meeses to repay him, Thomas did remind Meese to report the loan on his 1982 financial disclosure statement. Yet Meese somehow forgot to mention the loan. Later, when he came under fire from the press, Meese called the omission inadvertent.

Although his obligation to the Thomases was settled by the summer of 1983, Meese was hardly out of hot water financially. In June 1981, at the suggestion of his friend Deaver, he paid a visit to Deaver's crackerjack San Francisco accountant, John R. McKean, Jr.

Meese's principal financial problem centered on real estate. After buying a $260,000 house in the predominantly white, well-to-do Washington suburb of McLean, Virginia, Meese was saddled with his former residence in La Mesa, California, which seemed impossible to unload. To cover their down payment on the McLean house, they had taken out a complicated $130,000 bridge loan from the Great American Bank.

McKean analyzed the figures and suggested that Meese needed $60,000 to cover his shortfall. He offered a possible solution: He could arrange a $60,000 loan through client sources. Although the interest rate would be higher than bank rates—18 to 21 percent—the private loan would give Meese flexibility and confidentiality. Meese liked the idea but decided to start with a $40,000 loan and, if necessary, he would add another $20,000 debt later in the year.

A few months later, McKean received an unexpected phone call from the White House. It was his client, Mike Deaver, wanting to know if McKean would be interested in a presidential appointment to the Postal Board of Governors—a $10,000-a-year part-time job.

By 1982, Meese had borrowed the second $20,000 installment from McKean, and interest had come due on his first $40,000 note. Through a connection set up by Deaver, he had sold his La Mesa home at a disappointing price of $307,500 but still found himself unable to repay the loans. In the fall, McKean and Meese met and decided to defer interest payments on the loans until 1983.

In July 1983, the *Washington Post* uncovered McKean's loans to Meese and raised the prospect that his appointment to the Postal Board—by then full time—was linked to the transaction. Stinging from the negative press, McKean urged Meese to seek his own source of financing in the Washington area.

For help, Meese turned to his friend, Bob Wallach. As usual, Wallach had a solution. He had struck up a friendship with Jeffrey Cohen, the chairman of the board and major stockholder of the National Bank of Commerce in Washington. Wallach and Cohen were partners in real estate ventures, and they were also social friends. Wallach called Cohen and told him that Meese needed a quick $80,000 loan to pay off McKean—his only hope of quashing the negative publicity. Within the course of a day, the bank agreed to give Meese an unsecured, $80,000 loan, with the understanding it would be secured by a second mortgage on his McLean home as soon as the paperwork could be completed.

Wallach made no secret of his role in arranging the Meese loan when, in December 1983, he wrote Moreno and suggested that Wedtech deposit "significant funds" with the National Bank of Commerce. The matter, the letter said, was "of some importance to me as a matter of friendship and credibility."

Wedtech never did make the requested deposit, probably because it was too broke to do so.

On a hot July morning Moreno left his suite for the predawn meeting with Wallach. The streets were still silent, and the daily parade of placard-carrying protesters had not yet gathered on Pennsylvania Avenue as Wallach and Moreno strolled toward the White House, talking quietly. Wallach listened attentively as Moreno laid out the urgency of their problem with Campbell. If he could not be budged, they must go over his head with a direct appeal to Secretary Baldrige. Meese was the only one who could help them with that high-level contact.

With the clock approaching 6 A.M., Wallach headed across the street for his meeting with Meese, leaving Moreno to wait. The time passed slowly as pin-striped bureaucrats and perspiring joggers crisscrossed the sidewalks. It was almost two hours before Wallach reappeared. He brought good news.

Meese had made the requested phone call to Baldrige. Baldrige's wife, Margaret, told him the secretary was in the shower, but Meese waited while she fetched him.

Baldrige said such a move could be politically disastrous. Perhaps another assistant secretary could be found with the legal authority to sign off on the loan? It seemed unlikely that one could be found with both the legal authority and a willingness to get involved in the mess, but there was a chance that Baldrige could hastily fill a vacant assistant secretary slot with a new official sympathetic to the Welbilt cause. There were still problems with the agreement, Baldrige pointed out: The EDA was particularly concerned by Welbilt's unauthorized purchase of an Israeli factory, Carmo Industries.

Wallach told Moreno to stay in touch during the day with Mark Bragg, who would be closely monitoring developing events at the EDA. Anxiously, Moreno stationed himself by a pay phone and called Bragg every hour for updates. The news was not encouraging. By the day's end, the Commerce lawyers had nixed the notion of a new appointment. Welbilt was going to have to deal with Campbell, one way or another. A meeting had been set up for the following Monday.

Welbilt accelerated its efforts to pressure Campbell and his superiors. Bragg called Jenkins, and Wallach called Meese, leaving a message that "it's quite important." The two met at 11 A.M. that Saturday. Meese would later recall nothing of the meeting or the phone call to Baldrige, although he conceded on the witness stand that his diaries reflected that a call had been made.

The July 19 meeting was a show of power on both sides. Robert H. Brumley, a new EDA associate general counsel, attended the meeting. Brumley's instructions, as he later described them, were to "get the loan made or tell me why it can't be made." Welbilt also brought its top guns—Nofziger, Bragg, and Howard Squadron. (Bernie Ehrlich, left behind in New York, was infuriated when he learned Squadron was there.) Squadron pleaded Welbilt's case with convincing savvy. He argued that the EDA would suffer nothing from signing the loan agreement, since it would be promptly repaid in full from the proceeds of the public offering. He described the loan as a stopgap, to tide the company over until its defense contracts began paying off.

At first, Campbell would have none of the argument. He said Welbilt needed to improve its cost control system and to install an independent board of directors to strengthen its management—observations which few other bureaucrats had had the courage to state. But he was under considerable pressure. His phone had been ringing off the hook on the Welbilt matter, and the numerous calls from his superiors made him realize his actions were being too closely watched for his own good. At some point in the meeting, Campbell was called aside by Nofziger, and the two huddled in private conversation. When Campbell came back to the table, his position had abruptly changed. He agreed to approve the loan subordination deal.

Campbell later denied that Nofziger pressured him into shifting his position. He told me he merely came to see Welbilt's point of view. But his career started downhill within a few weeks of the July 19 meeting. In August, Meese and Jenkins went to Capitol Hill for a meeting with thirteen Republican congressmen who were disgruntled with Campbell's performance. Four months later, a congressional subcommittee announced its intention to question Campbell about staffing levels, grant recipients, and employee morale. Days before the hearing, Campbell received a call from Presidential Personnel Director John S. Herrington asking for his resignation. Herrington told him the White House intended to move him to another job as alternate executive director of the Inter-American Bank. But the White House never forwarded Campbell's name to the Senate.

While waiting for this nonexistent appointment, Campbell took a consultant's job with the Treasury Department. In late February 1985, on the day Meese was sworn in as Attorney General, Campbell went to pick up his Treasury Department paycheck and was told he had been removed from the payroll two weeks earlier.

With the EDA issue resolved, the Bank Leumi loan sailed through, and Welbilt's underwriters began preparing for the public offering. A preliminary prospectus filed with the SEC in July showed several significant changes in the company. First, in a settlement with the Welbilt Stove Corporation, the company agreed to change its name to Wedtech—a short, catchy title that suggested the company's growing emphasis on high-tech ventures. Secondly, under a section titled "Special Considerations," the company disclosed that with the sale of its stock it "will no longer be qualified to obtain new contracts under the Section 8(a) program."

Neuberger looked forward to the changes. He proclaimed to Moreno that the company would not "have to deal with those idiots at the SBA anymore" or conform to mandated restrictions in size and management. The other officers were not so confident. They spent hours researching their prospects of winning contracts under competitive bidding, and most of them knew it could be a losing proposition. Over the next few weeks, the company executives and their legal advisers made a subtle but highly significant change in the SEC filing. They revised the wording to show that Wedtech "may no longer be qualified" for the SBA program.

On August 25, 1983, Wedtech completed its initial public offering with its stock selling at $16 a share. Included in the sale were 400,000 shares owned by Mariotta, Neuberger, and Moreno. On September 1, the Wedtech officers, a team of lawyers from the Squadron firm, and representatives of Moseley, Hallgarten gathered at the Wall Street law office of Shearman & Sterling, Moseley's legal counsel, for the closing on the public offering. Mariotta was given two checks totaling $3 million. Neuberger got $3 million, and Moreno received more than $500,000. Although prohibited from selling their stock, the other officers were able to use their stock holdings as collateral on loans.

At a luncheon following the closing, the giddy soon-to-be millionaires from Wedtech began discussing Mariotta's pressing need for a new luxury car—something befitting the board chairman of a thriving corporation—to replace his battered old Lincoln Continental. Neuberger, Mariotta, Moreno, Bluestine, Guariglia, and Shorten trooped en masse to a Mercedes Benz dealership in Manhattan and paraded about the showroom like mischievous schoolchildren who'd just raided the cookie jar.

It was an unbelievably lucky day for an unsuspecting car salesman. Giddy with excitement, Mariotta decided that they should all have new, showy vehicles. They ordered six Mercedes, at a cost of $50,000 apiece, and charged them to the company.

Wallach would later insist that this show of opulence from the officers of the supposedly disadvantaged company was "a mistake that as much as anything cost them their relationships with a number of people."

10

THE PHONY STOCK DEAL

WEDTECH HAD BEEN a publicly traded company for a few weeks when the company's officers made an astounding discovery. They learned that the SBA was about to make available through its Section 8(a) program the largest defense contract ever set aside for a minority-owned business. The contract, which came under the Sealift Facilities Support Program of the U.S. Navy, was to manufacture simple boxlike pontoon boats to be used for unloading large naval supply ships. In shallow water, the boats could be lined up end to end to serve as a floating pier.

The shipbuilding job was so large and specialized that it was laughable to think Wedtech—which had no experience in the field whatsoever—would even consider applying for it. The company had no marine engineers, no shipbuilding facility, not even a location with access to water. But Neuberger was the only naysayer in the group. The contract had a staggering potential worth of anywhere from $500 million to $1 billion.

The White House saw the project as a meaty bone that could be carved up among a number of politically connected minority firms. Vice President Bush had claimed a stake in it for some Puerto Rican firm, as a concession to former Gov. Luis Ferre, his chief backer in the territory. Sen. John Tower, the stalwart chairman of the Senate Armed Services Committee, wanted part of it for a Texas constituent. And at least a slice of it was said to be reserved for a Chinese-American supporter and friend of President Reagan's in California.

For Wedtech, there was another major complication. By going public, Wedtech had cut itself out of the lucrative 8(a) program. Under the SBA's rules, Mariotta had to own at least 51 percent of the company's stock, but after the public offering, he held title to only 26.7 percent. Moreover, since Mariotta's net worth had zoomed overnight to $3 million, he no longer qualified, under even the most liberal definition, as a socially and economically deprived businessman. There also was the question of Mariotta's diminished control of the company. That June, he had been booted upstairs to board chairman and chief executive officer. Hands-on control of the company had been yielded to Neuberger, the president, and his band of scheming vice presidents—Moreno, Guariglia, Larry Shorten, and Richard Bluestine.

The Wedtech officers had gone into the stock offering knowing that their actions would end the company's ride on the 8(a) gravy train. Over the years, Mariotta and Neuberger had told the press repeatedly that they looked forward to the day they no longer needed the SBA. The stock offering had proved beyond a shadow of doubt that Wedtech was capable of attracting investors and surviving in the real world of competition.

Their early experience in the competitive marketplace had been discouraging, however. Wedtech had submitted bids on several contracts and lost out to lower bidders. New business was drying up. Consequently, word of the Navy contract convinced the Wedtech crew that the most certain way for the company to survive was to find a way to stay in the 8(a) program.

Peter Neglia, the SBA regional administrator, was the linchpin of their plan. Over the course of months they had wooed him with expensive dinners, managing to win his backing for the company. It was hardly a one-sided relationship, however, for Neglia's reputation within the SBA had been boosted by the rousing successes of Wedtech, the "model" company under the auspices of the SBA.

Not long after they learned of the pontoon contract, the Wedtech officers took Neglia along as their guest for an October black-tie fund-raiser honoring George and Barbara Bush. The tickets were $500 apiece, and the Wedtech officers picked up the tab. Ehrlich convinced them that this would be the perfect occasion to bring up the Navy contract again with Neglia. It also would be a test of Neglia's loyalty. Neglia, whose regional jurisdiction encompassed Puerto Rico, had been specifically instructed by Sanders that Bush was to get part of the contract for his Puerto Rican supporters.

As Moreno recalled, they had just finished cocktail hour and were ambling into the packed dining room when Moreno buttonholed Neglia and pulled him aside.

"Pete, I need to talk to you about something very important," Moreno said. "We have found a contract in Washington that seems like it can be obtained for Wedtech." Moreno reached into his pocket and pulled out two sheets describing the details of the enormous pontoon project.

Neglia glanced at the papers, and looked up with disbelief. He had felt this company tugging at his coattails since the day he took office, asking for impossible favor after impossible favor. "You people are crazy," he said, as he moved to his free seat at the Wedtech table.

Wedtech was the first company in the history of the 8(a) program to sell its stock publicly, but it had never bothered to ask permission from the SBA. One of the basic rules of the SBA program was that companies involved must notify the agency well in advance of any changes in management or corporate structure, even the most minor ones. The discovery of this company's pending stock sale had jolted the SBA out of its usual complacency and brought swift, determined action.

A meeting of the Review and Evaluation Committee, which was responsible for recommending punishments for flagrant program offenders, was hastily called at the SBA's New York district office. The three-person committee was chaired by Ming Yee, who already knew Wedtech was a special company. He had been warned that any matter involving the company should be forwarded directly "upstairs"—to the office of Regional Administrator Peter Neglia. Nevertheless, after reviewing the files, the committee voted to begin steps to terminate Wedtech from the 8(a) program.

The conclusion was communicated to Wedtech in a letter, which gave the company thirty days to explain in writing why it should not be kicked out of the program. The threat carried little weight, for Wedtech was already getting expensive assurances from Neglia that the company could circumvent the SBA's rules.

The plotting began in September 1983 over lunch. Neglia met Moreno and the General to share intelligence on the 8(a) matter. He warned them about the letter from Yee's committee declaring the company in technical default.

Ehrlich told Neglia that there must be a way for Wedtech to stay in the program. Perhaps the stingy Neuberger could be persuaded to transfer enough of his stock to Mariotta to remain in compliance with the 51 percent rule. Failing that, Ehrlich said, perhaps a collection of insiders could be persuaded to do the same. After all, Wedtech had been a model 8(a) company, scoring valuable points for the regional office. Surely, some way could be found to keep Wedtech in the limelight as the shining star of the 8(a) program.

A few days later, Moreno, Ehrlich, and John Mariotta trooped downtown to the SBA's New York office to state their case. Neglia called in his underlings to a meeting in his office. Moreno pleaded the company's case, assuring the SBA officials that with a little rejuggling of its stock, Wedtech could be brought back into compliance. The company simply needed a little time.

Shortly afterward, Ehrlich and Moreno invited Neglia to

dinner at a restaurant in Little Italy. Over the aroma of olive oil and simmering tomatoes, Moreno described the company's plight. Moreno told Neglia that he thought Wedtech could be brought back into compliance—as long as the company could be guaranteed a friendly interpretation of the SBA rules.

The Wedtech officers were considering a paper transfer of title to huge amounts of insider stock to Mariotta at a price he could never afford to pay. That would allow the company to squeeze more time out of the 8(a) program, but would not actually threaten their holdings, since the overpriced stock would eventually revert to the original owners.

Neglia listened and offered his legal analysis. The only immediate help he could offer was to grant Wedtech more time to reply to the SBA's eligibility inquiry. And shortly after the dinner, the officers received a letter giving them until January 16, 1984, to cure their problem or face immediate termination. The lengthy extension was a godsend, for at the time of the public offering, they had signed agreements promising that no insider shares would change hands within the company for up to 120 days. The extension enabled them to comply with that restriction, while giving them ample time to recomply with SBA requirements.

The notion of turning over stock to John Mariotta—whom most of the officers had already come to regard as a madman—rubbed all of them the wrong way. Nevertheless, at a stormy Halloween session of the board of directors at the Squadron, Ellenoff law offices, they decided there was no way around it. According to board minutes:

> The Board concluded after the discussion that the Corporation's Section 8(a) status could only be maintained if Mr. Mariotta were to be a 51% shareholder of the corporation. The officers and directors . . . indicated their willingness to transfer to Mr. Mariotta sufficient shares to accomplish such purpose.

On November 7, the officers and their advisers convened an all-day meeting at the Helmsley Palace Hotel to iron out details of the transaction. The deal would be written up as a stock purchase agreement, with Mariotta promising to pay for the stock in installments over a two-year period. If he did not pay, it was agreed that the stock would revert automatically to its original owners.

But the written agreement would not reflect an oral deal between Mariotta and the stock "sellers." In their discussions, Mariotta promised to let the purchase deadline pass and promptly return the stock to its rightful owners. In essence, he would hold their stock certificates for two years, then give them back, no questions asked. The SBA would never be the wiser.

Some aspects of the deal worried Wallach. He told the officers that, with nothing in writing, there was no way to guarantee legally that Mariotta would do what he said.

As the close of the year drew near, the Wedtech officers found themselves scrambling to come up with enough parties willing to engage in the transparent stock deal. They later testified that they asked the Squadron firm to participate in the transfer, but the lawyers refused. Wallach also backed out. Richard Biaggi was putting up so much opposition that Ehrlich seriously doubted he could get the congressman to go along.

Soon, as was their custom, Moreno and Mariotta found themselves at Biaggi's law office pleading for help.

To Biaggi, there was a significant irony in their visit. He listened cynically. "Every time you have a problem, you always come to us, and we always take you out of these situations. We will go along, but there will be some conditions to going along."

Unlike the other participants in the transfer, Biaggi demanded that he and Ehrlich regain title to their shares in one year instead of two. Mariotta agreed with Biaggi's terms.

Rushing to meet their deadline for submitting paperwork to the SBA, Neuberger transferred 1.4 million shares to Mariotta, Moreno 246,000, and Guariglia and Shorten 54,000 each. Ehrlich and Richard Biaggi ended up signing the agreement prepared by the Squadron firm on December 27. While the other officers scrambled, Mariotta was oblivious to the problem, sunning himself during a long Christmas vacation in Puerto Rico.

As their January 16 deadline drew near, Ehrlich and his

associates had been hard at work on imaginative legal briefs
for submission to the SBA, defending the stock transfer and
Mariotta's status as a socially and economically disadvantaged
businessman:

> Legislative history and case law provides that an individual
> who is prosperous may be allowed to participate in the 8(a)
> program. Mr. Mariotta competes in an industry which requires
> a tremendous amount of capital investment. Moreover, the
> type of assets owned by Mr. Mariotta are deceiving because
> Wedtech stock does not have an established market. Conse-
> quently, Mr. Mariotta's net worth is vastly overestimated. The
> 8(a) program was meant to assist entrepreneurs like Mr. Mari-
> otta, and thus, it would be consistent with established policy to
> continue Mr. Mariotta's membership in the 8(a) program.

Although Neglia had been apprised of the plan, Wedtech
still faced potential troubles at the SBA. Jack Matthews, the
legal counsel to Neglia, was dubious about the proposed stock
transfer. Other SBA lawyers raised concerns about the partial-
ity of Biaggi & Ehrlich's opinion, since the firm held stock in
Wedtech.

Bypassing Matthews completely, Neglia went to David Elbaum, Matthews' counterpart in the New York district office,
and asked him for a legal ruling on Wedtech's arguments.
Elbaum requested a second outside legal opinion, and Neglia
agreed to push for it. That same day, a letter from Squadron,
Ellenoff was hand-delivered to Neglia's office, assuring the
SBA that the stock transfer was legal and in full compliance
with Securities and Exchange Commission rules. Neither Elbaum—who was troubled by Biaggi & Ehrlich's conflicts in the
matter—nor Neglia rejected the Squadron opinion, even
though the firm also held Wedtech stock. Squadron and law
partner Arthur Siskind later testified that they had no knowledge of the corrupt intent of the stock transaction.

One day after he received the paperwork Elbaum gave
Neglia his written opinion that the stock transfer was legal.

Over a festive Italian dinner, Neglia passed on the good
news to Moreno and Ehrlich, who were ecstatic. It was a good

day for the company, which had just received indications from Washington that it was a shoo-in for the Navy contract.

Soon afterward, under the SBA's letterhead, Neglia sent along his formal opinion in the Washington office.

"My examination of the facts and recommendations leads me to conclude that Wedtech Corporation is in compliance with SBA's standards of eligibility based on Public Laws 95-507 and 96-481," Neglia wrote. "The firm is owned and controlled by individuals who are socially and economically disadvantaged and has not reached a competitive status in the private sector. The firm is eligible to participate fully in the Section 8(a) program."

"THE FIX IS ON"

ON A RAINY OCTOBER EVENING, Richard Ramirez, the young director of the Navy's small business office, was at home alone, when a car carrying three people pulled into his driveway. Earlier that day, he had taken an urgent call from Steve Denlinger, the LAMA lobbyist with whom he had frequent contacts on minority business matters. Denlinger was with officials of the Wedtech Corporation of the South Bronx, and they had just come from a meeting with what he called the "Big Man," one of their important contacts in Washington. Now, they wanted to see Ramirez to discuss a business proposition.

Ramirez was not fond of Denlinger, whom he had come to regard as arrogant and insulting. But he was well aware of LAMA's political clout; it was partly through the group's advocacy that Ramirez had been installed in a $58,000-a-year job with the stodgy Navy, assigned to change its minority hiring and contracting policies—then among the worst in the entire federal government.

Denlinger told Ramirez that Wedtech—along with virtually every other minority firm in the country—was interested in the Navy's giant pontoon contract. Ramirez was used to talking business at all hours. Since his elevation to the Navy job, he had moonlighted on the side, serving as a paid consultant to a variety of small businesses seeking government work. Ramirez needed the money.

By October 1983, he was drowning in a sea of personal problems. For several years, he had been involved in an expensive extramarital affair. To hide the affair from his wife, he had begun asking for consulting payments in cash and fudging on his tax returns. By the time the Wedtech officers came to call, Ramirez's wife had moved out with their children and virtually everything they owned, leaving him with a tattered old corduroy sofa, a couple of hard-backed chairs, and a piano whose notes echoed in the nearly empty house.

When they arrived, Denlinger led Mariotta and Moreno through a side door into a vacant family room. Ramirez offered them each a glass of cheap wine, and they sat down to talk. He was amazed at how much they knew about the pontoon deal. They were aware that parts of it were already promised to Puerto Rico and Texas. They knew that the Navy's key decision-maker, Everett Pyatt, was opposed to setting aside the contract for a minority firm. They also knew that Pyatt, whose appointment was only an acting one, was awaiting nomination for the job permanently. The sensitive appointment, although pushed by Navy Secretary John Lehman, seemed interminably stalled at the White House.

After a few minutes, Mariotta and Denlinger drifted into other rooms. Moreno grew quiet, studying Ramirez's face. He told Ramirez they were looking for an inside consultant, someone to guide them through the Navy contracting process. "How can we help you?" he asked, his tone deadly serious.

Ramirez laughed. "I'll take $100,000 in green," he joked.

"How about $60,000?" Moreno retorted.

Ramirez stalled, suspecting that this gold mine, coming at such a crisis in his life, was too good to be true. After all, he had no real authority in the pontoon contract. "Sure," he said finally. "I'll take the money in cash."

Moreno said the money would be paid in two installments—part up front, the rest once the contract was delivered.

Back in New York, there was skepticism. Neuberger questioned Ramirez's ability to deliver the huge contract. But Moreno assured the officers that Ramirez, because of his key influence in the 8(a) awards, would be the "most important mole we could install" at the Navy.

After the usual harangue, Moreno got the go-ahead. He drove home, where he kept a stash of ready cash, and threw together $20,000, a down payment on services to be delivered. Then, he boarded an Eastern Airlines shuttle to Washington.

Ramirez, who'd never imagined the riches that could lie in store for a government employee, was ecstatic. Over the next few years, Wedtech would pay him the rest of his $60,000, plus another $120,000 in consulting fees funneled through Repcon, a Pennsylvania consulting company. He also earned $125,000 as a commission for setting up Wedtech's purchase of a bankrupt Michigan shipyard, which he had learned about during his Navy years. After leaving the Navy in early 1984, Ramirez also took Wedtech with him as a client to his new job at the Washington lobbying firm of Gnau, Jacobsen, Carter, whose principal partner, John Gnau, had been Ronald Reagan's campaign manager in the state of Michigan and had connections at many agencies.

The Wedtech officers regarded the payments to Ramirez as a necessary insurance policy. They were prepared to pay—and pay well—for this giant Navy deal.

In late October, Mariotta summoned his secretary, Ceil Lewis, into Guariglia's office for a conference. Guariglia bluntly asked if she were still maintaining the FHJ slush fund. Lewis, who that year had deposited another $250,000 in kickbacks into the fund, said the account was still active.

"Good," Guariglia said. "We're going to use it."

*   *   *

In the fall of 1983, procurement officials at the Navy were dead set against reserving the contract for small business. Their position was that no existing small business was qualified to do the work quickly enough. It also saw no reason to set aside the contract for the SBA when major shipyards all over the country were idle and begging for work.

Pontoon causeways were not a new technology; the Navy had been using the floating piers since World War II to unload ships in hostile waters. But in 1983 the Navy, under the threat of mounting tension in the Persian Gulf, had decided to buy a large number of huge freighters, which would serve as supply ships for the Rapid Deployment Force. The pontoon boats or "lighterages" were a vital part of the plan for quick unloading in areas where a freighter could not find a friendly port.

The structure of the boats was amazingly simple. Each causeway consisted of a rigid metal frame encasing airtight steel boxes or pontoons, similar to ice cubes in a tray. But the Navy had left itself little lead time for acquiring the boats. The first squadron of prepositioned ships was scheduled to leave port in October 1984. The Navy wanted at least ten pontoons to send along with them.

As originally envisioned, the contract was to be divided into two portions. The most expensive portion was for the motor-driven pontoon causeways; the other, which would total no more than a few million dollars, involved building a much simpler, nonmotorized version, which was essentially nothing more than a barge. Given the tight delivery deadline, sentiment within the Navy procurement offices strongly favored awarding the entire contract to an established firm.

However, a number of 8(a) companies had learned of the pontoon program and were clamoring for it, soliciting help from their congressional representatives. Pyatt was also feeling pressure from the SBA, which argued that the Navy had done less than any other agency to reserve a portion of its contracts for minorities. He likewise had to answer to his boss, Navy Secretary John F. Lehman, Jr.

Lehman, a ferocious infighter considered one of the most "hands-on" Navy chiefs in recent history, had pushed his way into the Pentagon in 1981 determined to change the shape of the Navy radically. During his tenure, the Navy's budget grew from $70 billion to $95.3 billion, and its maritime force expanded from about 450 to more than 600 ships. But under Lehman's management style contract matters became more politicized than they had ever been, with many decisions ending on the busy secretary's desk.

Pyatt, a career civil servant who had climbed to one of the Navy's highest-ranking positions, had emerged as part of Lehman's hand-picked inner circle. But the confirmation of his acting appointment as assistant secretary seemed to be permanently stalled. It seemed to have landed, curiously enough, in Meese's office on the desk of Wedtech's ubiquitous ally, James Jenkins.

The delicacy of Pyatt's situation was not lost on the Wedtech gang. Nofziger and Bragg centered their lobbying efforts squarely on Pyatt and his boss, Lehman. Nofziger's pull at the Navy was well known. He counted among his clients the Marine Engineers Beneficial Association, a powerful, AFL-CIO-affiliated seafarers union which had been a major supporter of the Reagan–Bush team, and Nofziger's lobbying efforts on the union's behalf had frequently brought him into contact with Lehman and other top Navy brass.

Bragg had gone to work on the pliable Jim Sanders, and in November, Wedtech's strategy began to fall into place. Sanders contacted Lehman to appeal Pyatt's decision that the Navy would not use 8(a) firms to build the pontoons. A few weeks later, Pyatt did an about-face and decided to set aside the nonmotorized portion of the contract for an 8(a) firm. This conciliatory move only added fuel to the fire, however. It was seen as tossing a bone to minorities, and the 8(a) companies realized that they could now make a legitimate political issue of it.

Wedtech was hardly the only firm pushing for the work, but that autumn, mysterious things began to happen to its competitors. As Moreno aptly described in an affidavit given to Senate investigators: "In my view, Wedtech was able to obtain the contract because of the pressure and influence we brought to bear through our consultants and contacts within and without the federal government."

The first company to seek the Navy contract was the Univox Corporation, a black-owned California firm. Univox's owner, John Grayson, also had made what seemed to be all the right moves. He had hired Nofziger–Bragg, and he had solicited letters of support from Nevada Republican Sens. Paul Laxalt and Chic Hecht. He was also first in line to apply for the pontoon contract, and under normal SBA procedures, he would have had a proprietary claim on the contract.

But Grayson received a disturbing phone call from the SBA's associate administrator for minority small business, Henry Wilfong, who had supported Univox for the work. The Navy had decided the contract was too large to go to one company, so it was to be split into phases and divided among a number of eligible 8(a) firms.

Grayson was discreetly warned "not to make waves" if he was shut out of the initial phase of the Navy deal—this contract offered plenty of bounty that would be amply spread around the 8(a) community.

As Wilfong later testified, bleaker news soon came Grayson's way in a phone call from Nofziger. After talking to his lobbyist, Grayson called Wilfong, who later reported that Nofziger had warned Grayson to back off, that "the fix was on" and he "had no chance of winning that contract."

Another early contender was Lee Engineering of San Francisco, owned by Frank Lee, a Chinese-American backer of Ronald Reagan. When company officials heard about the contract, they too tried to retain Nofziger. They also contacted Sanders and Wedtech's newly recruited Navy "mole," Ramirez, and were encouraged to pursue the contract.

Taking the contract specifications seriously, Lee Engineering went to work to make certain that the firm could satisfy the Navy and meet the contract's unstated political prerequisites. Realizing that part of the job had been promised to Puerto Rico, they set up a Puerto Rican joint venture and lobbied Bush's ally, ex-Governor Luis Ferre, to look favorably upon the company. Ferre also encouraged their efforts. By mid-January 1984, when Lee Engineering got word that it had been dropped from consideration, the company had sunk so much money into trying to win the deal that it went bankrupt.

Meanwhile, Wedtech's officers had been working every other angle that they could think of. Through Biaggi, they solicited the help of D'Amato and Addabbo, who wrote personal appeals to Lehman pushing Wedtech. Denlinger had been working on the deputy associate administrator of the SBA, Robert Saldivar. After meetings with Denlinger, Saldivar began pushing Wedtech with such zeal that his underlings wondered if he had taken on the company as a private cause.

Wedtech believed it should reward Saldivar's loyalty. Wallach's memos reflect that Wedtech helped him get two jobs—first, promotion to SBA associate administrator after Wilfong was pushed aside and, secondly, a post as the Navy's small business director after Ramirez resigned to become a Wedtech consultant.

In addition, an appreciative Denlinger in 1985 showed up at Saldivar's door with a $10,000 cash gift. Saldivar turned the money down, but never reported the offer to authorities. According to testimony of the Wedtech officers, Saldivar later told Moreno there was another financial matter with which Wedtech could help him. His son was involved with a Washington restaurant that was desperately in need of a $25,000 loan.

Moreno testified that he went to the restaurant with Saldivar to discuss the transaction. The loan went through, and Wedtech never recouped the money. But Moreno said that while the deal was being worked out, Saldivar kept his ethical distance by sitting at a table a few feet away.

Republican politics had added a new complication to the pontoon deal. The word quickly spread among 8(a) companies that, at the behest of the Vice President, parts of the contract were earmarked for Puerto Rico and for South Texas. Texas was due a share of the contract as part of another administration economic revitalization program, the Southwest Border Initiative.

The Puerto Rican problem was one which the Wedtech officials addressed in their usual manner by hiring a new "consultant" with connections on the island. They found their man in San Juan native Rafael Capo, an articulate, Yale-educated lawyer with impeccable political connections. In his former job as director of the Office of Industrial Tax Exemption for the Puerto Rican government, he had spearheaded efforts to give substantial federal tax breaks to new industrial investors. He had also been the Vice President's point man on Puerto Rican issues. Although Wedtech still was making belated payments to Bush's relative, Dickey Dyer, for all practical purposes it had lost its entree to the Vice President's office. Capo, they reasoned, could be a way of reestablishing contact.

As Capo later described the job to me, he was to serve as the company's representative on Puerto Rican investments. Through his contacts in the Hispanic business community, he was familiar with the South Bronx firm. He insisted, however, that he never spoke to the Vice President about Wedtech while he was working at the White House.

Mariotta became enamored with Capo, convinced he could help not only with the pontoon deal but also with the coatings process that a new Wedtech subsidiary was working to develop. Capo's connections at the Export–Import Bank, where he had once been a top official, could also be valuable as Wedtech moved into international ventures. In compensation, Wedtech paid $44,394 in fees to his lawyer-wife, Ines, during the critical year of the pontoon negotiations. Moreno claimed that the indirect payments were requested by Capo because he was worried about the propriety of working for Wedtech less than a year after leaving the federal government.

When the Puerto Rican contingent heard through the grapevine that Wedtech was likely to win a large part of the Navy deal and that Nofziger was the man calling the shots, Luis Ferre's former aide Michael Govan called Nofziger immediately. "He denied everything. He said he'd never heard of Wedtech, that he wasn't involved in the Navy contract," Govan recalled. "We had no reason to doubt him at the time." But the information seemed so solid that Govan called Mariotta and arranged for Ferre to meet with him. Ferre went to the South Bronx to talk over the deal with the Wedtech officers and encourage them to subcontract part of the work to

Puerto Rican Dry Dock in San Juan. Ferre left with the impression that, should Wedtech get the job, at least part of it would come to Puerto Rico.

Unbeknownst to the ex-governor, however, Wedtech was determined by then not to share the contract with anyone unless absolutely forced to make a political concession. By the time the Navy turned over the pontoon work, the Puerto Rican commitment had disappeared. To the Wedtech officers, it was proof that the Reagan–Nofziger–Meese connection pulled considerably more weight at the Pentagon that the Bush–Ferre forces.

Bob Wallach was taking a special interest in Wedtech's efforts to win the pontoon deal. The company, from which he had acquired a block of stock but nothing more, had the potential to make him a very rich man. In September, Wedtech had paid him $125,000—$25,000 less than he requested—and, at Guariglia's suggestion, decided to "cook the books" to cover up the payment by disguising it as a charge for legal work. The cover-up allowed Wedtech to charge the expense to the shareholders instead of having to subtract it from the all-important profit statement.

The officers also had agreed to pay Squadron, Ellenoff a $150,000-a-year retainer, from which Wallach would get a finder's fee. The deal—which in essence left Wedtech paying Wallach twice for his sage counsel—had touched off concern at the Squadron firm because of ethical restrictions, which strictly limit fee sharing between lawyers. But, according to the officers, Mariotta agreed to an unorthodox billing arrangement, in which Wallach's cut of the Squadron bill was charged as fees for outside legal consultation.

Pyatt's decision to set aside the nonmotorized pontoons for a minority company caused the Wedtech officers to turn once more to Wallach. In their minds, it was clear the Navy intended to discriminate against minorities by handing over only the smallest part of the pontoon deal. Moreno called Wallach to complain about the Navy's "tokenism." The Navy was simply tossing the company a crumb, Moreno said, which would be meaningless in the contract's total magnitude. Wallach promised to see what he could do.

Wallach had been meeting frequently with Meese, often over dinner or breakfast. So, a few days after their phone chat, Moreno testified, he was not surprised to get a status report from him. He said Wallach told him he had reached Meese at an unidentified airport and that Meese promised to place a call to Defense Secretary Weinberger and ask him to pressure Lehman to set aside the contract.

Shortly afterward, Moreno said, he got another call from Wallach. "Everything's been more or less taken care of," he was told.

Within a matter of days, Moreno received word from Wedtech's "mole," Ramirez, that Pyatt "had changed his position completely on the pontoon, and that we were going to get the entire contract." Pyatt had decided the motorized portion of the contract would also be open to an 8(a) firm. Ramirez told Moreno that Wedtech was the likely "prime recipient" of the deal.

Wallach reportedly took credit for Pyatt's change of heart. Wedtech officers said Wallach told them that, through Meese, he had placed pressure on Pyatt either to approve Wedtech or risk losing his appointment as assistant Navy secretary. When Moreno called him with Ramirez's good news, Wallach was jubilant.

"I'm very happy, Mario. We did it," Moreno recalled him saying.

Wallach, however, was not the only one to trumpet his influence. The Wedtech officers were also led to believe that Nofziger and Bragg had leaned on Pyatt through a barrage of phone calls to his office. Lehman would later deny that any such political pressure was brought to bear, and James McKay, the special prosecutor appointed to investigate Nofziger's and Meese's ties to Wedtech, said he found no evidence to indicate Pyatt's nomination was linked to the Wedtech talks.

Curiously enough, however, Pyatt's nomination won White House approval on April 16, 1984. One day later, Wedtech received final word from the Navy that it had been awarded a $24 million pontoon deal, with two unpriced options on future work.

Almost as an afterthought, Pyatt convened a January 19, 1984, meeting of uniformed Navy officers to get their feedback on a decision he had already made and communicated to the SBA. "We were asked to prove negatives, to show him why this couldn't be done," recalled Capt. David de Vicq, the assistant commander whose responsibilities included the pontoon contract. Pyatt heard warnings from at least two admirals—Tom Hughes and John Paul Jones—that a set-aside could be disastrous for the Navy. Admiral Hughes described problems the Navy was having with an experienced boat builder, Jeffboat Company, in delivering an earlier pontoon order. "The trouble would be compounded by giving the work to someone who has no nautical experience," he said.

But by then, the SBA had already started its search for the perfect 8(a) shipbuilder. Other minority firms were ostensibly in competition for the contract, but on January 25, the same day the SBA approved the bogus stock transfer allowing Wedtech to stay in the 8(a) program, the agency approved Wedtech as the contractor whose name would be forwarded to the Navy.

As part of the arrangement, Wedtech agreed to subcontract part of the motorized pontoon work to Medley Tool Company, a firm in Philadelphia, and another company in Arlington, Virginia. For the nonmotorized pontoons, it agreed to work with Martinez Custom Builders of Brownsville, Texas, a newly formed joint venture. The Texas firm had been added as a last-minute concession to Senator Tower, whose aide, José Martinez, later went to work for Wedtech as a consultant.

Even so, Wedtech was doing what it could to push out Medley, which it regarded as an interloper. In the latter part of January, Moreno brought up the matter with Wallach and soon received word that "Mr. Medley . . . was under some kind of investigation by the Justice Department." Ultimately, Moreno received notice through Bragg that Medley had been conveniently disqualified after the SBA resurrected some old charges against the company, which were never proved.

Sanders communicated the SBA's choices to Pyatt by letter, and the Navy, under the gun to get things moving, undertook a hurried inspection of the facilities of Medley and Wedtech. When Navy contract officials showed up to conduct a site inspection, they were led by Mariotta through the company's showcase headquarters, with its spotless factory floors and expensive machinery, then driven to the new plant site at 149th Street and Bruckner Boulevard, which was to serve as the pontoon production facility.

The Wedtech officers, in need of a building to comply with the contract requirements, had found a nearly gutted 215,000-square-foot structure through Pat Simone, who had acquired it from the state Urban Development Corporation. It had no electricity or plumbing and was missing a roof. The building had no capacity for overhead cranes, which would be needed to lift the pontoons. The company also still had to build a giant plastic bubble outside to serve as a painting center.

De Vicq then asked how Wedtech would get the boats to the water for testing, which was a requirement of the contract. As his notes from the meeting indicate, "Contractor proceeded to lead party over railroad track, along a road owned by a trucking company, then onto a private junk area to look at 35,000 feet of waterfront property owned by Wedtech."

Wedtech didn't actually own the waterfront property; it was merely renting a slice of land from Con Edison. The Navy inspectors, particularly De Vicq, departed with serious reservations about Wedtech. But the Wedtech officials assured the skeptical Navy inspectors that they were ready to begin an elaborate $3 million renovation that would make the 149th Street building a model factory site. The Navy inspectors, unable to prove that Wedtech *couldn't* do the work, issued a guarded opinion that the company could do it—although it would probably fall behind schedule.

What the Navy did not know was that the Wedtech officials were planning to cash in personally on the new pontoon facility. They testified later that the deal was worked out in a series of meetings at Simone's Hunts Point Auto Wreckers. The

Wedtech officers decided to form a leasing company called Jofre Associates and enter a partnership with Simone's PDJ Realty Company, for which they would pay Simone almost $1 million. Their partnership, which they named PJ Associates, then would sublease the building to Wedtech at an inflated price, enabling them to skim a share of the payments for themselves. In addition the extensive renovations were to be carried out by Simone's family-owned construction company, so that, in Guariglia's words, "we could make some money on the construction side."

When Biaggi heard about the officers' secret deal with his friend Simone, he was furious.

"Why didn't you let us know about this?" he demanded of Moreno in a meeting at the Biaggi & Ehrlich law firm.

". . . We should have gotten our 5 percent of whatever you did there!"

Guariglia testified that one day he walked into Simone's office just as Simone was finishing a heated talk with the congressman. "That S.O.B. just asked me for 5 percent of the building," Guariglia remembered Simone saying. But he urged Guariglia not to fret about the dispute. "Don't worry about it. I own him."

Even after the contract announcement ceremonies on April 23, 1984, the political bloodshed still lay ahead. The original piece of the contract was worth $24.2 million. Wedtech knew it would lose money on the deal; its price could not cover the costs of setting up a completely new shipbuilding operation and delivering the finished boats. But the agreement included options for up to $150 million in 1985 and 1986 and the prospect of a similar contract with the Army, which was also acquiring pontoons. Wedtech banked its hopes of a profit on receiving all possible contract options. To secure them, Wedtech would have to keep its political network happily in place—just in case it had to use politics to pressure the Navy.

Tensions between the company's New York and Washington support factions had escalated sharply during the contract negotiations. Each side wanted credit for delivering the deal. Wallach had made it clear that he, through his well-connected friend, had effectively used the Pyatt nomination to force the Navy's hand. Nofziger and Bragg had delivered Sanders and, with Wallach's help, John Lehman.

The New York faction let it be known, however, that it was ultimately responsible for Wedtech's good fortune, since the firm would be nowhere without the persistent efforts of Biaggi, D'Amato, and Addabbo. If the company abandoned them, it could expect serious problems with its hope for lucrative add-ons.

D'Amato made that clear when he showed up along with Biaggi and Congressman Robert Garcia for the well-attended press conference at 595 Gerard Avenue. D'Amato had just come into the plant with his aide, John Zagame, when he spotted Moreno chatting with Mark Bragg, who had flown up from Washington to attend the event.

The senator looked Bragg square in the eye. "Tell Mr. Nofziger that we control the government, not him. Make sure that you tell him this," Moreno recalled him saying. Then, D'Amato turned and stalked down the hall.

12

SIMPLE SIMON

WHILE WEDTECH WAS BUSILY raking in federal contracts, Bronx lawyer Stanley Simon was establishing a reputation as perhaps the stupidest man ever to serve as Bronx borough president. The Machiavellian Democratic party boss, Stanley Friedman, had plucked Simon from well-earned obscurity on the New York City Council in 1978 to fill the unexpired term of Borough President Robert Abrams, the new state attorney general. Friedman was looking for a willing puppet to carry out his wishes on the all-powerful city Board of Estimate, and Simon, the Riverdale district leader, was a longtime cipher of the party machine.

Born in the Bronx, Simon grew up on West Tremont Avenue where his parents ran a "mom and pop" candy store. A product of the Bronx public schools, Simon gained his first political experience as student body president of DeWitt High School. After graduation from New York University, he picked up a law degree in 1952 from Brooklyn Law School, and shortly afterward, he joined the heavily Jewish and Irish Northend Democratic Club in the Bronx.

Simon worked to get out the vote, shaking hands and making small talk, and in time his party loyalty paid off in a series of patronage jobs with the state legislature.

He was appointed to a vacant slot on the City Council in January 1973, representing a district that encompassed the well-heeled Riverdale section. From a cubicle at 250 Broadway, opposite City Hall, Simon each week held court for Bronx constituents seeking help for their problems. Simon relished the chance to organize a street cleanup or intervene with the Parking Violations Bureau on behalf of an important constituent. These were matters that Simon could handle with distinction.

With his elevation to the borough presidency, however, Simon overtaxed his limited abilities. "At the time I became borough president," he testified at his federal trial, "the Bronx was looked on by the world as a devastated area. . . . The unemployment records were very high. The delivery of essential services was in a terrible state. . . ."

Simon was hardly up to the task of revitalizing a borough wracked by poverty, blight, and pervasive corruption. A man of mechanical smiles, blank stares, and twisted syntax, he seemed baffled by the city's budget deliberations and, to the chagrin of his aides, put his foot in his mouth with virtually every public pronouncement. As *Daily News* columnist Ken Auletta described in a 1979 column on Simon's reelection campaign, "working for a candidate like Simon could induce heart attacks. Aides tremble not that he will say the wrong thing, but that he will have nothing to say."

Nonetheless, Simon's reelection effort brought support from not only Friedman but also Rep. Mario Biaggi, who signed on as his campaign chairman. It was the first time the popular congressman had ever campaigned for someone other than himself. Friedman, who tried to polish Simon's image by sending him to a Manhattan speech therapist, drummed up financial support from a host of backers who were in need of city favors. The donors included developers Donald Trump and Peter Kalikow, express-bus operator Edward Arrigoni, and parking lot baron Paul Dano. Brooklyn longshoremen's boss Tony Scotto contributed $5,000 on the eve of his Federal racketeering trial, while Friedman's law partner, Roy Cohn, signed up as a loan guarantor.

While Friedman and Biaggi pulled strings to bring out Simon's base of white Jewish supporters, they kept Simon closemouthed as much as possible. In public appearances, he showed a startling lack of energy and charisma, reading blankly from prepared statements and stumbling through short press conferences.

There was really only one area in which Simon truly excelled. He discovered early on that he could translate the pull of the $80,000-a-year borough presidency into a comfortable life-style for himself, his wife Irene, and their two daughters. Largely through his influence, Irene was given two simultaneous part-time jobs: one as a $25,000-a-year consultant with the Bronx-based Alexander's department store, the other a $300-a-week job as an "outside commissioned agent" with the politically connected Castle Fuel and Oil Company. Irene seldom showed up for her fuel oil job, but the company contended later that her salary was based on number of gallons sold. Castle just happened to do $9 million a year in business with city agencies.

One of Simon's first orders of business was to install on the public payroll a personal manservant, Ralph Lawrence. Lawrence held the lofty title of assistant to the borough president, but his job was to serve at Simon's beck and call from sunrise to midnight. His duties included bringing Simon the soup that was a part of his not very successful weight-loss diet and feeding Simon's cat, Ziggy, and cleaning its litter box. He would also carry Simon's luggage, buy his groceries, have his clothes laundered, and arrange for theater and dinner outings. A walkie-talkie and beeper kept him tethered to his boss.

Over the years, Lawrence's salary rose from $34,200 to $52,000, but the raises could hardly be considered merit increases. Instead, Lawrence was expected to pick up the tab for his boss for meals at various fancy restaurants, car rentals, and other services. The government eventually charged that Simon extorted $13,000 from Lawrence through the unorthodox kickback scheme.

It became a truism in the Bronx that anyone with business before Simon could expect to pay some sort of tribute. Most were hit up for contributions to Simon's President's Club, a select group of $1,000-and-up campaign donors managed by his economic development aide, Kathy Zamechansky. Businessmen in need of city-backed loans or property were referred to Zamechansky, and they complained openly that their requests for help had barely reached her desk before she suggested the political advisability of their joining the President's Club. Others contributed more tangible goods and merchandise. One contractor spent $8,000 making improvements to Simon's Riverdale home and paying expenses for the borough president's 1984 holidays in Rome and Las Vegas. He also paid for a car for Simon's teen-age daughter, who had just learned to drive.

Even his one-time supporter, Mayor Ed Koch, eventually made light of Simon's avarice. Testifying before the state anti-corruption commission in 1989, Koch was asked about his relationship with Simon, who by that time had been sentenced to prison for his role in the Wedtech conspiracy. Koch said Simon was only interested in the workings of city government if it meant that somehow "we could build a bathroom for him. I mean, it was things like that that you discussed with Stanley Simon."

It was only natural that Wedtech eventually would come to need Simon; such was the way New York City government worked. Through his seat on the Board of Estimate, Simon exercised clout in city land deals, leases, and contracts. In 1984, after the Navy had rejected Wedtech's half-baked plan to launch the pontoons from the inaccessible waterfront property, Wedtech's only hope of meeting the Navy's strict deadline was to use its city connections to arrange a lease on a waterfront parcel owned by the city's Department of Ports and Terminals. As usual, the firm would have to overcome a rather formidable obstacle. Most of the city's valuable waterfront land was obligated under long-term leases that were virtually unbreakable.

Ehrlich had wisely counseled Moreno several years earlier that the newly installed borough president was a "person who deserved to be cultivated." Simon had first showed up on Wedtech's doorstep in 1979 as part of a tour of his fiefdom. Soon, Mariotta and Neuberger were featured on the front of a brochure with Simon for the Bronx Democratic dinner.

At one such function the subject of Simon's sixty-five-year-old brother-in-law, Henry Bittman, came up in casual conversation. Simon had a special fondness for Bittman, his elder sister's husband and a jeweler by trade who had fallen on hard times because of a foot ailment. Bittman had been a good provider for Simon's handicapped niece and ailing sister, who died in 1984. As several Wedtech officers testified later, Ehrlich told them Simon was looking for extra income for his brother-in-law, who also held a patronage job with a state legislative commission. He wanted Wedtech to hire Bittman, with one condition. Every week, Bittman had to show up at the state offices in the World Trade Center to sign for his weekly government paycheck. He could only make it to the South Bronx four days a week.

Mariotta and Neuberger fumed. "I don't want any of those politicians bringing me deadbeats over here," Moreno recalled Mariotta saying.

But at the time, the officers were awaiting word from the Board of Estimate on their purchase of a city-owned building at 350 Gerard Avenue, which they needed for the Army engine contract. They could not afford to cross Simon, so they hired Bittman on April 13, 1981, at a salary of $15,000 per year, as a payroll clerk. Ironically, the man holding a no-show legislative job was the keeper of Wedtech's employee time-clock.

In August 1983, to the outrage of other Wedtech employees, Bittman was granted a $10,000 merit raise at Simon's request. Wedtech had wanted to give him $2,000.

"That guy is a problem here and has created a lot of morale problems among other employees," Mariotta said. But the amount was increased after Simon, encountering the officers at a Democratic fund-raiser, complained that it was not enough.

By the summer of 1985, Bittman was earning $35,000, and his supervisors were on notice not to irritate him. When one supervisor unwisely placed Bittman on a layoff list—figuring the company could hire two competent employees with the money from Bittman's salary—Guariglia instructed him that Bittman could not be fired.

Simon's fondness for Wedtech grew when he discovered that he and Moreno shared a mutual interest in the Atlantic City casinos. For several years, during efforts to bring legalized gambling to New York, Simon had enjoyed high-roller's treatment when visiting the glitzy Boardwalk gaming halls. All he had to do was call, and the red carpet was rolled out for him, with free transportation, rooms, meals, and entertainment for the asking.

For Moreno, the casinos had become the fuel for a passionate $1 million gambling habit. He spent so much time at the blackjack tables that he talked Neuberger and Mariotta and his sisters into investing in several expensive co-ops, which could be used for their own pleasure outings as well as to house the government officials who sometimes went along as Moreno's guests. At one point, Moreno owned seven apartments in the fancy Ritz-Carlton on the Boardwalk.

Amid the bright lights, squeals of ecstasy, and moans of anguish on the casino floor, Simon gambled away with plodding, methodical technique and low stakes. Whenever possible he liked to gamble with other people's money; it was much safer that way.

In November 1983, Moreno invited Simon and Ehrlich to accompany him on a weekend gambling junket. Moreno, Simon, Ehrlich, and their wives piled into a Wedtech station wagon for the trip. Another of their good-time buddies, SBA regional chief Peter Neglia, and his wife, Marian, were to join them there.

With Moreno behind the wheel, they whiled away the four-hour Friday morning drive telling gambling stories. Moreno dropped off the Simons at the Ritz-Carlton, where they were to stay as guests in a Wedtech apartment, then drove the others to the Tropicana, where they had booked a luxurious two-bedroom suite. That night, they dined and attended a Neil Sedaka concert, then went to the gambling tables. Like a jovial Santa Claus, Moreno handed out chips; he estimated he gave the Simons $2,000 to $3,000 that weekend. All told, the group spent about $10,000 in Wedtech money—low losses by Moreno's standards. Well-known at the high-roller's tables, he had blown $43,000 a few weeks earlier.

The junket sealed the friendship between Simon and his most dependable corporate benefactor. It was a cordial and mutually beneficial relationship. When Moreno needed zoning variances to excavate for an underground pool for his home, Simon's office interceded. When Simon threw a $500-per-person fund-raiser, Wedtech could always be counted on to buy a table.

Then, in June 1984, when Wedtech faced its crisis with the Navy, Simon saw a golden opportunity. Wedtech needed a waterfront lease by July to satisfy the Navy's requirements; Simon needed a nest egg of cash. On June 20, Simon ran into Neuberger and his third wife, Eileen, at Yonkers Raceway. The borough president explained that he was facing a tough reelection campaign and needed Wedtech's help, suggesting a figure of $75,000 to $100,000.

The stingy Neuberger said the amount was ridiculous. "The best I can do is $50,000."

They agreed the money would be placed in a ready-access account maintained by the tight-lipped Ceil Lewis, out of funds withdrawn from the FHJ slush fund. When Simon needed money, all he had to do was contact Lewis through Ralph Lawrence. He used the account almost like a twenty-four-hour cash machine. Once, in his largest single withdrawal, Lawrence showed up at Lewis's desk to collect $10,000 in cash.

Simon made good on his part of the deal after Ehrlich learned it might be possible to lease part of a parcel of riverfront property at One Loop Drive in Hunts Point. It was already occupied, but the Department of Ports and Terminals was in the process of evicting the leaseholder for nonpayment of rent.

Wedtech had begun making moves to take over the property. While at the Yonkers race track, Neuberger happened to see Susan Frank, the young, Koch-appointed commissioner of the ports agency who would be deciding on Wedtech's application. He took the opportunity to buttonhole her and ask for a status report on One Loop Drive. She urged him to relax; the matter was being taken care of.

Simon became upset when he saw Neuberger chatting with the city official. Pulling him aside, he scolded Neuberger: "Don't talk to her. That's being taken care of by me and Bernie Ehrlich."

Businessman Henry Thomas was in a delicate position. A black entrepreneur whose small food-processing business, Freedom Industries, had been plagued by problems, he had earned a reputation as a troublemaker by the city and federal agencies with whom he did business. He was a rabble-rouser who complained so much that no one wanted to take him seriously.

Thomas was in the midst of a long-running rent war with the city. He was trying to snare a potential $20 million contract with the Department of Defense to make rations for the Army, a deal expected to create up to 400 new jobs in the Bronx. As with all defense contracts, Thomas had to prove he had the facilities to do the work, a matter he thought he had taken care of in 1982 when he leased a 200,000-square-foot building in the Hunts Point area from the Department of Ports and Terminals.

For more than a year, Thomas had withheld rent payments in a protest of conditions in the building. He claimed that the city had rendered the building virtually unusable by digging a trench through the property to separate the sanitary drain from the sewer line. The trenches, he said, had become foul-smelling pools of human waste, so gross a violation of U.S. Department of Agriculture standards that Freedom could no longer cook its specialty, beef stew, on the premises. The city said he owed $171,000 plus $27,000 in gas and electricity costs, and demanded that he pay.

In January 1984, the department took the first step in eviction proceedings, serving Thomas with a notice to quit the premises. He had begun to panic when a white knight came to his rescue: Bernie Ehrlich, dressed in a National Guard uniform.

Thomas had hired Ehrlich in 1983 and paid the Biaggi law firm a $5,000 retainer. But now, in Thomas's moment of crisis, Ehrlich offered him a proposition, which was drawn up on paper and left at his factory for a signature. Ehrlich's law firm would agree to bring its undeniable clout to bear on the Department of Ports and Terminals. It also would help Thomas win city contracts and represent the company before the Neglia-controlled Small Business Administration, where Freedom had had little success on its own.

In return, Biaggi & Ehrlich wanted 10 percent of Freedom's stock. It also expected an initial retainer of roughly $2,000 a month. When the time was right, after Freedom had sealed its Department of Defense deal, Thomas was told that Biaggi & Ehrlich wanted to take the company public.

Thomas was considering the stock proposal when the city stepped up pressure, filing an eviction proceeding in the Bronx courts. In a funk, he agreed to hire Biaggi & Ehrlich to represent him in the eviction matter while details of the stock agreement were under negotiation. Thomas was vainly trying to barter for a reduced sum of stock and for more specific promises of government contracts before signing the papers that Ehrlich had left on his desk.

Meanwhile, the Department of Ports and Terminals, while trying to kick Freedom out, was negotiating with another company, Hebrew National Corporation, the kosher foods manufacturer, to take over the lease on the waterfront building. In early 1984 when the company launched plans to relocate its Queens offices, the city tried to accommodate the company, fearful it would flee elsewhere. Soon, the company was in line for a lease and a $2 million loan from the city's Industrial Development Agency. Hebrew National also became part of the President's Club with contributions to the Simon campaign. Simon and Zamechansky had given Hebrew National assurances that it could obtain the prime lease on the so-called Vita Foods Building occupied by Thomas.

At that point, in June, Wedtech got word from the Navy that it had to produce a prime lease on a waterfront parcel.

The officers first called Pat Simone, their helpful landlord and business partner, who referred the matter to Tartaglia. Then, they called Bernie Ehrlich. It just so happened that Ehrlich knew about a possible site—a spacious parking lot at One Loop Drive. The building's leaseholder, he explained to the Wedtech crew, was about to be evicted. Maybe Wedtech could take over part of the property if a deal could be worked out with Hebrew National.

Ehrlich seemed untroubled by the fact that he also served as a lawyer for Henry Thomas, who was fighting tooth and nail to keep the building. One day, he took Moreno, Mariotta, and Zamechansky on a tour of the Vita Building, sneaking about to avoid areas where Thomas might spot them. Ehrlich explained to Moreno that he had a secret agreement with Thomas to own part of his company, but had decided nonetheless to drop Freedom Industries as a client.

A few days later, Ehrlich lowered the boom on Henry Thomas, informing him that the firm was now representing Wedtech. Thomas left the meeting in a state of shock. He had thought he had the most powerful law firm in the Bronx working on his side, only to find out it was also representing a client trying to kick him out. Suddenly, he remembered the unsigned stock deal gathering dust on his desk. Ehrlich, he believed, was getting his vengeance.

Thomas called the office of Rep. Joe Addabbo and succeeded in getting a letter sent to Koch, confirming that Freedom was waiting for a major contract that would allow it to settle its debts. On June 26, Koch wrote back to assure Addabbo that, if Freedom sealed the contract, he would help Thomas find a suitable building.

In July, Thomas decided to appeal directly to Susan Frank. He wrote a letter alleging that he had been a victim of "extortion and shakedown" by certain unnamed political officials— "local politicians who have actually predicted we would lose our premises if we do not 'play ball.'" He cited a blatant conflict of interest by the Biaggi & Ehrlich firm and said Koch had been misled about Freedom's status.

Frank considered Thomas's charges for exactly one day before responding in writing that she considered them "to be without merit." The shakedown charge was never forwarded to the city's Department of Investigation, and Koch aides insisted that the mayor never saw Thomas's letter.

On June 5, Frank wrote a letter to Mariotta agreeing to rent the 100,000-square-foot parking lot to Wedtech at $50,000 a year for three years, with a four-year renewal option. Wedtech used the "letter of intent" to convince the Navy it would soon hold a lease on the property.

The highly unusual circumstances under which the letter was written showed just how rapidly the juggernaut of city government could roll, once enough political grease was applied. Within a single working day, Wedtech officers, Hebrew National executives, and city officials toured the One Loop Drive site; an agreement to oust Freedom Industries and bring in Wedtech was negotiated; and Wedtech had in hand a written commitment from the city for the lease.

The process by which the lease was approved by the powerful Board of Estimate also was unusually speedy. Any contract involving more than $10,000 required approval by the Board of Estimate, consisting of the five borough presidents, the controller, the city council president, and the mayor. The board met regularly on Wednesday and Thursday of every other week. Its practice was to "calendar" proposals on Wednesdays and vote on them the following day.

The first attempt to get the board to vote on the Wedtech lease was made on Wednesday, June 13, 1984, the first day it could possibly be on the calendar. But city Controller Harrison "Jay" Goldin had great reservations about calendaring and voting on the lease on the same day.

Carlos Cuevas, an associate in the Biaggi firm, called Richard Biaggi and told him of Goldin's concern, and Biaggi told Cuevas to call his father. Cuevas phoned Mario Biaggi at his Bronx office, and the two had a very succinct conversation. Cuevas described the problem in less than a minute and hung up.

The board took no action on the lease that day, because, in Ehrlich's words, Simon had failed to "move his ass." But

Ehrlich told Moreno that the congressman had made known his displeasure, threatening to withdraw his support in the next election if Simon did not move quickly. By the time the July meeting of the Board of Estimate rolled around, Biaggi also had placed a call to Goldin, and the lease sailed through with hardly a ripple of discussion.

Thomas still was refusing to budge, while the city was pressing its case in eviction court. In August, in a highly unusual intrusion in the judicial process, Koch wrote a letter to Freedom's new attorney, state Sen. John Calandra, protesting Freedom's refusal to leave the building. He also sent a copy of his strongly worded protest to Israel Rubin, the administrative law judge handling the case.

Not long after Koch's letter prodded the city judge, Thomas showed up at work one day to find city marshals loading his belongings into trailers. He was even more astounded when he looked in the mailbox and found among his monthly bills a $2,196 invoice for the August legal services of Biaggi & Ehrlich.

Thomas called a DOD fraud hotline, spilled out his story of Bronx corruption, and soon was visited by the FBI. But as usual, his charges, which seemed to amount to little more than hot air, were duly recorded and quickly forgotten. A few months later, his DOD contract down the drain, Thomas filed for bankruptcy.

Thomas had given up on telling his story by the time our paths crossed in the fall of 1986. He could hardly have known that his interview with me then would drive a nail into the coffin of the corrupt Bronx political machine.

13

BUYING JUSTICE

WHILE WEDTECH WAS CELEBRATING the pontoon award, Bob Wallach was preoccupied with other matters. An event of great importance to the nation—and, more immediately, to Wallach's career—had consumed his undivided attention. On January 19, 1984, Ronald Reagan's trusted friend and personal lawyer, William French Smith, resigned as Attorney General to return to private law practice. On the same day, Reagan decided to nominate as Smith's replacement the man who had served at the President's elbow—Edwin Meese III.

For Meese, then fifty-two, the nomination was the culmination of a lifetime of loyalty to Reagan. He had asked Reagan repeatedly for the Attorney General's job and left little doubt about how he would run it. Viewed by right-wing activists as the last true conservative left in the White House, Meese had engineered administration drives against funding for the Legal Services Corporation, which provides legal counsel for the poor, and pushed to reshape the fractious U.S. Civil Rights Commission to give Reagan greater control. He was also the architect of a failed administration effort to weaken the 1982 Voting Rights Act, a position which ultimately so embarrassed the Reagan administration that it ended up supporting a much stronger bill. On civil liberties issues, Meese sent shivers through the liberal criminal justice community with his out-spoken opposition to the exclusionary rule, which says any evidence improperly obtained by police is inadmissible.

Meese told reporters he expected no problems in winning Senate confirmation. But his nomination, announced by the White House only days before the President was to unveil his intentions to seek a second term, was quickly seized upon by hungry Democrats. Presidential candidate Walter Mondale urged the Senate to reject Meese. A Meese-led Justice Depart-ment, he said, would "make government secrecy, not the Bill of Rights, its top priority, and make the Justice Department into the defender of privilege, large corporations, and the wealthy few." Meanwhile, the congressional leadership pre-dicted a tough examination of Meese's views on civil rights and privacy.

Certain lingering issues were bound to be thorns in Meese's side as he faced the Senate Judiciary Committee. One was his acceptance of the $60,000 loan from his accountant, John McKean, while supporting McKean's nomination for the Postal Board of Governors. Meese's attempt to quell the criti-cism by hurriedly taking out a loan in order to repay McKean had not satisfied his critics.

Meese's nomination and the prospect of intense Senate scru-tiny added a new dimension to Wallach's role as Meese's best friend and counselor. Wallach had rented a Georgetown apartment and virtually abandoned his San Francisco law prac-tice to be closer to Meese and Wedtech. As soon as Meese's nomination was announced, Wallach ended his casual flirta-tion with Washington and came to town prepared to do battle. His life had been given new purpose. Meese now needed him not just as an intimate friend and dinner partner but as a lawyer to guide him through the inevitably rough seas of confirmation. Wallach made it clear that he, like many of the lawyers who represent administration nominees, expected no payment for his services. However, it was clear that Meese might soon have a suitable place in government for Wallach's talents.

In January, while Wallach was preparing to represent Meese pro bono, the Wedtech board, grateful for his contacts with Meese on the pontoon negotiations, voted to give Wallach options to purchase 50,000 shares of common stock at $21.88 per share. Wallach received more than double the shares granted anyone else during the meeting. Although Meese later testified that he knew as early as 1981 that Wallach served as a paid consultant to Wedtech, he said he was unaware of these negotiations.

By the end of 1983, Wallach had seen that the work he did for Wedtech—initially at no charge—could have significant financial benefits. The company's stock was booming, as Wallach discovered when he sold stock he'd purchased over the counter that year for an $11,802 profit. He also had convinced the Wedtech officers that the company was now prosperous enough to enter a formal consulting agreement with him at suitable rates for his service. He had Squadron, Ellenoff draw up a one-year renewable consulting agreement with a salary of $100,000 per year and another $50,000 in expenses. The agreement was approved without objection by the Wedtech board.

Not long after Meese asked Wallach to represent him, Wallach contacted the Wedtech executives. It was likely he would follow Meese to the Justice Department in a senior executive position, he said, but in the meantime, he had left his lucrative San Francisco practice and would be spending much of his time representing Meese without charge. Would it be possible, the officers recalled him asking, for Wedtech to prepay him under the recently signed retainer agreement to help supplement his strained income?

The Wedtech executives were more than happy to accommodate. They were ecstatic over Meese's elevation, which could only work to the company's benefit. So on February 2, while Wallach was meeting with Meese at the White House, the officers prepared a check for $150,000 and handed it over to Wallach the next day.

As expected, the upcoming confirmation hearings brought a new closeness between Meese and Wallach, who, as in their old college debating days, began closeting themselves for hours in Meese's office to prepare for the savage questions of the press and hostile Democratic senators on the Senate Judiciary Committee.

The hearings kicked off on March 1, and promptly turned into a bloodbath. While Sen. Edward Kennedy (D-Mass.) focused on Meese's civil rights blunders, Sen. Howard Metzenbaum, the thick-skinned Democrat from Ohio, emerged as the chief critic of Meese's ethics and personal business dealings. He started the fireworks by questioning the McKean loans and disclosing that Meese in early 1982 owed $420,000 to the Great American Federal Savings and Loan Association, whose president, Gordon Luce, was the California secretary of transportation when Reagan was governor. At that time, Meese was fifteen months delinquent on mortgage payments on his California home and four months behind on his $1,659-a-month mortgage in McLean, Virginia. In most cases, Metzenbaum pointed out, homeowners who fall four months behind in their payments soon find themselves on the street. "While Meese allowed his mortgage delinquency to grow, the country was in the middle of one of the deepest recessions in history." Meese's excuse for the loans—that his finances were strained because of a move from California for which the government refused to pick up the tab—hardly satisfied his critics.

The next day, Metzenbaum questioned Meese's veracity, suggesting that, under questioning, Meese had pretended to know less about the sale of his La Mesa home than the facts indicated. After two years on the market at a $330,000 asking price, the luxury home had been sold through the efforts of Thomas Barrack, a Los Angeles attorney and real estate developer who was appointed deputy undersecretary of the interior in late 1982.

Barrack's performance in the sale of Meese's home was so extraordinary that, when he finally met the Meeses for the first time, Mrs. Meese referred to him as "the one with the halo around his head."

Meese had told the Judiciary Committee he knew nothing about a less-than-market-rate loan obtained by the purchaser through the Great American Bank. But Metzenbaum confronted him with handwritten notes from a conversation Meese had with Barrack outlining the deal. Meese railed at the notion that he had withheld information from the committee: "The facts are exactly as I stated them yesterday. I don't know the amount of the note. I didn't know the amount then. . . . There is no discrepancy whatsoever, Senator!"

But Meese's fumbling left enough doubt in the committee's mind that it extended the hearings through March 6 to allow time to question Barrack and McKean under oath. The next week, the hearings were postponed indefinitely pending conclusion of a special prosecutor's investigation into the charges which had surrounded Meese since he came to Washington.

The appointment of an independent counsel raised the specter of a lengthy, potentially destructive investigation, which would require Meese to retain a masterful criminal lawyer in order to defend himself. But the Independent Counsel Act—the law setting up the mechanism for special prosecution of executive branch employees—included a helpful provision. Under the act, if criminal charges investigated by a special prosecutor were unsubstantiated, the targets of an independent counsel's probe could submit legal bills for payment to the U.S. Court of Appeals. The court would then decide whether the government would pay all or a portion of the bills.

Around this time, Wallach paid a call on powerful attorney Leonard Garment of the prestigious Washington firm Dickstein, Shapiro & Morin. Their association dated back to Wallach's early days in Washington, when he had paid a respectful introductory visit to Garment's office seeking advice on the ways of Washington. Briefly outlining the charges against Meese, Wallach asked Garment if he would be willing to represent Meese on a contingency basis. The challenge was

Judgment Day: Flanked by law enforcement officials, Fred Neuberger (wearing hat), Mario Moreno (wearing striped tie) and Anthony Guariglia (at rear, in dark coat) leave the Bronx County Courthouse after pleading guilty to state charges as part of a deal struck by U.S. Attorney Rudolph Giuliani and Bronx District Attorney Mario Merola. Their decision to cooperate was the turning point in the federal probe of Wedtech payoffs.
(Photo by Robert Rosamilio, used with permission of the New York *Daily News*)

Four More Years: Over an expensive meal at an Italian restaurant in Washington, Wedtech officer Fred Neuberger (far right) and SBA regional administrator Peter Neglia (seated next to Neuberger) celebrate the inauguration of President Ronald Reagan's second term of office. (Photo introduced as evidence in the Biaggi trial, used with permission of the U.S. Attorney's office)

A Valued Friend: During happier days, Wedtech officer Fred Neuberger (right) poses with Bronx Democrat Rep. Mario Biaggi in the congressman's Washington office. Later, Neuberger grew so disgusted by Biaggi's constant efforts to collect retainer fees that he compared him to a cop on the take.
(Photo introduced as evidence in the Biaggi trial, used with permission of the U.S. Attorney's office)

Thumbs Up: San Francisco attorney E. Robert Wallach forces a smile at his arraignment in federal court in Manhattan. After a jury convicted him for peddling his influence with Attorney General Edwin Meese III, Wallach told a judge that his life demonstrated that "too much success can bring failure." (Photo by Bill Turnbull, used with permission of the New York *Daily News*)

Missing: Fred Neuberger's emotionally troubled third wife, Eileen, disappeared from the couple's home in Manhattan's posh Sutton Place as investigators began closing in on Wedtech. A prosecutor opened a homicide investigation, but the case was eventually dropped because no body could be found. (Photo used with permission of the New York *Daily News*)

Hero for the '80s: Wedtech founder John Mariotta leaves the federal courthouse in Manhattan after his August 1988 conviction on racketeering charges. Mariotta portrayed himself as an innocent pawn used by associates scheming to enrich themselves at Wedtech's and the government's expense.
(Photo by Dan Cronin, used with permission of the New York *Daily News*)

He Made It: Investment counselor Wayne Frank Chinn, whose attorney called him the "five-foot-t drop-out kid from China," was known around Francisco for his fast and loose trading practices. ability to turn a quick profit earned him an import client in Edwin Meese III.
(Photo by Bill Turnbull, used with permission of the N York *Daily News*)

On the Rise: Mario Biaggi poses in 1973 outside Gracie Mansion, where he hoped to live as mayor of New York. Biaggi's law-and-order candidacy was derailed when the facts came out about his heated denial that he had refused to testify before a grand jury. At Biaggi's urging, a judge released a transcript that showed Biaggi had repeatedly invoked his Fifth Amendment right against self-incrimination before a grand jury investigating his finances.

(Photo by Richard Corkery, used with permission of the New York *Daily News*)

Presidential Retreat: As the day of John Mariotta's ouster as president approached, he spent most of his time at Wedtech's Mount Vernon, New York, plant, where his hand-picked Russian scientist, Dr. Eduard Pinkhasov, worked on a top-secret coatings formula that Mariotta considered the key to Wedtech's future.

(Photo from a Wedtech annual report)

Something for Henry: At a fund-raising banquet, Bronx Borough President Stanley Simon (left) and his favorite brother-in-law, company bookkeeper Henry Bittman (right). Simon arranged for his brother-in-law to be put on the Wedtech payroll as a payroll clerk. Fred Neuberger looks solemn while his wife, Eileen, laughs.
(Photo introduced as evidence in the Biaggi trial, used with permission of the U.S Attorney's office)

The Gang's All Here: Wedtech vice president Mario Moreno drapes his arms around New York National Guard Commander Bernard Ehrlich (top row, right) and Bronx Borough President Stanley Simon at a dinner. Moreno's longtime companion, Caridad Vazquez (front row, center), was paid $35,000 a year to accompany him to what he called "boring" Wedtech social events.
(Photo used with permission of the U.S. Attorney's office)

Seeds of Friendship: Attorney General Edwin Meese III plants one of the trees donated by his friend, attorney E. Robert Wallach, for a memorial in Israel to Meese's son, Scott, who was killed in an automobile accident. Wallach arranged for the American Friends of Tel Aviv University to underwrite Meese's travel expenses for the May 1986 dedication. On a stopover in Jerusalem, Wallach introduced Meese to his client, Wedtech officer Fred Neuberger.

(Photo by Keren Kayemeth LeIsrael, used with permission of the Jewish National Fund) twofold. First, they had to clear Meese of groundless criminal allegations, which was a matter of law; then they had to resurrect his nomination, which was a matter of public relations. Wallach explained that he, too, would be part of the defense team and perhaps other prestigious lawyers like Washington's Max Kampelman and Howard Squadron in New York. After a cordial three-hour lunch with Meese and his wife, Garment agreed to accept the job as lead counsel.

Garment's services did not come cheaply, and Meese faced the prospect of staggering legal fees. Briefly, there was talk among senior Republicans of starting a Meese legal defense fund, but Garment advised against it, fearing further backlash from the Democrats. Instead, Garment agreed to represent Meese at his usual hourly rates but to delay billing him until the independent counsel probe was completed.

Wallach followed suit, and drew up a retainer agreement for Meese to sign. It provided that Wallach would keep a running tab of his legal fees and expenses and, if possible, submit an application to the court for reimbursement. If the court did not provide compensation, he would bill Meese for any remaining fees.

Wallach went to work with a vengeance, carrying out Garment's instructions and raising no objections to his number two role. For a while, the day began with Garment conducting a 9 A.M. detailed grilling of Meese in his White House office, sessions attended not only by Wallach but also loyal Meese aides like Jenkins and Ken Cribb. The location changed abruptly to Garment's downtown law office when White House aides began reviewing Garment's letters and legal briefs to ensure that they had the proper political perspective.

Wallach's role in the sessions was to help "put the client at ease," Garment recalled. On his frequent trips back to California, Wallach also took statements from important witnesses in the case, showing delicacy and patience in interviewing the web of Meese's close friends whose names surfaced during the probe.

Independent Counsel Jacob Stein, who was sworn in on April 2, 1984, was asked to examine Meese's loans from his former assistant, Ed Thomas, and his accountant, McKean, and the Thomas Barrack real estate deal. He also was asked to look into the relationships between loans made to Meese and the appointment of various individuals to federal jobs. Stein also was presented with a mishmash of allegations, including charges of possible insider trading by Meese and his wife, Meese's failure to report loans from friends on his financial disclosure forms, and his successful efforts to secure an unwarranted promotion in the Army National Guard.

Curiously enough, Stein was also asked to investigate a charge which had surfaced in the newspapers concerning possible special treatment from the SBA for a company in which the Meese family held stock: Questech, a firm owned by Meese's friend, Dr. Earl Brian, the former California health secretary. Mrs. Meese had bought stock in the company in January 1981, using the $15,000 that she borrowed from Ed Thomas, who also owned stock in the firm. The question was whether or not Questech had received favorable treatment from the SBA in 1981 as a result of phone calls from Meese's White House office.

Stein's probe of the charge eventually would prove that Thomas had made calls from the White House to the SBA to inquire about the company. But he could find no violations of criminal law. And, despite a lengthy probe into Meese's personal associations, finances, and dealings with federal agencies, Stein would uncover no hints that another scandal with close parallels and a web of interconnections was lurking in the corners of Meese's tangled finances. Nor would he discover that the man defending Meese, E. Robert Wallach, had been lobbying Meese for three years on behalf of another SBA company in which the lawyer had a personal financial stake.

Meese's stalled confirmation hearings were the only negative news on the horizon as Ronald Reagan left Washington on March 6, 1984, for a hectic day of campaigning with evangelicals in Ohio and business leaders in New York. Meese had been condemned by the government watchdog group, Common Cause, as "unfit" to hold the Attorney General's post, an example of Reagan's blind cronyism and bad judgment. But Reagan, brushing off reporters' questions with a wave and a smile as he boarded a plane, said his confidence in Meese was unshaken.

In Columbus, on a day when the Senate was debating a plan to allow organized prayer in the public schools, Reagan told a gathering of friendly fundamentalist church leaders that "Americans are turning back to God. . . . Today our country is seeing a rebirth of freedom and faith—a great national renewal." He spoke with a confidence confirmed by the polls. With the election eight months away, Reagan was enjoying a ten-percentage-point lead in the polls over his closest Democratic challenger.

Reagan's New York visit that evening was intended to raise $1 million for his already bulging war chest. The event, staged by the New York State Republican Party, was a $1,000-a-plate fund-raiser in the elegant Grand Ballroom of the Waldorf Astoria. The crowd of 1,400 that night was a virtual Who's Who of New York movers and shakers, the *crème de la crème* of the city's business and political leadership. It included socialites Ivana Trump and Brooke Astor, businessman David Rockefeller, HUD Secretary Samuel Pierce, and a bipartisan collection of New York's political leadership, including Senator D'Amato and crusty Meade Esposito, the longtime boss of Brooklyn's Democratic Party, whose support for Reagan had helped him carry the heavily Democratic state in 1980.

After an introduction by state chairman George Clark, Reagan stepped to the podium at 8:38 P.M., leaned into the microphones of the hotel's $1 million sound system, and began with a pep talk. "The Republican victory in 1980 was no aberration," he said confidently. "It marked a turning point in New York politics, and we're going to prove that in 1984. . . ."

After a long recitation of his administration's accomplishments, Reagan turned back to New York matters, lauding the accomplishments of retiring upstate Republican Rep. Barber Conable and the cooperation of Senator D'Amato, whom he called a "real plus in the Senate." The President liked to add a personal touch to his speeches, often singling out an unsung hero as a lasting example for his audiences.

He had almost finished his address when suddenly, almost as an afterthought, he focused his attention on one of the more obscure guests of the evening, a round-faced, bespectacled businessman who looked more at home in a machinist's coveralls than the black tuxedo he was wearing. The Hispanic entrepreneur and his corporate associates, elated by their most recent federal contract victory, had coughed up $10,000 for the chance to bask in Reagan's company. The President began:

> Real progress in this country can be traced to the work of conscientious and hard-working individuals like Congressman Conable. One such person is John Mariotta, who's providing jobs and training for the hardcore unemployed of the South Bronx. Born of Puerto Rican immigrants, and having served in the United States Army, Mr. Mariotta has had all the ups and downs associated with entrepreneurship. And today, through Wed-Tech, he not only has built a successful corporation, he's helping hundreds of people who would otherwise be condemned to menial jobs or a life on the dole. And what gave Mr. Mariotta the courage to keep going when others quit? He tells us it was his faith in God. Now his faith has moved mountains, helping hundreds of people who'd almost given up hope. People like John Mariotta are heroes for the eighties.

Wedtech was still such an unknown quantity that the company's name was not only mistakenly hyphenated by a White House speechwriter but also misspelled by the New York *Daily News,* which called the company Medtech.

In the eyes of the Wedtech crew, Reagan's speech once again validated Wallach's value to the company. Guariglia recalled that Wallach took credit for having the Mariotta tribute included in the Reagan speech, which Wallach said was part of his continuing appeal to Meese for presidential recognition for the firm. Sadly, Wallach had missed Mariotta's grand moment. A few days before the speech, Wallach noted that the demands of the Meese confirmation hearings had created a conflict between his two "major East Coast clients" and would prevent him from attending the ceremonies.

Jacob Stein issued his 385-page report clearing Meese of criminal conduct on September 20, 1984, and on January 29,

1985, the Meese confirmation process resumed in the Senate Judiciary Committee. The hearings lasted two days. Democrats argued that, while Stein's report found no criminal violations, it unearthed voluminous evidence of conduct unbefitting the Attorney General. When the final Senate vote finally came on Saturday, February 23, 1985, after a week-long filibuster on a farm bill, it split 63–31 along party lines. Common Cause noted that it was the largest vote against a nominee for Attorney General since 1925.

A relieved Meese, tackling reporters' questions outside the White House, said he was not at all embittered by the grueling confirmation process and expected no problems working with the sharply divided Senate. He was sworn in by a notary public the next day to move into the long-vacant job.

Like a true friend, Wallach had been at Meese's side constantly during the long period of uncertainty, and when victory came, they celebrated it together at a party in Meese's honor.

Wallach had thought for some time that, once Meese was confirmed, he would be in line for a top Justice Department position, and the days after the confirmation were a testament to his influence. The two had breakfast together on the twenty-fifth, lunch on the twenty-sixth, breakfast on the twenty-eighth. They went together to Meese's farewell party at the White House, and celebrated again at a party hosted by Wallach at a cost of $1,894.50. On February 28, they left for three days in San Francisco; on March 19, they flew together to Orlando. Meanwhile, the stream of memos to Meese picked up again, with Wallach offering his thoughts on the organization of the Department of Justice and recommending candidates for key slots. On March 7, he sent along his personal "wish list" of "rewards for services contributed." The list included his desire for pictures with President Reagan and for White House mess privileges, which he described as "the most important 'perk' one could have."

Although Wallach had set his heart on following Meese to Justice, to do so would clearly bring an end to his profitable retainer agreement with Wedtech. Conflict of interest laws would bar him from accepting further payment.

In September 1984, Wallach once again met with the Wedtech officers to discuss his financial dilemma. Meese's confirmation was inevitable, but the long wait, which seemed likely
to stretch into 1985, had further drained Wallach's tight finances. He told the Wedtech officers that he was going back
to San Francisco to finish work on several pending trials scheduled for that fall and "that I was simply not going to be able
to participate with them in a continuing relationship on the
East Coast. They were upset about that." The conversation,
Wallach said, ended when the officers agreed to pay him in
advance so that he "would then . . . remain with them."

According to the officers, Wallach proposed a new payment arrangement—one that would allow him to take Wedtech's money before the tight constraints of government
ethics laws came into play. According to Neuberger, Wallach asked Wedtech for an advance payment of $500,000, a
sum that would cover his future representation of Wedtech
during the years 1985 and 1986. In return, from his anticipated slot at Justice, he would watch out for Wedtech's interests and provide the company even greater access to the Reagan administration.

The Wedtech executives tried to barter with him. Such a
huge payment would drain the company and have a terrible
impact on the firm's financial statements. Wallach also would
be faced with a major tax liability, they argued, since he had
already received $150,000 earlier that year.

Neuberger objected to the size of Wallach's request. After
all, the retainer agreement called for $150,000 per year, so a
two-year advance would be $300,000, not $500,000. For
once, his argument prevailed, and Wallach agreed to accept
the $300,000 called for in the original deal.

The Wedtech executives also objected to making the payment because it would have to be subtracted from the company's profits at a time when it was desperately important that
Wedtech attract new investors and keep the firm's income
statements as high as possible. The more income the company
could show, the more its stock prices would be worth. It was
decided that the way to address the problem was to find a way
to capitalize the payment as a company debt, using the same

accounting trick they had used in 1983 when they made their first $125,000 payment to Wallach.

The company's purchase of the bankrupt shipyard in Ontonagon, Michigan, provided a vehicle for the coverup. The officers had kept Wallach well-informed of their plans to purchase the facility, a matter they were handling largely through a network of newly cultivated political contacts in Michigan. They decided to disguise Wallach's advance payment as a fee for his counseling services on the shipyard purchase. He submitted an invoice, and on the weekend of October 27, Guariglia hand-delivered the $300,000 check to him in a hotel restaurant.

Wallach soon turned the money over to a brokerage account, ERW Partners, which he had set up with a hotshot San Francisco investment adviser named Wayne Franklyn Chinn, whom he had met through his landlord and friend, Rusty Kent London.

Meese would repeatedly deny any knowledge of Wallach's fee arrangement with Wedtech. But the Wedtech officers were convinced that through their payments to Wallach, they had, in essence, picked up the tab for Meese's legal representation throughout his long fight to become Attorney General.

On the day of Meese's confirmation, Moreno showed up at the offices of Dickstein, Shapiro to meet with Wallach, who was closeted at the time with a much-relieved Meese. Wallach came out to greet Moreno and urged him to wait for a moment, saying he wanted to introduce him to someone.

According to Moreno, a few minutes later, Meese came out to shake Moreno's hand warmly. "I want to thank you for all the help you've been to the company," Moreno told Meese, genuinely proud to be in such close contact with the next Attorney General on the day of his sweet victory. Moreno later claimed that Meese chatted with him for a moment, then moved back behind closed doors.

Moreno and the other officers did not know at the time that Wallach, while appealing to them for money, had petitioned another source for reimbursement. In December, the same month he was squirreling away his Wedtech money in the Chinn account, Wallach filed a joint appeal with Dickstein,

Shapiro to the Court of Appeals for reimbursement of legal expenses. Garment, who had served as lead counsel, sought reimbursement for $578,361; Wallach asked for $142,562. He also filed an affidavit with the court in which he stated:

> Commencing with my retention by Mr. Meese in March 1984 until September 20, 1984, when the Report of the independent counsel was released, I earned no income from any source, including the practice of law, due to my inability to participate in matters in which I would have participated and which I would have concluded had I been engaged in my private practice. . . .

Wallach made no mention of the money he had received from Wedtech during his representation of Meese. When the court entered an order granting Wallach $76,870—or 54 percent—of his request, Wallach announced to reporters that he considered the court award substantial compensation for his services. In fact, he never did bill Meese for the remainder of his fees.

When Meese took office on February 25, 1985, one of the first documents to cross his desk was a long memo from Wallach concerning the reorganization of the Justice Department and possible roles for himself. He explained that he would be ideally suited to help Meese interview candidates for high-ranking Justice jobs and could provide a "major assist" to Meese in keeping up his contacts at the White House, a role Meese himself had suggested. Wallach wrote that for "obvious reasons, I have a particular interest in your activities there."

Wallach, in fact, did play a role in interviewing key Justice applicants. However, he was frustrated in his desire for a Justice Department post of his own, which he knew would remain in limbo until his claim for reimbursement of legal fees was resolved. He wrote Meese:

> More and more, as this time has elapsed, I have been struggling with my own ego. Quite frankly, and I know you will accept this as being somewhat humbly stated, I didn't interview

a single person whom I didn't feel superior to as both a lawyer and a person of judgment and experience.

After Wallach's fee claim was resolved, the two talked again about possible Justice appointments. But it was still not feasible. As Meese later testified, "There were a number of people who didn't think it was a good idea. . . . He had financial needs that were beyond what the department would bear, what salary would bear. . . . In addition to that, his ability to do a lot of things he was interested in would have been severely curtailed."

Wallach decided to bide his time. Meese clearly wanted him with him, so much so that he became "a piece of furniture" in the department, according to one high-level aide. He sat in on many of Meese's meetings and was with the Attorney General constantly.

Wallach came to visualize himself not only as the ideal candidate for chief of staff but as a lawyer of such stature that he should serve as solicitor general, representing the Justice Department before the Supreme Court of the United States.

14

FOUR MORE YEARS

ON A FRIGID JANUARY WEEKEND in 1985, the Wedtech officers left New York for a trip to Washington. This time, there were no crises to attend to, no bureaucrats to cajole, no pressure-packed White House meetings to attend. Instead, this was a time to give thanks to the administration which had financed the good life for them all.

Ronald Reagan was scheduled to be sworn in for a second term on Monday, January 21, and thousands of Republicans were streaming into the city for a 50th Inaugural extravaganza of parties, parades, and balls that had cost roughly $12 million to put together. The weather was not cooperating. A vicious cold front, nicknamed the Arctic Express by local weathermen, had swept into the city, and the whipping winds were so vicious that for the first time in 196 years, the Inaugural Parade up Pennsylvania Avenue was canceled.

The Wedtech officers checked into the Sheraton Hotel in a rare show of collegiality. They had done as much as anyone to put Reagan back in office with $200,000 in contributions to the Reagan–Bush team. Neuberger showed up with his two adopted toddlers, a nanny, and his wife, Eileen. Mariotta, Moreno, Guariglia, and Shorten came with their wives and escorts, and, as usual, Bernie and Maggie Ehrlich tagged along. The group also included Richard Biaggi and his wife, Toni, Ehrlich's National Guard buddy and Wedtech consultant, Vito Castellano, with one of his two wives, and a new addition to the group, Bronx developer Zacharias Gertler. Gertler, a Biaggi client, was using the law firm to smooth the way for housing deals from the city's Department of Housing Preservation and Development. Also with the group were the SBA's Peter Neglia and Neglia's father, Joseph. The younger Neglia by that time had moved to Washington to serve as Jim Sanders' chief of staff at SBA headquarters, one of the agency's top jobs.

On this weekend of revelry, the Wedtech officials were determined to do things first-class. They bought $4,800 worth of Inaugural Ball tickets for themselves and their guests. Guariglia rented limousines for the weekend, and the group made reservations at Il Giornale, a fancy Italian restaurant on Pennsylvania Avenue. The dinner cost them $1,926, which included a $250 tip.

A number of parties were of special interest. On Saturday, they showed up for an entertainment gala at the Kennedy Center that was attended by President Reagan; on Sunday morning, they had invitations to a breakfast in a Senate office building sponsored by their friend Senator D'Amato. The President also was due to drop by their hotel, where one of several inaugural balls was to be held. This one was in the Sheraton's Grand Ballroom, where 5,000 dancers were to be serenaded by the Count Basie Orchestra and Guy Lombardo's Royal Canadians.

The bad weather forced them to take refuge in the Sheraton

bar on Sunday, and around noon the General brought up a subject they had kicked around before but never resolved: Some means had to be found to reimburse one of their most faithful allies—Peter Neglia of the SBA.

Ehrlich broached the idea of a gift of stock, the company's usual mode of compensation. But Moreno nixed the idea. Now that the company had gone public, it was no longer that easy to dole out packages of stock. There were stock options, however, a means of reimbursement that they were using with increasing regularity. Wedtech could grant Neglia the right to purchase a block of stock at a set price—say, $15 or $20 per share. With Wedtech's stock prices climbing and possibly reaching as much as $50 or $100 per share, Neglia could purchase his stock at a bargain-basement price, then turn around and sell it for a small fortune. The only problem was that some means would have to be found to cover up the gift of options. After all, he was still a high-ranking government official.

Ehrlich had another suggestion. It was already agreed that, when he left the federal government, Neglia was going to come to work for the Biaggi & Ehrlich firm. Wedtech could show its appreciation to Neglia by kicking in half of his $50,-000 salary. Moreno was receptive to the idea; he saw no problem with supplementing Neglia's salary.

Later that day, Moreno joined the other officers who were crowded into one of the hotel suites partying and watching Super Bowl XIX. While the TV blared in the background, Moreno briefed Guariglia, Neuberger, and Shorten on the plan to grant Neglia options for 20,000 shares of stock and pay half his salary at Biaggi & Ehrlich. They talked of putting Neglia's stock options in the name of a friend, Ronald Betso, a former Brooklyn cop who worked as a right-hand man to George Clark, the state Republican chairman. (Betso would eventually be indicted as part of the racketeering case, but was acquitted of the charges.) No one objected.

On Inaugural morning, the weather had forced Reagan's swearing-in ceremonies inside the Capitol Rotunda. Some 140,000 guests who had been invited to watch the outside ceremonies were shut out, with only a handful of top dignitaries allowed inside.

Reagan took the brief oath of office, then moved on to shake hands with his family and the few trusted aides. Among those reveling in the moment were his deputy chief of staff, Michael Deaver, his national security adviser, Robert "Bud" McFarlane, and the right-hand aide who would soon be leaving the White House to become Attorney General after a grueling investigation of his conduct, Edwin Meese III.

That night, dressed in tuxedos and drinking the finest wines, the Wedtech party toasted Reagan's inaugural and the prospect of continued prosperity. Four more years! they must have said to themselves as they lifted their glasses high. Four more glorious years!

By the dawn of 1985, Wedtech had become a corporate version of *Pygmalion*. Its officers—who once brazenly begged, borrowed, and stole simultaneously to keep the company afloat—now found themselves overseeing the affairs of a far-flung empire of subsidiaries, boarding Concorde jets to negotiate complex deals in Europe and the Middle East.

"You'd be sitting at their conference table," said one Albany businessman of Wedtech around this time, "and one would be on an urgent call on the red phone, another on the yellow phone. All this while they were trying to deal with you." The company had subcontracts in Italy and England and was involved in sensitive business negotiations with the French, the Saudis, and the Israelis. One of its new consultants, James Jenkins, the former Meese deputy who had set up his own consulting firm, was trying to market an experimental Wedtech engine in Red China. Baffled by the complexity of these global ventures, the Wedtech officers were depending more and more on their highly paid Washington consultants: Wallach, Bragg, Jenkins, Denlinger, Capo, José Martinez, and a host of others.

Wallach, to whom they owed the greatest allegiance, assumed a coach's role, trying to bring the company into sync with its newfound status. The company had clearly arrived at the big time; now, it had to start acting like it.

On paper, it appeared that the strength of Wedtech's management was keeping pace. Respect-worthy names began showing up on the firm's board of directors: Frederick Moss, a director of Moseley, Hallgarten, Wedtech's underwriters; Paul Hallingby, Jr., a Manhattan socialite who was a managing director of Bear Stearns & Co.; Gen. Richard Cavazos, the retired commander of the U.S. Armed Forces Command; Verne Orr, the recently retired Air Force secretary, recruited for the company by his friend, Jenkins.

A number of other changes were shaking Wedtech to its foundations. With the award of the pontoon contract, Wedtech had experienced a year of explosive growth, its revenues jumping 168 percent, from $27 million in 1983 to $72.4 million in 1984. It had negotiated a new $35 million revolving credit line with four major banks, paving the way for expansion.

But many developments looked better on paper than they were in real life. Through its political connections in Michigan, for example, Wedtech had bought the Ontonagon shipyard for $5.3 million, which included among its assets a gargantuan $28 million tug barge, which the state of Michigan had built to transport rail cars across Lake Superior. The barge system, abandoned long before it was finished, had been a foolhardy use of state money, but Wedtech's executives rationalized that they only had to sell the tug barge to recoup the firm's entire investment several times over.

Over the next two years, they tried to market the barge as everything from a containerized cargo carrier in Texas to a floating Manhattan restaurant. They hired agents, among them Richard Ramirez, and offered a small fortune in commissions if they could find a buyer. Finally, when all prospects fell through, they began trying to unload the tug barge as scrap for $200,000.

In Israel, Wedtech had bought out its partner in Carmo Industries and now had a full-fledged international subsidiary, which it was using to make engine castings. The Israeli plant, bordering a desert and staffed by hundreds of displaced Ethiopian Jews, certainly sounded prestigious in the company's annual reports. But as a business proposition, it made no practical sense to ship engine parts back and forth from Israel to the South Bronx. Worse yet, Carmo's internal management was a Middle Eastern nightmare. Wedtech appointed lawyer Howard Squadron, with his wide-ranging Israeli government contacts, to the Carmo board of directors and dispatched Larry Shorten to monitor the company. Shorten finally threw up his hands, devoting most of his time to high living on the Wedtech expense account.

All of Wedtech's corporate maneuvers were made in the interest of diversification. The firm's Wall Street advisers had theorized that Wedtech's stock would remain at a stalemate unless the company could break its almost total dependence on DOD contracts. Working toward that goal, Wedtech courted Representative Garcia, who sat on the House Post Office Committee, for help winning a $5 million contract from the U.S. Postal Service to make mail-box containers. Wedtech then listed the contract in its SEC filings as proof of growing corporate diversity. Nowhere did the company mention that in order to win the contract, it had paid a $20,000 bribe to a Post Office contracting officer, Jerrydoe Smith.

On the advice of Wallach and the company's new accountants and advisers, Touche Ross & Co., Wedtech's officers placed more emphasis than ever on its research and development subsidiary, Vapor Technologies Incorporated in Mount Vernon, where Dr. Eduard Pinkhasov's remarkable coating process was being developed. The officers' theory was that a $1 million coatings contract would do more for the company's future than $50 million in new work from the Pentagon.

The process involved placing industrial materials like pipes, blades, silicon wafers, and batteries in a sealed chamber and coating them at room temperature with ultra-thin layers of metal or other protective materials. But after a lifetime of experimentation, Pinkhasov had been unable to perfect the formula. Every sample that went through Wedtech's lab came out marred by bubbles, glitches, and cracks. Despite this, Wedtech told potential customers that the problems were only steps away from resolution.

Pinkhasov had come to be viewed as the firm's most prized possession. Wallach and the Wedtech officers fretted over the state of his health, the possibility that a heart attack could, in the flash of a moment, wipe out their key to future riches. They believed it was imperative to treat Pinkhasov like pampered royalty. Pinkhasov had brought the formula with him from the Soviet Union when he left the country with his wife, Bertha, and two children. Struggling to make ends meet, he started at Wedtech in 1980 as a lowly tool-and-die maker, while Bertha tried to learn enough English to find some sort of medical job. But in 1981, Pinkhasov enthralled Mariotta with tales of his top-secret formula. He was elevated that year to Wedtech's director of research, but it was in 1983, when Wedtech went public, that his value to the company became apparent. He was given a five-year contract, with a salary climbing from $80,000 to $117,128 a year, plus bonuses. Pinkhasov also was to receive a cut of any royalties received from marketing the process. Wedtech put him up in a $500,000 Scarsdale home, and charged him $1,000 a month to rent it with a purchase option. Years later, he was sued by Wedtech for charging the company for expenses of his daughter's college tuition, his parking tickets, gardening bills, and $500 lunch tabs, a claim he resolved in an out-of-court settlement. When Pinkhasov dumped his wife and moved out of their apartment for a posh Scarsdale life-style, Wedtech's attorneys, Squadron, Ellenoff, represented him in a highly favorable divorce settlement.

At great cost, Wedtech hired a network of national salesmen to hawk Pinkhasov's process to Fortune 500 companies. In theory, the idea sounded too good to be true, and major corporations wanted proof before considering large orders. The coatings salesmen found a few takers willing to sample the process, but the results were uniformly disappointing.

Whenever possible, the Wedtech salesmen brought prospective clients to the secret Mount Vernon laboratory. There Pinkhasov's staff—comprised of so many exiled Soviet Jews that the plant's Hispanic workers complained of discrimination—paraded about in protective garb, funneling colorful liquids into test tubes. No one was allowed to discuss the process in detail, and the salesmen were warned to keep viewers at a distance. As proof that the process worked, the salesmen showed off the few samples Wedtech had perfected—a dollar bill coated with a thin layer of silver, a sheer lady's stocking dipped in nickel. Major companies, however, could not buy the logic that a nickel-plated stocking would necessarily translate into a usable nickel-plated battery or jet engine blade.

Although the coating-process gold mine remained elusive, Wallach and the company executives were convinced that a megacontract was just around the corner. They speculated that the technology-conscious Japanese were salivating for a chance to get their hands on Pinkhasov's secret formula.

Largely for that reason, Wallach introduced the company during the week of April 15, 1985, to two California friends who he believed could produce enormous results for the coatings process. One was his former landlord and jogging partner, Rusty Kent London, a lanky, bespectacled, red-haired physician and waterbed company executive, who had made a fortune as an investment adviser and blackjack expert.

Born Irving Louis Lobsenz in Jersey City, New Jersey, on January 19, 1943, London had seen his life transformed by his move to the laid-back environs of Berkeley, where he graduated with honors from the University of California in 1963. He had gone to court twice to shed himself of his stodgy given name, first changing Lobsenz to London, then dropping Irving for the more lyrical Rusty Kent. He immersed himself in a California regimen of health foods, herbal tea, meditation, and exercise.

Although licensed in 1969 to practice pediatrics in California, he left the medical profession to pursue his business talents. For three years, he marketed waterbeds and eventually moved on to a profitable career in real estate and investments. He set up two California corporations domiciled in Hawaii—International Financial Consulting and Investments, Incorporated, and National Consulting and Management, Incorporated.

London met Wallach in September 1983, when he rented him an apartment beneath his own in San Francisco. Wallach, by that time, was riding high in the Reagan administration and contemplating his relocation to the Washington area. He quickly let his landlord know of this big connection. In August 1984, at Wallach's instigations, London sent to the White

House a memorandum he had written on a national sales tax. A week later, Wallach escorted London to lunch at the White House with Meese's deputy, Bruce Chapman, and an introduction to Meese.

London had married a Japanese woman and split his time between California and Honolulu, where he eventually was to build a spectacular ancient Japanese farmhouse. In introducing his friend to Wedtech, Wallach touted London's Japanese contacts. Even more intriguing to the Wedtech officials, however, was London's skill in the casinos. He was widely considered the best blackjack player in the world and, under the pseudonym Ian Anderson, had written three books about beating the system.

Wallach also introduced Wedtech to London's friend and business partner, Wayne Franklyn Chinn, an unorthodox high-stakes investment counselor with whom Wallach had set up an account and entrusted with his most recent $300,000 Wedtech retainer. Chinn, who stood only 5 foot 2, was an animated character with darting eyes, a playful, schoolboyish grin, and expressive gestures that reflected a quick wit and sharp mind. Wallach told the Wedtech officials that Chinn was perfect for helping Wedtech bone up its investment contacts and increase the value of its stock. As an investor for several institutional clients, Chinn was plugged into defense analysts and brokerage houses, and had a worldwide network of financial connections. He ran a business, Financial Management International Inc., out of a high-rise residential building atop San Francisco's elegant Nob Hill.

Despite his prestigious address and the Rolls Royce and driver he kept to wheel him around town, there was certainly nothing snooty about Frankie Chinn, as he was known in the Bay City financial community. A war refugee born in Shanghai in 1945, he came with his mother, Essie, and his two sisters to San Francisco when he was only four. Bunked in one room, they struggled to get by, and by the time he was six, Frankie was shining shoes on the street. He dropped out of high school in the tenth grade to become a bicycle messenger, bellhop, and dishwasher. Finally, he signed up to dig ditches with a Filipino work crew in the Marshall Islands.

The menial job instilled in Chinn a thirst for travel, and back in San Francisco, he took a job that would enable him to see the world. He became a crackerjack encyclopedia salesman, peddling the books in Asia, Africa, Europe, and the Middle East. Along the way, Chinn met and fell in love with Shahdan el-Shazly, the daughter of an Egyptian defense minister. Before they married, he took an Islamic name and became Wayne Franklyn Mohamed Farid Chinn, a title stamped into his bulging passport.

They had two children and were ready to settle down, when Chinn began looking for another line of work. He had developed a fascination with the mercurial ups and downs of the stock market. He was a risk-taker, not afraid to lose $100,000 in a day and regain it two days later. Chinn answered an ad for a brokerage house, lied and said he had a high school diploma, and went to work learning everything he could about the market. He dabbled in everything from retail and institutional sales to over-the-counter trading; among his clients were a number of wealthy Middle Eastern families whom he had met through his wife. He later boasted that he handled $1 billion for individuals living in the Middle East and doubled the amount.

Chinn became known in the Bay City financial district as a flamboyant figure, who often showed up for work with flowing black hair, blue jeans, and a backpack. Straitlaced investors did not know how to take Chinn and his lovely Egyptian wife. When Chinn and el-Shazly divorced, she married David Meid, a securities broker with whom Chinn had numerous business contacts. Chinn also remarried, but the turbulent marriage ended nine months later. His estranged wife, Barbara, charged that Chinn attacked her, tore her blouse, and grabbed her by the throat in front of a restaurant while she was hailing a taxi, and that he possessed at least one handgun.

Chinn and Meid were involved in two partnerships—Hillsborough Partners and Dynasty Partners—before Meid became a broker at Bear Stearns & Co., where he handled Chinn's accounts. Meid introduced Chinn to his principal client, Marymount Palos Verdes College near Los Angeles. The college hoped Chinn could place its money in speculative investments as a way to drive up the value of its endowment. Among the investments Chinn selected was a chunk of Wedtech stock.

Chinn's trading techniques were fast and loose, causing some brokers to refuse to do business with him. A common Chinn technique was to dump blocks of stock on several different brokers without indicating that he was splitting his order—a tactic that allowed him to unload his stake at a higher than average price while the brokers were left to absorb substantial losses. He also specialized in a practice disparagingly known in the securities industry as flipping. Chinn targeted hot new stock issues that he could buy and sell in a day. Relying on this highly speculative technique, he managed to make $12,869 for Wallach in the short period between January 23 and April 30.

Wallach told the Wedtech officers that Chinn and London served as money managers for highly placed individuals in the Reagan administration, and the Wedtech officers regarded this as a veiled warning that they should hire the men—despite negative feedback that they were getting about Chinn from some of their own Wall Street advisers.

On April 30, 1985, the Wedtech board voted to retain London and Chinn as consultants and entered agreements to grant stock options to the two. The agreement called for both London and Chinn to purchase up to 50,000 shares of Wedtech common stock at a price of $13.875 a share, a potential gold mine if they succeeded in bolstering its value to $50 or $100 a share.

The signing of the Wedtech agreement came at the end of a climactic month for Frank Chinn. A few days earlier, Chinn had found a broker in Hong Kong willing to assist him in filing phony reports of London gold transactions—a means Chinn could use to cover the movement of large amounts of illicit cash from Hong Kong to the United States. Through Wallach's recommendation, he also had retained that month an impressive new private client. The client had little money, but his name carried such clout that, at the very mention of it, Chinn and his staff could open doors on Wall Street.

Newly appointed Attorney General Ed Meese had been

backed into a corner by the Senate Judiciary Committee, and
had promised as a condition of his appointment to place his
convoluted investments into a blind trust as a means of ensur-
ing no conflicts of interest. On April 12 Wallach introduced
Ed and Ursula Meese to Frank Chinn and gave him a glowing
recommendation. Meese never bothered to check Chinn's credentials before selecting him to manage his life savings, an
amount he estimated at close to $60,000.

Frankie Chinn was justifiably proud. He had been chosen
out of all the investment specialists in America to handle the
financial affairs of the top law enforcement official in the nation.

Despite these distractions, the Navy contract was Wedtech's
immediate bread and butter, and things were not going well
at the chaotic pontoon factory on East 149th Street. To win
the contract, Wedtech had practically written in blood that it
would meet the Navy's October 1984 delivery deadline. But
as the date approached, it became obvious the company could
not meet the schedule. The Wedtech assembly plant—populated by Rastafarians and warring street gangs plucked from
the unemployment lines—seemed incapable of putting the
simple boats together. The Navy had made it clear that the
floating pontoons must fit easily into their metal casings, but
Wedtech's workers made a mockery of precision engineering
by using sledgehammers and wrenches to try to bang the
pontoons into shape. They seemed unable to straighten the
corners of the boxlike boats. It took months for the workers
to discover the problem: In trying to make a perfect 90-degree
angle, they were dropping the plumb line against a floor that
wasn't level.

The production building was still without electricity, and
workers were complaining to the Environmental Protection
Agency about toxic fumes from the huge generators that Wedtech was using. Pervading the factory was the stench of human
waste, a problem traced back to the company's failure to pay
the subcontractor servicing its portable toilets. Fred Neuberger had moved his office to the plant, but he clearly had
lost interest in the business. He punched out every afternoon

before four—because, as he often boasted, that was his favorite time for sex.

At the Navy, program manager Captain De Vicq was losing his patience. An experienced civil engineer who had managed Navy projects all over the world, he had been disturbed by Wedtech's attitude from day one, when he spelled out the particulars of the Navy contract in a briefing at the SBA. The Wedtech delegation hardly listened, as if it couldn't care less what the work entailed. Mariotta kept interrupting the presentation to give what De Vicq considered a "sales speech." Later, he would come to realize that Mariotta was the equivalent of "an R2D2 jukebox with four or five records"—a man who delivered his "God and country" speech anytime he had the chance.

As Wedtech's delivery date neared, De Vicq saw no evidence that the company would be able to meet the time requirements. The assembly line was laughable, so bad that the Navy stationed experts at the site to do on-the-job training. De Vicq began to realize that the company, to his estimation, was running about a year behind schedule. He put the company on "red status"—a warning that it should move quickly to get its act together. He also began communicating the bad news to other offices in the Navy.

Unbeknownst to De Vicq, the Wedtech officers had come to the conclusion in the summer of 1984 that he was not just an officer trying to do his job; he was the new archenemy, out to destroy their chances of winning the vital contract options. They had taken up the matter with Wallach, who, in a long memo to the officers, urged them to invite De Vicq in for a private meeting and make him aware of the company's "ally structure." He also advised the officers to "make an implicit suggestion that if he wants his record to look good, obtain a promotion, etc., that by working with you and your working with him, that is the most efficient way to achieve everyone's common goal." De Vicq "should be aware of Wedtech's general ally structure. He doesn't have to know it in detail. The fact that you have it, and his awareness of it, ought to be gently indicated . . ." Wallach said.

In November 1984, Wedtech carried out Wallach's advice.

Moreno and Mariotta invited De Vicq to a meeting at Wedtech headquarters along with the SBA's Bob Saldivar. Moreno warned De Vicq that unless he played ball with them "we would have to do other things."

De Vicq told me later that he had no recollection of such a session, although he did recall being led on several occasions to the Wedtech "trophy room," where the most senior of photographed officials just happened to be the President of the United States.

Since Wedtech had performed so badly, De Vicq and his boss, Admiral Tom Hughes, were convinced the Navy should cut its losses and look elsewhere for a company to take over the pontoon contract. Hughes began writing memos to Everett Pyatt, in which the wording progressed sequentially from "I am concerned" to "I am deeply concerned" to "I am gravely concerned." However, the memos fell on deaf ears.

Around the same time, Pyatt's nomination as assistant secretary had finally won Senate confirmation, and Lyn Nofziger was one of the first to congratulate him. A few days after his appointment, Pyatt named as his principal deputy Wayne Arny, a former aide to John Tower's Senate Armed Services Committee.

As soon as he took office, Arny's phone began ringing with phone calls from Wedtech lobbyist Mark Bragg, who was inquiring about the pontoon options. In late August, Arny attended a meeting to discuss the situation with De Vicq and SBA officials. He decided that he could not rely on De Vicq's judgment, that instead what he needed was an independent analysis of Wedtech's performance capabilities. He assigned the job to Capt. Charles Piersall of the Naval Sea Systems Command.

Unlike the irascible De Vicq, Piersall took a friendly approach to his mission. He told the Wedtech officials he was there to troubleshoot and to help them improve their performance. Within a few weeks, Piersall filed an interim report to Arny suggesting that Wedtech could complete the causeways on schedule provided the Navy stepped up its deliveries of government-furnished equipment.

Nevertheless, time was rapidly running out for Wedtech.

Under the contract, the Navy had ninety days in which to negotiate the options or else they would be automatically dropped. And even if the Navy accepted Wedtech's sorry performance, the company and the Navy were miles apart on the cost of the pontoon options. Wedtech wanted $68 million; the Navy had budgeted only $42 million. But Arny came to the rescue. In mid-November, he sent a memo ordering the pontoon options to be granted to Wedtech immediately by letter contract—a seldom-used method that allows a company to begin work at a price to be negotiated later.

When De Vicq heard about Arny's actions, he was incredulous. Except in wartime or other emergencies, when crisis work had to commence immediately, he had never heard of a letter contract being used. Under the present circumstances, it was nothing more than a "license to steal." De Vicq's assessment was shared by several admirals, who objected vociferously to Arny's approach. Adm. John Paul Jones, the commander of NAVFAC, dashed off a message to Arny asking him to reconsider the issue. His superior, Adm. Richard Miller, called Pyatt directly to complain.

While the letter contract was under discussion at the Navy, the Wedtech officials were involved in negotiations of their own. As Moreno testified, in December he, Mariotta, and Wallach had met in Washington for a conference with Bragg on the pontoon options. But in Nofziger & Bragg's waiting room, Bragg asked that Wallach stay behind. He wanted to talk to the Wedtech officers privately, Moreno testified.

Inside, Moreno briefed Bragg on their problems and said he would be willing to do something really big for Bragg if he could help them through the maze at the Navy.

"What are you willing to do?" Bragg reportedly asked him.

Moreno and Mariotta huddled in a corner for a moment, then returned to their seats. Moreno outlined an attractive proposition. If Nofziger & Bragg could deliver the options at their asking price, they would reward them with $400,000. If the price was negotiated down, they would still kick in $200,000.

When they emerged from the room, Moreno said, they found Wallach fuming at having been shut out of the meeting.

He demanded to know what had gone on behind closed doors.

So they made him a similar offer: If the pontoon options went through, they would give him an additional $150,000.

Back at the Navy's executive offices, Arny's letter-contract plan had met with such opposition that he backed off. But the Navy had lost so much time debating the idea that it could no longer afford to seek a second source for the boats. After haggling over the price, the options were awarded at $51.5 million on March 15, 1985. At the time, Wedtech still had not delivered a single acceptable pontoon, and its first delivery was not yet in sight.

Soon after the talks were completed, Admiral Hughes and De Vicq continued their efforts to drop Wedtech before the next set of options came up for negotiation. At Hughes's urging, the Navy began talks with Bay City Marine, an established shipbuilder. But in early 1986 the Navy abruptly cut its budget for the Sealift Support Program, and the cuts made it unfeasible to seek a second source.

When Wedtech saw the reduced figures, it doubted it could continue to produce the boats. The company decided that it would have to bypass the Navy and have an appropriation for the company written into the annual funding bill passed by Congress. It called on Biaggi, Addabbo, and D'Amato to push for the firm, and also hired two new influential consultants— John Campbell, a former aide to Republican Sen. John Warner of Virginia, and Jim Aspin, the businessman brother of powerful Rep. Les Aspin of Wisconsin, the chairman of the House Armed Services Committee. This strategy was successful. The full funding was tacked onto the House–Senate appropriations conference report.

The early months of 1986 also were difficult ones for Captain de Vicq, an intense, hard-working officer whose job evaluations had been glowing. He had been awarded three Navy Legions of Merit in his career, including one for his management of the pontoon job. But in January, he was abruptly removed from his program manager job and moved to a less prestigious one. This followed a session with Saldivar and Arny in which he was told he was "riding too hard" on

Wedtech. His replacement in the job was Capt. Tim Kelley, a personal friend of former White House aide Jenkins, who was then working as a Wedtech consultant.

Not surprisingly, Captain Kelley came in with a more tolerant attitude toward Wedtech. In his six months on the job, he recommended the award of a second set of options to Wedtech and told the Navy that the company was performing well. When a preaward survey recommended against giving the contract to Wedtech, he ordered that a second review be performed. As he was about to leave the Navy, Kelley also gave a favorable report to Wedtech's underwriters, Bear Stearns & Co., which was preparing for a $75 million bond offering for the company.

When a defense contract officer, Col. Don Hein, suggested that Wedtech's finances were in dreadful disarray, Kelley told him to mind his own business. Hein had grown increasingly alarmed by Wedtech's sloppy paperwork and misleading financial reports and had discovered that the company was misrepresenting its financial picture to the Department of Defense. The company dealt with Hein by sending Ehrlich to tell him of his regular meetings with Senator D'Amato and of Wedtech's ability to go over his head. When that intimidation attempt didn't work, Wedtech called Hein's boss and threatened to file a $10 million lawsuit unless he was removed from the case. Hein was promptly replaced.

De Vicq kept a good attitude about his fate, but the events gave him cause for contemplation. In March 1986, he went on leave status and then retired.

Ironically, De Vicq had a job offer from Wedtech, which tried to lure him with a hefty salary to serve as a consultant. When he went to talk to Hughes about it, De Vicq learned—to his amazement and amusement—that Wedtech had also approached Hughes.

"What are they offering you?" Hughes asked.

"Oh, about twice what they're offering you!"

The two sat in Hughes' office and shared one of the best laughs they had had in a long time.

*   *   *

In September 1985, the Wedtech officers were back in Washington with their tuxedos for the annual Ambassadors' Ball, sponsored by the National Multiple Sclerosis Society. They bought a table for $15,000 at the behest of Bob Wallach, who was pushing the cause. Nofziger & Bragg had kicked in $5,000 for a table, and banker-developer Jeffrey Cohen had made a similar contribution.

The Ambassadors' Ball pulled together most of Wallach's developing circle of influence for an important cause. It was a chance for Ursula Meese, the cohostess of the event and a longtime volunteer, to shine outside the shadow of her famous husband. Mrs. Meese had suffered something of a career crisis after the tragic death of her son, Scott, in a 1982 car accident. At the time, she had been holding a full-time job as director of a research program at the William Moss Institute of American University, a $53,333-a-year position, financed by private donations, that she had won through one of her husband's political friends, Bob Gray, a Washington consultant. After the family tragedy, she had cut back her hours and reduced her salary to $40,000 a year. When the research program ended, she decided to stay at home until her daughter graduated from college.

Wallach had been concerned about Ursula Meese's plight and had begun circulating word to some of his business contacts that he was looking "with some urgency" for a job for Mrs. Meese. He told one contact that he felt compelled to help the Meeses improve their financial status, which had suffered greatly from Ed Meese's commitment to public service.

In June 1985, he introduced Mrs. Meese to Howard Bender over dinner at a Washington restaurant. Sondra Bender and Mrs. Meese already knew one another, having served together on the American University Board of Trustees, and the conversation quickly drifted to Mrs. Meese's job search. The Benders had a great idea: They proposed that Mrs. Meese go to work for a radio station they owned in Washington, doing public interest programs. The proposal for the radio job later fell through, but Wallach by then had come up with a better plan. He proposed to Bender that the Bender

Foundation, a charitable trust, donate $40,000 to the Multiple Sclerosis Society, which could be used to fund a full-time salary for Mrs. Meese, who would work as development director of a program called Operation Job Match.

The Benders were receptive to the plan, and soon the Benders were lunching with the Meeses at the White House and hosting the Attorney General and his wife at their horse farm in Frederick, Maryland. Wallach had made everyone happy.

Around the same time, Wallach had taken a special interest in a lease renewal that Bender's Blake Construction Company was negotiating. Two divisions of the Department of Justice were housed in the building, and Blake was hoping for a ten-year renewal at a substantially higher rental—a deal which would inevitably increase the value of the building for future sale. Instead, Justice's Data Center, which occupied 100,000 square feet of space, wanted out of the lease altogether.

Wallach had interceded with a brilliant suggestion. He recommended a Washington consultant who could help in the lease negotiations—James Jenkins, Meese's former deputy. Bender and Jenkins met and entered a handshake agreement for a $75,000 retainer. After a series of phone calls by Wallach, the lease renewal was finally executed in May 1987. Immigration and Naturalization agreed to a ten-year lease, and the Data Center headquarters signed a five-year deal, which upped the value of the building by more than two thirds. Meese, questioned later about the lease deal, said he had no knowledge of Bender's interest in government buildings.

On the night of the Ambassadors' Ball, Wallach escorted the Meeses around the crowded dance floor, introducing them to various people. He was clearly in his element. When he spotted the three Wedtech tables, he beamed and proudly came over. He had arranged for the group to be seated with distinguished ambassadors from Egypt, Pakistan, and Israel. Wallach asked them if they would like to meet the Meeses.

In the presence of Meese, they stood humbly while Wallach introduced them and boasted of their success: The company was growing, employment was high, and there was only hope for the future.

According to Moreno, Meese wanted to know how the firm was doing with the huge pontoon contract: "Are you on time with your deliveries?"

"Fine," Mariotta said.

Ursula was more exuberant. The officers later testified that when Wallach led the group to her side, the bubbling co-hostess exclaimed, "Oh! This must be the Wedtech clan!"

For the officers, it was one more sign of their comforting intimacy. Mrs. Meese had made them feel that they were almost like family.

15

THE LAST IN LINE

In the spring of 1984, Mario Moreno took a call from an irritated Rep. Robert Garcia, the Democratic congressman from the poorest district in America, whose boundaries included the Wedtech plant. Immersed in the affairs of Washington, where he was one of the leading Hispanics in Congress, Garcia had taken only a lukewarm interest in Wedtech and lost track of his district's most important defense enterprise. But when Wedtech won the pontoon contract, Garcia picked up word that Wedtech had gone public the previous fall and was making Biaggi a fabulously wealthy man. According to Moreno, Garcia was disturbed by the reports: "Why did I have to hear this from strangers?" Realizing they could not afford to alienate their own congressman, Moreno agreed to

178

meet Garcia and his elegant wife, Jane Lee, over dinner to discuss their concerns.

Bobby Garcia was something of a sore point at Wedtech headquarters. John Mariotta adored him; it was Garcia, after all, whose Urban Enterprise Bill introduced in 1980 had won Mariotta an invitation to the White House to deliver his "God and country" speech to President Reagan. As early as 1981, Mariotta had raised $4,000 for Garcia's campaign—telling his cohorts he needed to reward Garcia for his help on the company's first loans from EDA.

Although the Mariottas had honored Garcia with a wedding gift at the time of his 1980 second marriage, Mariotta's wife, Jennie, did not care for the congressman's new bride, Jane Lee, a Puerto Rican socialite who had worked on Garcia's congressional staff. Jennie Mariotta was still friends with Garcia's first wife, who had moved to Rockland County with their two teen-age sons.

Neuberger disliked Garcia for other reasons. The 18th district congressman was a philosophical enigma, a Democrat who dressed in Republican clothes whenever it fit his purpose. Moreover, Neuberger objected to what he saw as a pacifist voting record; in 1982 alone, Garcia had cast votes against funding for the MX missile and in support of a nuclear freeze. Neuberger made his position clear. He wanted no Wedtech money to go to Garcia. To do so would be an insult to Wedtech's customers.

As Moreno met with Garcia, he needed to be convinced there was something Garcia could offer Wedtech. Jane Lee Garcia emphasized her husband's credentials and committee assignments as well as her own network of connections to the pro-statehood leadership in Puerto Rico. She and Bobby were close friends of then-Gov. Rafael Hernández Colón, who offered an entree to big contracts on the island. Moreno listened carefully. By the end of the meal, they had drawn up an agreement in which Wedtech would hire Jane Lee as a consultant for a regular monthly retainer. The money would be funneled through the law firm of another of their Puerto Rican friends, Ralph Vallone, Jr., a San Juan lawyer and businessman.

Moreno testified that the payments began in August 1984 and continued for two years, amounting to $86,100 over a two-year period and including a $10,000 commission for Vallone. Garcia did little for the money. Investigators found evidence that he interceded for Wedtech with the U.S. Postal Service to thwart the transfer of their bribed contracting officer, Jerrydoe Smith. Garcia also arranged for Mariotta and Moreno to meet with Governor Colón to discuss a major Puerto Rican ferry contract, which evaporated as the company's financial affairs deteriorated.

The favors to Garcia steadily escalated, however. Mariotta contributed $60,000 to Garcia's sister, the Rev. Aimee Cortese, a Pentecostal minister, to pay off the mortgage on her humble storefront church. Later, according to the officers, the sister provided a cover when Garcia sought a secret $20,000 Wedtech loan.

In 1985, Mariotta told the other officers that Garcia needed more money and that he intended to make it available. The payment showed up in the form of an odd business investment between Jane Lee Garcia and Jennie Mariotta. On December 14, Mariotta's wife wrote a check for $45,000 to Mrs. Garcia, ostensibly for a part-interest in a clothing store in San Juan's Old Town shopping district. His wife never worked in or made a dime from the shop, but Mariotta later claimed that he made the investment because he wanted her to have her own business interests.

The Mariottas also ran into the Garcias while visiting the teeming shopping district in the Caribbean island of St. Thomas, where Wedtech maintained its offshore accounts. Strolling along the long aisle of discount linen and jewelry shops, the foursome ducked into an emerald shop, lured by the glittering display cases. Mariotta was overcome by impulse. He bought a $75,000 diamond and emerald necklace to adorn the neck of the lovely Jane Lee Garcia, a woman of exquisite taste. All told, the Wedtech cooperators later calculated that the firm paid $185,000 to the Garcias over the course of two years, money that had no major effect on Wedtech's business.

The November 1988 indictment of Garcia—along with his

showy wife and their friend Vallone—ranked as one of the most distressing developments of the Wedtech scandal. Garcia, then fifty-five, a Bronx street kid who grew up to be one of the city's most influential congressmen, was for years the great Hispanic hope, a role model whose voice carried clout from City Hall to the White House. The son of a minister, he had an unblemished career in the state legislature and a superlative ethical record. His constituents looked up to him as one of the city's last honest politicians.

Garcia's popularity was such that a few weeks before his indictment—which came after months of public accusations from the witness stand—he was reelected by a landslide. His constituents never quite understood how Bobby Garcia could surrender his principles to the lure of power and money. They could not even accept the government's charge that Garcia, the last in line for a Wedtech handout, came to see the defense contractor as an open checkbook, just like all the rest.

Bobby Garcia made his way to the corridors of power the hard way, climbing flights of bleak tenement stairs in the South Bronx to check the pulse of his constituents. Desperately poor and stripped of hope, they found they could identify with the humble Garcia, who walked the streets in cheap wrinkled suits and scruffy shoes. Garcia was a politician, as columnist Jack Newfield once put it, "who seemed emotionally inseparable from his community."

Born in the South Bronx in 1933, Garcia, a church deacon, was the son of the Rev. Rafael Garcia, a Pentecostal preacher at the Thessalonica Christian Church on St. Anns Avenue. He grew up in the Bronx, attending city schools, and he served in Korea as an Army infantryman before enrolling in City College. He did not graduate and eventually trained as a computer programmer at RCA Institute, a vocational school. Married, with two sons, he worked for eight years with firms like IBM and Control Data before entering politics, a field that seemed suited to his sincere, caring nature.

He was elected in 1966 to fill an Assembly seat, and two years later, moved up to fill a state Senate post. He was the first man of Puerto Rican ancestry elected to the Senate.

Garcia quickly emerged as one of the legislature's work-horses, climbing to deputy minority leader. His early legislative efforts concentrated on tenants' rights and prison reform, a special concern after his appointment to the Attica Observers Committee, in the wake of the violent 1971 prison uprising. A year later, the Citizens Union rated him a "humane legislator with a deep personal commitment to relieving the ills of his underprivileged constituents." Affable and popular, Garcia, a stocky man of medium height, prided himself on his ability to bring together the disparate interests of blacks and Hispanics for worthwhile community projects like drug rehabilitation centers and programs for the handicapped. "My claim to fame has always been to get the commissioners and my community leaders together. . . ." he once told an interviewer.

Garcia's heavily Puerto Rican 30th district spanned an area from Hunts Point in the Bronx to Fifth Avenue and 94th Street in Manhattan's Yorkville section. Half of his 315,000 constituents earned less than $5,000 a year, while at least a portion of them earned in the millions. Garcia himself stuck to his modest Senate salary, reporting a meager 1973 income of $15,000. Money seemed of little concern to him, except for the constraints posed by his tight legislative budget.

Besides his Puerto Rican ancestry and broken Spanish, Garcia shared similar viewpoints with John Mariotta, an emerging Bronx industrialist. Garcia also believed in giving the down-and-out a second chance. A key member of his legislative staff was a reformed junkie and stick-up man out on parole. Garcia fought savagely against a tough drug package, proposed by Gov. Nelson Rockefeller, setting up severe penalties for pushers and users.

Garcia's performance was so highly rated and his record so clean that in 1978 he seemed a natural to move into a congressional seat when his friend and political ally, the Puerto Rico–born Herman Badillo, stepped down from Congress to become Koch's deputy mayor. But then–Democratic Party boss Pat Cunningham pushed instead for Assemblyman Louis Nine. Garcia responded by running for Congress on the Republican and Liberal tickets and recruiting a coalition of blacks, Jews, and Italians. The deciding factor in the race proved to be Badillo, who walked arm in arm with Garcia through the South Bronx streets to demonstrate his ringing endorsement. That act of loyalty turned the tide in the election, but Garcia did not return the favor in 1985, when Badillo tried to summon support for a mayoral candidacy against Ed Koch. Without so much as consulting Badillo, Garcia gave his unsolicited support to Koch.

In Washington, he quickly emerged as a leader, heading the Congressional Hispanic Caucus from 1978 to 1982. Speaker Tip O'Neill considered him a coalition builder, one of the best in the chamber. He became chairman of the Census and Population Subcommittee of the Post Office and Civil Service Committee, using the position to press the point that 1980 Census figures should be adjusted to compensate for counting deficiencies that often caused blacks and Hispanics to be underrepresented. In 1980, he joined forces with conservative Republican Jack Kemp in sponsoring the Urban Enterprise Bill, a plan to use tax breaks and other incentives to spur development in depressed areas. The odd alliance with Kemp was a philosophical leap that some of his supporters found hard to swallow, but Garcia defended it as simply a way to get things done. Their proposal brought Garcia into favor at the White House. Congress passed the measure but never backed the bill with the tax breaks needed to make it work. The administration did little to press the point.

Radical changes in Garcia's personal life also disturbed some of his supporters. Garcia and his wife separated three years before his election to Congress, and Garcia began seeing a twice-divorced wealthy Puerto Rican, Jane Lee Matos, a mother of four. The cultured daughter of one of the island's most prominent families, she had studied at the University of Puerto Rico and the American Academy of Dramatic Arts. Horses were her great love. Her second marriage was to a horse breeder, and during the union she raised horses and raced them at El Comandante race track near San Juan.

In 1979, the glamorous Jane Lee, with flowing hair and a brilliant smile, moved to Washington to work for Garcia's census subcommittee and later transferred to his congressional office. They married in 1980 and soon became immersed in the social and political whirl of Washington, attending all the right parties and finding less and less time for visits to the squalid surroundings of Garcia's district.

Jane Lee also had connections to Puerto Rico's pro-statehood faction and was a friend and political supporter of former Gov. Carlos Romero Barceló. After her marriage, she turned her political ties to her advantage by setting up her own consulting firm, Leesonia Enterprises, and recruiting clients with Puerto Rican interests to push.

Jane Lee Garcia also was appointed president of the Board of Trustees of the newly formed Bronx Museum of the Arts, founded in a renovated synagogue by Irene Simon, the borough president's wife. Among those named to the museum board were Wedtech's Mario Moreno, Jack Bronston, an influential lawyer and former Queens state senator convicted in a city bus shelter scandal, and Ralph Vallone, a well-connected San Juan lawyer. Under Jane Garcia's tenure, the museum, which received $3.9 million in city funds, adopted a peculiar habit of making political contributions, including donations to Stanley Simon's campaign. The practice brought the museum and its five satellite branches—including one in Borough Hall—under federal investigation in 1987.

Soon after their marriage, Garcia underwent what his friends detected as a makeover both in appearance and personal values. His cheap, ill-fitting suits were tossed aside for expensive, designer cuts; his full head of graying hair took on a softer, blow-dried look. At Jane Lee's insistence, he took Spanish lessons to improve his broken dialect. The address he claimed to live in—a modest apartment on the Grand Concourse—appeared deserted most of the time. Instead, the Garcias took up residence in a two-story home on a sixty-five acre horse farm named Moccasin Kill Farm in Rotterdam, 180 miles north of the South Bronx. They bought the farm in October 1983 for $156,502, financed with a $150,000 Veterans Administration loan. Garcia also borrowed $10,000 from a Bronx businessman, Johnny Torres, the owner of Metro Food Stores at the Bronx Terminal Market.

Garcia's financial disclosure forms gave a picture of the couple's escalating debt, extravagant tastes, and rising income through Jane's consulting services. In his 1984 filing, the congressman reported free Las Vegas trips from the letter carriers' union and the League of United Latin American Citizens, free trips to Puerto Rico from the Bronx Museum and the Mondale Campaign Committee, a free diamond ring for Jane from a Brooklyn supporter, and honoraria from a number of concerns with interests in postal legislation. The Garcias owed money to five banks, with a debt somewhere between $50,000 and $100,000 to the Simone-controlled New York National Bank.

Garcia's disclosure statements also noted that Jane received consulting fees from her lawyer friend, Vallone. They did not reveal, as the Wedtech officers charged, that the $4,400-per-month payments had been devised as an indirect way to purchase the influence of Garcia's office.

The same year that Bobby Garcia allegedly began making arrangements to cash in on Wedtech, his sister, the Rev. Aimee Cortese, was involved in secret negotiations of her own. A longtime board member of the immensely popular and profitable Praise The Lord–People That Love television ministry, based in faraway Fort Mill, South Carolina, Cortese was taking care of a messy personal problem tormenting her spiritual mentor, the Rev. Jim Bakker. Trying to unwind before an important TV taping, Bakker had found himself in a compromising position in a Florida motel room with a toothy young Long Island church secretary named Jessica Hahn. The two had sex, which Bakker later admitted and blamed on Hahn, whom he described as a young woman of worldly ways. Hahn had a different account. Four years after the incident, she told her lawyer that she had been drugged and raped by Bakker, a charge the PTL leaders considered tantamount to blackmail.

Hahn's allegations cut to the heart of Bakker's incredibly popular and successful $129 million television ministry, headquartered in a Biblical Disneyland called Heritage Village. His longtime marriage to Tammy, a bleached blond whose abuse of mascara and rouge spawned a cottage industry of TV parodists, was a central part of Bakker's television appeal. His allies at PTL had decided to take care of Hahn's un-Christian allegations in a diplomatic way—by pressuring her to sign a retraction and, if need be, by paying her off.

Cortese, a PTL board member for six years and one of Bakker's closest allies, played a central role in pressuring Hahn—according to Hahn's version of events as related in a transcribed interview with her attorney, Paul Roper. Hahn said she had at least two meetings with Cortese, a licensed minister since 1951, and Richard Dortch, Bakker's right-hand man, to discuss the terms of a settlement. The first meeting, in March 1984, was at a motel near La Guardia Airport, followed that autumn by a meeting at Cortese's Bronx church.

While bodyguards waited outside the church door, Hahn claimed, the church leaders accused her of extortion and defamation. Hahn was handed a $20,000 cash payment as an installment of a negotiated financial settlement. Finally, Hahn said, Cortese thrust a retraction in front of her and demanded, "Sign the papers or you will never have any peace."

The allegations brought Cortese under scrutiny by her church leadership and, eventually, by federal law enforcement agents. Cortese's elders found Hahn's allegations difficult to fathom. Cortese, ordained in 1974 by the Assemblies of God, which was unaffiliated with the PTL organization, won the favor of church elders for her tireless work in the deprived surroundings of the South Bronx, where her father had also ministered. Like her brother Robert, she took a special interest in prisons and became chaplain of New York's Bedford Hills Correctional Institution. In the Bronx, she served as pastor of the Cross Roads Tabernacle, a 400-member church that became a gathering place for the poor and disadvantaged, who often called upon her brother's legislative office for help.

In March 1987, the *Charlotte Observer* broke the story of Jim Bakker's sexual misadventures, and federal law enforcement agents in North and South Carolina began tracing the source of the $265,000 in hush money that PTL gave Hahn to buy her silence. They established that the ministry paid Hahn with funds derived from charitable contributions, then covered up the payments with phony construction bills from a prominent church builder.

But revelations coming out of New York in the developing Wedtech scandal were intriguing and posed a fascinating, though distant, possibility that Wedtech money had somehow ended up in the hands of Jessica Hahn. New York investigators learned about a suspicious $20,000 loan made by Wedtech to Robert Garcia, which company officials claimed was laundered through his sister. They also discovered that Mariotta, a PTL supporter, had donated $60,000 to Cortese's church to pay off its mortgage. After subpoenaing the Cross Roads' records, they were puzzled when they could not properly account for the Wedtech donation. The mystery was heightened with revelations that Bakker also donated $50,-000 to Cortese in July 1985 as a "bonus" for her services to PTL. Ministry officials said they could find no purpose for the payment in PTL's records.

In June 1987, with a swirl of questions still surrounding Cortese's financial dealings with PTL and Wedtech, FBI agents paid a visit to Jessica Hahn at her apartment to question her, not about the Rev. Jim Bakker, but about the Wedtech Corporation. She had never heard of the company. They told her to prepare to be subpoenaed by a Wedtech grand jury to testify about her dealings with Cortese. The warnings came to nothing. Hahn put the odd collision of scandals behind her as she moved into Hugh Hefner's Playboy mansion for a new, liberating life as a national sex symbol.

As the Wedtech investigation of Garcia continued over the course of months, the Rev. Mrs. Cortese occasionally gave status reports on subpoenas and grand jury testimony to her concerned supporters, asking them to "pray for us."

By that time, the church was suffering from such crowding problems that it had begun meeting in an electronics warehouse in a Bronx industrial park. On the front row every Sunday, taking solace in his family's deep Pentecostal roots, sat her brother, the congressman, often accompanied by his wife, Jane Lee. Stripped of her job at the Bronx Museum because of questions about her management of city funds, she seemed under considerable strain. Garcia told friends that he had been "born again" in the midst of his legal difficulties, an act of salvation that enabled him to get through his stressful days.

As his sister appealed to God for a legal victory, the Garcias stood out among her concerned followers. Their heads bowed in supplication, they seemed to be praying harder than anyone.

THE
BALTIMORE-WASHINGTON
CONNECTION

BIDING THEIR TIME in prison, Richard Strum and Lenny Lockhart had plenty of time to think about what they would do when they were free men. It was 1983, and the two were cell mates at the Allenwood Federal Prison Camp in south-central Pennsylvania.

Strum, a fifty-five-year-old marketing representative, had been convicted of fraud and sentenced to fifteen months in prison in connection with a loan scam. A married grandfather of four with a drinking problem that often clouded his memory, Strum had only three years of high school education. But during three decades as a marketing representative, he had developed an enviable business savvy and a long list of business contacts. He counted among his friends Wedtech's cunning cofounder, Fred Neuberger, whom he had met when Neuberger was trying to resuscitate Fleetwood Metals.

Lockhart, a thirty-one-year-old former college basketball star turned businessman, was the black sheep of a politically active family on Maryland's rural Eastern Shore. He had been convicted of writing bad checks in Delaware and of mail fraud in Baltimore. His gift for gab was more impressive than his career, however. After spending from 1971 to 1975 at American University, he left without getting a degree—"another athletic casualty," as a prosecutor would describe him.

At Allenwood, Lockhart tried to impress Strum with his connections, telling his cell mate that if red tape had to be cut, he knew the people who could do it. His contacts, Lockhart claimed, extended far beyond bucolic Cecil County, where his father, Leonard H. Lockhart, Sr., was a prominent attorney and behind-the-scenes political player.

Strum and Lockhart left Allenwood later that year, but their paths would soon cross again, thanks to a company that had made a name for itself by hiring and rehabilitating ex-cons—Wedtech. In the summer of 1984, facing the threat of a congressional investigation, Wedtech turned to the two ex-cons for help.

In October 1983, Wedtech was looking for a marketing supervisor to coordinate salesmen in Los Angeles, Baltimore, Long Island, and Rock Island, Illinois. Neuberger immediately thought of his friend, Strum, who had landed in a halfway house after leaving Allenwood and was looking for work. Neuberger pushed Strum as a man who knew his way around the business, had friends in the right places, and didn't mind working hard. Neuberger's prediction proved correct. Wedtech hired Strum and he did so well in his new job that he was promoted to assistant vice president for marketing and ultimately vice president.

Strum also used his position to return favors to a few of his old friends in need of work. One of his many contacts was a fellow marketing representative by the name of Anthony Loscalzo. Loscalzo was living in Davenport, Iowa, across the Mississippi River from the Rock Island Army Arsenal. According to Strum, Loscalzo's usual place of business was a bar called the Sundance Club in Davenport, where he would hang out, pushing his clients and buying drinks for the bureaucrats who manned the arsenal's procurement office.

Loscalzo touted his own political connections, particularly to a prominent Baltimore family that had been a leading force in the American civil rights movement. He told Strum that he was especially close to Michael and Clarence Mitchell III, the sons of pioneering NAACP leader Clarence M. Mitchell, Jr. Strum filed away this information and persuaded Wedtech to hire Loscalzo as a consultant. Initially his Executive Marketing Services got a monthly retainer of only $1,500, but the fee skyrocketed to $20,000 after he helped Wedtech land a contract from the Rock Island Arsenal for smoke grenade launchers.

Strum soon brought another friend on board—his former cell mate, Lenny Lockhart, then serving out the last six months of his prison term at the Volunteers of America halfway house in east Baltimore. Strum told Lockhart he might have a client for a business that Lockhart was forming, International Assistance Corporation. Soon, IAC was also working for Wedtech for an initial retainer of $10,000 plus $5,000 a month.

Before long, Strum, Loscalzo, and Lockhart became central players in a new drama that was threatening Wedtech. U.S. Rep. Parren Mitchell, the Baltimore Democrat who served as chairman of the House Small Business Committee, began an investigation into allegations from anonymous sources that Wedtech had used illegal means to stay in the SBA's 8(a) program. The complaints were an outgrowth of jealousies within the intensely competitive 8(a) community, which had divided into two distinct factions—the blacks and the Hispanics. Black entrepreneurs were upset by the rising percentage of set-asides going to Hispanic-owned firms, particularly to Wedtech. Mitchell had become a champion of wounded black businessmen. The Hispanics, through their aggressive lobbying group, LAMA, had turned more frequently to influential Reagan administration figures.

For the first time, Mitchell's investigation brought Wedtech under hostile scrutiny by an unfriendly government entity. It posed the risk that Congress, with its broad investigative powers, would expose Wedtech and force government agencies to end the company's history of favored treatment. The unanticipated probe threw Wedtech for a loop. In all of its perfectly calculated payoffs, the company had failed to anticipate the potential damage that could be done by an aggressive black congressman from a district hundreds of miles from the South Bronx.

Wedtech, by then fat and supremely self-important, had to rejuvenate its street-fighter instincts to ward off this new potential disaster. Parren Mitchell would eventually terminate his inquiry as suddenly as he began it, but not before his nephews Michael and Clarence accepted $110,000 in bribes from Wedtech—payments that would lead to their November 1987 convictions on federal charges of wire fraud and attempting to obstruct a congressional investigation.

Parren Mitchell himself was not indicted, but a wave of negative publicity followed him as he retired from Congress in 1986. Stymied by a lack of cooperation from a protective Congress, federal investigators dropped their pursuit of Parren Mitchell, while never quite coming to terms with his committee's decision to end the Wedtech probe in close timing to the company's retention of the Mitchell family law firm.

The scandal centered in the slums of the South Bronx would bring a cloud of shame upon one of Maryland's most illustrious and respected black families. The congressman's brother, Clarence M. Mitchell, Jr., who died in March 1984, was one of the nation's best-known civil rights leaders. For three decades he was the chief Washington lobbyist for the National Association for the Advancement of Colored People. Clarence Mitchell's reputation on Capitol Hill was so highly regarded, and his presence so keenly felt, that he was nicknamed "the 101st senator." Mitchell was instrumental in the passage of the Civil Rights Act of 1964, the Voting Rights Act of 1965, and the Fair Housing Act of 1968. As chairman of the Leadership Conference on Civil Rights, which he cofounded, Clarence Mitchell helped to persuade the Senate to reject the nominations to the Supreme Court of judges Clement Haynsworth and G. Harrold Carswell. His wife, Juanita Jackson Mitchell, became the first black woman to practice law in Maryland. The

Mitchells' modest brick house on Druid Hill Avenue in Baltimore served as the fertile setting for the early seeds of the civil rights movement. In it were also launched the political careers of the Mitchells' two eldest sons, Clarence M. Mitchell III and Michael B. Mitchell.

Parren Mitchell also had a long and distinguished career in public service. Born in 1922 in Baltimore, he earned a Purple Heart in World War II and returned to Baltimore to work as a probation officer. In the 1950s, he brought a successful lawsuit to integrate the graduate school of the University of Maryland. Mitchell was supervisor of the domestic relations division of the city's Supreme Court before becoming executive director in 1963 of the Maryland Commission on Interracial Problems and Relations. He also served as director of Baltimore's Community Action Agency.

In 1968, Mitchell launched his political career with an unsuccessful race for Congress against longtime machine Democrat Samuel Friedel. Mitchell carried the inner city but was knocked out in the predominantly white suburbs. The influx of blacks into formerly white neighborhoods gave Mitchell the courage to try again, and he was elected in November 1970 in a squeaker rematch with Friedel that was decided by 38 votes.

In the House, Mitchell emerged as a voice of indignation against policies and programs that hurt the poor. He lashed out at Reagan-era military spending as a waste of government resources in a country desperately in need of housing and other domestic aid programs. As chairman of the Small Business Committee, he channeled his advocacy into efforts to increase the percentage of federal contracts available to minority firms. He set up a legal defense fund to help minorities challenge discriminatory contract decisions and once threatened to sue Interior Secretary James Watt.

Michael Mitchell, a lawyer, and Clarence Mitchell III, a realtor, followed their uncle's footsteps into politics. Clarence served in the state legislature for twenty-four years, longer than any other black in Maryland history, until he stepped down in 1986 to run unsuccessfully for his uncle's congressional seat. Michael gave up his City Council seat in 1986 to campaign for, and win, the state Senate seat that his brother was vacating. The brothers had unblemished records until that year, when suddenly, they found themselves pummeled by negative publicity. First, reports surfaced that Clarence was under investigation for his ties to a reputed drug dealer, "Little Melvin" Williams. Then, word filtered out that the brothers were under scrutiny for their dealings with Wedtech, where a scandal was just being uncovered.

The careers of the Mitchell brothers took a precipitous tumble. Their family—full of the fury of the civil rights years—reacted to their federal indictment by organizing protest marches through the streets of Baltimore that cast the brothers as victims of racism and discrimination. But the damage had already been done.

In late 1984, the Wedtech officers first learned that Parren Mitchell was on their trail. The House Small Business Committee chairman had taken great pains to protect the confidentiality of his probe, but Wedtech's ties to the SBA paid off once again.

Shortly after he became chairman of the Small Business Committee early in 1984, Mitchell began receiving a number of complaints about Wedtech, mostly anonymous. Since Wedtech was then getting multimillion-dollar federal contracts and had gone public, the complaints said, the Bronx firm clearly should be removed from the protective wing of the SBA's 8(a) program. It was also alleged that Wedtech was a "front" company, unqualified to do the work for which it had government contracts, and in addition, Mitchell was alerted that President Reagan's former political affairs director, Nofziger, was lobbying the White House on Wedtech's behalf.

By July, the complaints against Wedtech had become so numerous and so insistent that Mitchell decided he needed to do something about them. He wrote a letter to the head of the SBA and instructed an aide to hand-deliver it with great secrecy and suspense.

According to the SBA's regional counsel, Jack Matthews, in mid-July word filtered up from SBA headquarters in Washington that Mitchell's committee was ready to dispatch some of its staffers to New York to investigate an unidentified 8(a) firm there. Not until their arrival would they divulge the name of the company.

A few days later, the committee's chief investigator, Tom Trimboli, who was an expert on the 8(a) program, and another aide showed up in New York. About 12:15 P.M., Trimboli glanced dramatically at his watch, picked up a phone, and dialed a colleague at the Small Business Committee in Washington. Trimboli advised his listener that, at that moment, he was turning over the letter to the SBA's acting New York district director, Mervyn Shorr. Reading the letter, Matthews and Shorr saw that the company in question was Wedtech, the star of the 8(a) program.

The letter, addressed to "the Honorable James C. Sanders, Administrator, Small Business Administration," requested that Sanders supply the committee with any SBA records about Wedtech and the names of all SBA employees who were dealing with the firm. It also asked that, within two weeks, Sanders provide the committee with the names of all "agents" who had appeared on Wedtech's behalf before the SBA since March 1, 1981.

Trimboli told Matthews he wanted to take back to Washington any documents on Wedtech's 8(a) participation that the SBA had readily available. But he had no idea what a mountain of paperwork awaited him. Among the reams of documents that the SBA had on Wedtech were five files on business development expenses, each 8 to 10 inches thick. Trimboli filled his two briefcases, and Matthews lent him two more. Matthews then loaded up several boxes with documents and mailed them to Washington. He also prepared the lists of SBA employees and Wedtech agents, and forwarded them to Sanders in Washington. At the top of the list of SBA employees was the name of Peter Neglia, then Sanders' acting chief of staff.

Mitchell said later there were two reasons he went to the SBA, instead of Wedtech, for answers to his questions: The SBA was responsible for overseeing the 8(a) companies, and he didn't want to deal directly with Wedtech in resolving the serious allegations.

Despite Mitchell's precautions, Wedtech's officers learned

about the letter almost immediately. Neglia apparently saw the letter the day it was delivered to Sanders' office. Within several days, Moreno had a copy on his desk.

The questions seemed fairly innocuous to the Wedtech officers. But the letter was troubling enough that the Wedtech officers began a concerted effort to lean on Mitchell. He soon found himself besieged by expressions of concern from members of New York's congressional delegation.

One day, while Mitchell was on the House floor, Representative Garcia approached him and asked: "What's this going on with the Wedtech company?" Garcia told Mitchell that the company had been a boon to his economically struggling district by providing much-needed jobs, and that he was concerned about the damaging effects of an investigation.

"Look, I got no problem with this particular company," Mitchell reassured Garcia.

Then came a similar entreaty from Representative Biaggi. Cornering Mitchell on the House floor, Biaggi said, "Hey, Parren, what's going on with the Wedtech company? That's a splendid company. It has won a presidential award. . . ." As he had done with Garcia, Mitchell assured Biaggi that he was not out to destroy Wedtech.

The congressman was also coming under pressure from the Hispanic business community. Mitchell was accustomed to hearing often from Steve Denlinger of LAMA and didn't think it unusual when his secretary announced that Denlinger was in the congressman's outer office. But when Mitchell went out to usher him in, he found not only Denlinger but about a dozen other people. Mitchell became furious, convinced Denlinger was trying to intimidate him.

Denlinger told Mitchell that the people with him were representatives of the Hispanic community who wanted to express their concerns about Wedtech. He was interrupted by a man with gray hair and a beard who launched into a speech about how Wedtech was the flagship of the Hispanic business community. Irately, Mitchell cut the man off.

"Look, I am sorry, I am not going to meet with you," he said. "There is an investigation under way. If [it] clears this outfit, fine. . . . But I am not going to discuss it, because I don't think it would be proper. . . ."

Then, Mitchell turned to Denlinger and told him he wanted to see him, alone. Denlinger went into Mitchell's personal office, where he got a tongue-lashing for bringing the crowd, unannounced.

"Well, you don't understand how deeply these guys feel about the flagship company. . . ." Denlinger told him.

By late August or early September, Mitchell decided that his committee didn't have the manpower to investigate Wedtech adequately. The logical solution was to have the investigation conducted by the Small Business Administration, with guidance from his committee. He decided to write a tough letter to the SBA asking it to resolve questions about Wedtech's status and special treatment. Later, at his nephews' trial, he said he knew of no special relationship between Wedtech and the SBA that would have prevented the agency from doing its job.

Mitchell tried to soothe the fears of Garcia and Biaggi by telling them that the SBA had taken over the case. "If the Small Business Administration clears it, that's fine with me. I don't want to try to hurt the company," he told them.

But the fears of Wedtech's officers were not so easily relieved. They tried every means they could think of to stop the investigation. Moreno had talked to just about anyone who would listen to him, including Ehrlich, Wallach, Addabbo, Nofziger, and Bragg. He had a number of conversations with Neglia. But the consensus was not good. Everyone he consulted said there was really not much they could do to stop Mitchell's investigation.

By September, Moreno and the other Wedtech officers realized that their efforts were getting nowhere, and Mitchell was still hot on their trail. The officers' concern turned to alarm when, in the middle of September, Neglia told them that an even more devastating letter from Mitchell to the SBA was in the works. He warned Moreno and Ehrlich that the committee was preparing a "very strong letter demanding critical answers to critical questions," as Moreno later told investigators.

The Wedtech officers realized how loudly publicity about a congressional investigation into a publicly held company would echo throughout Wall Street. They needed a quick, effective way to stop the investigation dead in its tracks. But no one in Wedtech's upper management boasted any pull whatsoever with the black political leadership in Washington. In the midst of their panic, a bell went off in Neuberger's mind. He remembered that Richard Strum once told him that his friend Loscalzo was friendly with the Mitchell family. Neuberger suggested to Moreno that Strum be put in charge of getting the Mitchell investigation stopped.

Soon afterward, Moreno called Strum into his office. Strum immediately noticed that Moreno looked "terrible" and "very upset." Moreno told him about the congressional investigation headed by Parren Mitchell, and the name clicked in Strum's mind.

"Is that Parren Mitchell from Baltimore?"

Moreno nodded. Strum told him that throughout the years, Loscalzo had often mentioned the Mitchells and said he was close to them, especially the congressman's nephews, Michael and Clarence. Strum went to his office and called Loscalzo, who said the way to get to Parren Mitchell was through his nephews.

Over the next few days, Strum left half a dozen phone messages at Michael Mitchell's law office, but he was unable to get either Clarence or Michael Mitchell to return his calls. Moreno also tried his hand, but his calls likewise were not returned.

Temporarily stymied, Strum realized he needed an intermediary. He remembered the boasts of his old cell mate, Lenny Lockhart, that he was tight with Baltimore politicians. Strum called Lockhart and described the situation, and the younger Lockhart asked if there was any money in it for him. "Most definitely," Strum replied, telling Lockhart that he could name his price if he could get the letter stopped.

Lockhart recommended that Strum come to Baltimore, convinced he could arrange a quick meeting with the Mitchells. Strum hopped on a plane and met Lockhart at the new Hyatt Regency Hotel, where Lockhart introduced him to his father and to former state Sen. Harry McGuirk, a powerful Baltimore political figure. Strum later testified that the Lockharts and McGuirk assured him that they could have the Mitchell brothers "get rid of the problem."

According to Strum, he and the elder Lockhart then walked over to a phone in the lobby. The contact that had eluded Strum came easily for the well-connected Maryland lawyer, who got Michael Mitchell on the phone and handed Strum the receiver. Strum gave Mitchell a brief rundown of their problem, and the two agreed to meet face to face the following day.

The helpfulness that the Lockharts and McGuirk showed was not free of charge, Strum later testified. He said they told him they wanted $5,000 each plus an equal payment for Michael Mitchell. Strum also stood to profit from the deal. Strum and Lockhart had a long-standing arrangement for Lockhart to kick back to Strum part of any money he got from Wedtech. They figured Strum could also get $5,000.

Despite assurances from the Lockharts and McGuirk that the problem was easily resolved, Strum had a queasy feeling when he left the Hyatt that night, not at all certain the Lockharts could deliver what they promised. Worried, he placed a call to Tony Loscalzo, who warned Strum that he should deal directly with the Mitchells, rather than use the Lockharts as intermediaries.

The next morning, Strum had breakfast with the Lockharts at the Omni hotel. Later he walked over to Tug's, a restaurant in the same building as the Mitchell family law firm. Strum introduced himself to the hostess and asked her to point out Michael Mitchell when he arrived. Strum ordered a vodka and tonic, which he said he nursed because he realized that the upcoming meeting would be extremely important to Wedtech's future. Strum's caution was well-advised. Even drinking in moderation, he was not able later to recall whether Clarence also attended the restaurant rendezvous.

Soon Mitchell walked in, found Strum at the bar, and introduced himself. The two walked over to a table and sat down.

Strum told Mitchell that Wedtech had a serious problem because of the investigation initiated by his uncle, and asked Mitchell if he could help "to get Parren Mitchell off our back." Mitchell's response, according to Strum, was that "he can get rid of the problem but it would be for a fee. A fee of 25 or 50 thousand, I don't recall." Mitchell said he wanted the fee paid in the form of a retainer to his law firm. Strum said he would report that to his superiors and would be back in touch with Mitchell.

If the Wedtech officials thought their troubles with Parren Mitchell were over, they had a rude awakening. Unbeknownst to Michael Mitchell and Strum, on the very day that they first met, the congressman had mailed the dreaded letter to Sanders, asking the SBA to investigate and report back to him on a number of controversial questions.

The letter seemed carefully crafted to destroy Wedtech, as if it were written by someone with intimate knowledge of the company's shenanigans. In the document, Mitchell asked the SBA to answer twelve questions that concerned whether Wedtech broke the law by its participation in the 8(a) set-aside program, the issuance or trading of stock, and the solicitation or performance of federal contracts. The letter asked the SBA to investigate whether any present or former SBA employees gave preferential treatment to Wedtech in violation of federal law, or acted on Wedtech's behalf as a result of White House pressure. It also asked if any former White House employees were representing Wedtech.

The letter could not have been more devastating, targeting virtually every skeleton in Wedtech's closet. As word spread among the company officers about the letter, the feeling of dread grew palpable. The only way Wedtech could survive the SBA scrutiny, they reasoned, was somehow to assure that their friend Peter Neglia was the one responsible for answering the questions.

Strum had barely arrived back at his Staten Island home from Baltimore on September 26 when he got a phone call from a panic-stricken Larry Shorten. Shorten said Parren Mitchell had already mailed the letter, and he ordered Strum to set up a meeting with Michael Mitchell as soon as possible.

Strum immediately called Mitchell and arranged to meet with him in Baltimore late in the afternoon on the following Monday, October 1. Moreno and Mariotta decided to go along so that they could meet the man who held the key to Wedtech's future. Loscalzo, who had convinced Strum he was the only one who could pull real weight with the Mitchells, arranged to fly into Baltimore from Iowa for the meeting. He informed Strum that the Mitchells had agreed to give him a one-third cut of any business he brought their way—an amount he was willing to split with Strum. Strum then followed some advice that Loscalzo had given him. He called Lenny Lockhart and told him that, since he had failed to stop the letter, their $25,000 deal was off.

The following Monday, Strum caught a flight to Baltimore and sat in the airport lounge waiting for Loscalzo's flight to arrive. He sipped the first of many drinks he would consume on that stressful day. After Loscalzo arrived, the two each had a drink before driving to downtown Baltimore, where they checked into the Tremont Hotel. After drinks at the Tremont, the two went to Tug's and had more cocktails while waiting for the arrival of Moreno and Mariotta, en route from New York in a limousine. In a while, the four went to Michael Mitchell's law office, where they met the Mitchell brothers.

The meeting began casually, with general discussions of Wedtech. Like a proud father, Moreno bragged about Wedtech, describing its work on the Army engines and the Navy pontoon assemblies. Then Moreno got down to the more pressing business at hand—the Mitchell letter to the SBA.

Moreno told Michael Mitchell that Wedtech had a "serious, serious problem" and that he wanted to be sure that the Small Business Committee investigation was stopped. Clarence Mitchell, sitting behind Michael, began talking about other potential joint ventures that Wedtech and the Mitchells could develop. But Moreno quickly cut him off. Everything else must wait, he said, because if the probe wasn't quashed, Wedtech could be out of the 8(a) program.

According to Strum, "Michael Mitchell said it would be stopped; and Mario and John Mariotta were very happy about that." Mitchell didn't say how the investigation would be halted—only that "arrangements had to be made"—and he requested $50,000 for his help, Strum said.

Moreno said the group decided to create what appeared to

be a standard retainer agreement between a law firm and a client, because "the real agreement had to be covered." A retainer agreement was typed up that night, and Moreno read it and signed it before leaving the meeting.

Strum recalled the meeting ending with documents, which he assumed were just "window dressing to cover up for the fee." Then he and Loscalzo walked across the street to their hotel, went into the cocktail lounge, and had a few drinks to celebrate their successful meeting.

Back in New York the following day, Tuesday, October 2, Moreno issued, he said, a $50,000 check that Mariotta's protégé Mario Rosado carried to Baltimore and delivered to the Mitchell, Mitchell & Mitchell law firm. Three days later, Michael Mitchell wrote a check in the amount of $16,666.66 to Loscalzo, who then wrote a check for $8,333.33 to R&R Marketing that was Strum's cut of the referral fee.

Within a few days of its arrival at SBA headquarters, the letter marked "CONFIDENTIAL" made its way to Wedtech headquarters, leaked by Peter Neglia, as usual. Wedtech could depend on its friends in the SBA, a fact once again demonstrated when Neglia was put in charge of the SBA's response to Mitchell. Neglia asked Wedtech to begin drafting answers to Mitchell's questions.

But even then, the matter was moot. Shortly after the meeting, the Wedtech officers were informed that the investigation had been quashed. There was never any explanation of why Parren Mitchell's bloodhounds, who seemed so determined to expose the company once and for all, disappeared without a whimper.

Wedtech thought of the Mitchells again in the winter of 1985, when the company began hearing about a competitor who could give Wedtech problems. A former professional football player, Ernie Green, was trying to get an Army contract from the Rock Island Arsenal to build M13 kits, which were to be used to decontaminate clothing and gear. Green, who ran Ernie Green Industries of Dayton, Ohio, was the first to solicit the contract from the SBA—beating Wedtech by about a month.

According to Strum, when Loscalzo called to deliver the bad news, he suggested that Wedtech consider asking the House Small Business Committee to investigate whether Ernie Green Industries was a front for a white organization.

Strum liked the idea, even though they had no evidence of such a scam. He went to Baltimore to meet and confer with the Mitchells, who assured him such an investigation could be initiated for a fee. They suggested another $50,000 retainer. Strum told the Mitchells that he would sound out the other Wedtech officers and be back in touch.

Strum said the Wedtech executives agreed that since the M13 contract could mean "many, many millions of dollars for the company," and since "everything seems to be going good," they would pay the Mitchell brothers $50,000 to get an investigation started.

Guariglia, as the company's chief financial officer, approved the payment of $50,000 to Mitchell, Mitchell & Mitchell on February 26, 1985. As with the previous $50,000 payment, Michael Mitchell on March 9 wrote a check for $16,666 to Loscalzo, and Loscalzo split the money with Strum.

The House Small Business Committee never investigated Ernie Green Industries. Prosecutor Gary Jordan of the Baltimore U.S. attorney's office said federal authorities never found any evidence that Clarence and Michael Mitchell ever contacted their uncle, either to ask him to stop investigating Wedtech or to launch an investigation of Ernie Green.

The Mitchell brothers knew a good thing when they saw it. Even after collecting the second $50,000 payment, they seized the opportunity to milk Wedtech for another $10,000—a payment for so dubious a service that the Wedtech officers considered it pure extortion.

On March 7, 1985, five months and ten days after asking the SBA to take over the Wedtech investigation, their uncle forwarded another confidential letter to Sanders. Mitchell said his committee staff had been trying, without success, to learn the status of the SBA's investigation, and he demanded a full written report within thirty days.

When Larry Shorten heard about the letter, he tackled Strum. What in the hell was going on? he demanded. The

Wedtech people had paid $50,000 to have Parren Mitchell's investigation stopped, and here the problem was raising its ugly head again.

Strum said he needed another $10,000 to give to the Mitchells. When Shorten complained about the expense, Strum told him it could have been higher; he had talked the Mitchell brothers down from $25,000.

On March 29 Moreno asked Guariglia to write a $10,000 check. When Guariglia asked what the money was for, Moreno told him that it was needed to keep the unguided missile, Trimboli, from retriggering the investigation.

The Wedtech officers needn't have worried. When the SBA finally responded to Parren Mitchell's September 25 letter, the answers—crafted and approved by Neglia—were tailor-made to get Wedtech off the hook: The SBA said it knew of no preferential treatment given to Wedtech by present or former SBA employees in violation of federal law. It said there was no indication that SBA acted as a result of directions or suggestions from the White House. The SBA conceded that, while it *may* have taken actions concerning Wedtech that had been suggested by former White House employees, that was just coincidence. Nofziger's name was not mentioned. Point by technical point, the letter cleared Wedtech of even the suggestion of impropriety.

Mitchell accepted the pat answers unquestioningly and never again raised the prospect of investigating Wedtech.

The most troubling aspect of Parren Mitchell's role in the Wedtech investigation was this unquestioning acceptance of the SBA's exoneration. The questions he had asked the SBA to answer, prosecutors believe, would have resulted in Wedtech's removal from the 8(a) program—had they been answered honestly and accurately.

For Wedtech to "fix" Mitchell's investigation, according to prosecutor Jordan, involved a two-pronged effort: "You had to have somebody like Neglia making sure that the answers on paper were pretty harmless. And then, at the other end, you had to try to make sure that somebody like Parren Mitchell . . . is going to be satisfied with the response."

For Wedtech, however, the bottom line was that the company had masterfully thwarted its first federal investigation. The turn of events left Wedtech's officers convinced that, should they ever again fall under scrutiny of investigators—including ones from Meese's Justice Department—there were friends in high places willing to help them out—for a price.

THE SLICKS MOVE IN

THEY REALIZED IT was all out of control when Mario Moreno found himself huddled over the blackjack tables in Atlantic City with a Saudi Arabian prince, trying to seal a deal to deliver Wedtech cooling kits to the Saudi army. Already, they had paid $400,000 to an intermediary to smooth their way with Saudi decision makers, but they also hoped to sign a joint venture agreement with the prince that would guarantee more business. Moreno took the prince to Atlantic City, but the potentate, unfortunately, was on a depressing losing streak. As Moreno later testified, the prince first blew $150,000, then borrowed $40,000 in chips and promptly lost that. When Moreno, eager to please, persuaded the casino to extend his own credit line and came to the rescue with $20,000 more, plus $12,000 in cash, the eager prince was properly appreciative. At the evening's end, they signed the joint venture deal atop the blackjack tables of Caesar's Palace.

Then there was the trip to Italy in the summer of 1985. Mariotta and Moreno went to meet with an engine subcontractor, who had agreed to pay them kickbacks in return for business. Moreno went to the factory to pick up a large sum of cash and was astounded when the company turned over the money not in American dollars but in lira, enough to fill a treasure chest. They were on their way to the airport when Moreno made a routine call to Guariglia back in the South Bronx to report their success. Guariglia screamed at him, warning him not to attempt to go through customs with all that cash. Somehow, they had lost their grasp of the most basic sort of logic.

Simple arithmetic also was working against them. They knew there were only so many people one could pay off before someone got caught or squealed to the authorities. Until that point, Wedtech's Ponzi scheme had worked like a charm, keeping the gluttonous beast well-fed. Wedtech's accountants, first Main Hurdman and then the equally respectable Touche Ross & Company, had attested to the company's glowing financial picture, and none of its soiled linen had appeared in reports filed with the unquestioning SEC. Squadron, Ellenoff had counseled them through their public offerings and complicated stock transactions. The SBA had never dared to strip away the thin skin of success masking the company's cancerous center.

But their behavior was becoming more flamboyant and risky. They were stealing with such abandon that one officer could not begin to keep up with the nefarious acts of the others. Mariotta hit the ceiling when he found out that Moreno's meticulous secretary, Deborah Scott, had typed a detailed, computerized ledger of their political contributions paid for with the FHJ account. If anyone so much as spotted it, the list was a dead giveaway of some of their illicit acts.

One day at a business meeting, when the officers were trying to devise yet another scheme, Mariotta pensively picked up a rubber band and, using two fingers, stretched it as taut as it would go.

"One of these days," he said, his voice trailing off. All of them knew exactly what he meant.

With the arrival of smooth operators Chinn and London, it became obvious that Mariotta's Wedtech career was on its last legs. Control of the company was moving increasingly toward what came to be known as the California Mafia, headed by Wallach. "Listen carefully to our friends from the west coast," he wrote Guariglia. "I feel very certain about their ability to contribute in a meaningful way to the future economic benefit of this company."

From the time they arrived on the scene, Chinn and London had been pushing for a restructuring of Wedtech's management. To Guariglia's mind, there seemed to be an ulterior purpose behind their advice. It was as if Wallach, Chinn, and London were determined to take over Wedtech by driving apart Mariotta and Neuberger and breaking up their huge controlling block of stock. The efforts, Guariglia would later tell investigators, intensified through the summer and fall of 1985 as Wedtech prepared to make its second offering of common stock.

Clearly, Mariotta's usefulness to the company was running out. Wedtech's days in the 8(a) program were numbered, and with Neglia leaving the agency to work for Biaggi & Ehrlich, the company's chances of remaining with the SBA had considerably weakened. Even more disturbing, Mariotta's moodiness and unpredictability had inspired deep concerns among the more sophisticated thinkers. How could the company afford to send as its representative to Washington a man so out of control that he might slug a government contracting officer?

None of them needed to be reminded that Mariotta also posed another formidable threat. Under the terms of the phony 1983 stock purchase agreement, Mariotta still had the legal right to buy the stock to which he held title and regain majority control. This was a distressing prospect, especially when word filtered out that Mariotta had been meeting over a long lunch with the well-connected Puerto Rican lawyer, Ralph Vallone, to explore ways to come up with the financing before the January 1986 deadline.

In early July 1985, treading delicately around Mariotta's temper, the insiders tried to address Wedtech's obvious management deficiencies by electing a new slate of officers. Mariotta remained as chairman of the board, and the increasingly bored and remote Neuberger continued as vice chairman. But Guariglia assumed real control of the company as its new president. Unlike the others, Guariglia, with his expensive, Italian-cut suits and keen calculator of a mind, could confidently match wits with the savvy investors and foreign businessmen whom Wedtech would be courting under the guidance of Chinn and London. It was also decided around that time that Chinn would also move onto the company's board of directors, a plan accomplished on August 13, 1985.

With his new legal demands and continuing efforts to be of service to the Meeses, Wallach seemed to have abdicated his growing control of Wedtech to his two California friends. Just that spring, while still banking on a high-level Department of Justice job, Wallach had taken on another major client, a wealthy Swiss oilman named Bruce Rappaport. Once again, his work required that he call upon his lofty contact in government for help.

In January 1985, Rappaport heard about a problem the Bechtel Corporation was having with its plans to build an oil pipeline from the Iraqi city of Kirkuk to the port of Aqabah on the Red Sea in Jordan. Bechtel urgently needed to give written assurances to Iraq that the government of Israel would not sabotage the pipeline project. Rappaport offered to obtain the written guarantee if Bechtel would agree to sell him oil from the pipeline at a 10 percent discount. He planned to pay Israel a percentage in cash or oil in return for its promise not to destroy the pipeline.

It took Rappaport only a few weeks to get assurances from Israeli Prime Minister Shimon Peres that the government would sign the letter, but then Bechtel imposed another condition. It also wanted Israel to promise to pay the construction debt if it violated its commitment and to insure the vow with a $400 million insurance policy. This was not so easy to deliver. Rappaport determined that what he needed was a financial commitment from the United States government and the assistance of the U.S. Overseas Private Investment Council in putting together the insurance package.

Rappaport began shopping for a consultant who could shake trees in the Reagan administration. A French lawyer offered the names of two of the most influential consultants in Washington—Lyn Nofziger and E. Robert Wallach.

Rappaport met with Wallach in late May over an expensive dinner in Georgetown and agreed to retain his services at an hourly rate. Wallach assured him he could set up a meeting with National Security Adviser Robert C. "Bud" McFarlane. At 8:20 P.M., as soon as their early dinner was over, Wallach called Meese to brief him on his new client and to seek help with the McFarlane meeting. Meese wrote a note in his diary to remind himself of the conversation. It read "Bruce Rappaport—Richest Man In Israel."

As an independent counsel's investigation later disclosed, there were several reasons why a more careful Attorney General would have turned Wallach away in his request for assistance with yet another private client. Technically, Meese still owed Wallach money, since Wallach's legal fee request was pending before the Court of Appeals. Secondly, Meese had signed a recusal statement at the Department of Justice that month, specifically stating he would not get involved with matters involving Wallach until all legal bills were settled.

Undeterred, however, Meese promptly placed a phone call to his friend Bud McFarlane and asked him to help Wallach arrange a meeting on the pipeline project. McFarlane, responding to what he considered an extraordinary request by the Attorney General, agreed to the meeting and assigned an NSC staffer to help Wallach obtain the insurance package.

Throughout the summer of 1985, Wallach was intensely involved in the pipeline negotiations, devoting what little free time he had to the escalating management crises at Wedtech. On July 9, a few days after arranging a possible radio job for Ursula Meese, Wallach invited Chinn, London, Nofziger, Bragg, Jenkins, and the Wedtech officers to meet him in Washington for a strategy session on the 1986 pontoon options. He squeezed in the Wedtech crew between a meeting with Rappaport's lawyer, Julius Kaplan, and a former national security adviser, William P. Clark, whom he was trying to retain as a $500-per-hour consultant for Rappaport. Clark agreed to attend a pipeline meeting in Baghdad but soon dropped out of the project, concerned about Wallach's indiscreet behavior and incessant name-dropping.

That afternoon, Wallach also met with Meese. He took Chinn and London along with him to the Department of Justice for the 3 P.M. private session. The substance of the meeting has never been publicly disclosed, and Meese later claimed a lack of memory when asked for details of the session. A few weeks after the session—on July 26—Chinn made his first two trades at Bear Stearns for the newly activated Meese Partners account. He bought securities in Reebok and Union Exploration Partners for a $3,679 net profit. Although Meese only had $50,587 in his account at the time, Chinn purchased $61,000 worth of securities that day and made up the difference later, a practice forbidden by most brokerage houses.

A few days later, Wallach accompanied Meese to the American Bar Association convention in London, where the two were virtually inseparable. The ABA paid Meese's way, and Rappaport picked up the tab for Wallach's airfare and expenses. Their long discussions during the trip led Wallach to write to his daughters, "I suspect I know more about the intimate workings of this Administration than probably any outsider in this country."

In London, they checked into the luxurious Grosvenor House, where Rappaport coincidentally maintained a flat. On Tuesday, Wallach devoted most of his day to pipeline business and arranged for Meese to meet two officials of the Overseas Private Investment Council, who were in London to consult with Lloyds of London about insurance for the pipeline project. They chatted briefly, but no one questioned later about the meeting could recall whether Meese discussed the pipeline project.

With Wallach as his coach, Meese delivered a luncheon address to the ABA convention, then the two sped off for a garden party in Meese's honor at Buckingham Palace. It was a grand event, and the Queen mingled graciously, showing special attention to Meese.

Back in the United States, the month of August brought a round of good fortune to Wallach. With Meese's backing, President Reagan appointed him on August 9 to a second term on the U.S. Advisory Commission on Public Diplomacy. A day earlier, his new client, Rappaport, wired a $150,000 retainer for Wallach directly to his money manager, Franklyn Chinn.

Lastly, Wallach's generous friends at Wedtech voted to raise his compensation by $150,000, in keeping with the deal hatched at Mark Bragg's office the previous year. As usual, Wedtech was reluctant for the payment to show up as a reduction to its profits, so a scheme was devised to charge it off as an expense that could be amortized over a number of years. The Wedtech officers said they arranged to make the payments not directly to Wallach, but to IFCI, the company owned by his friend Rusty London.

London submitted an invoice to back up the payments, charging the company for consulting services on the sale of Wedtech's infamous tug-barge in Michigan.

Bob Wallach's delicate pipeline negotiations demanded most of his time in late 1985, a heady period in which he traveled in the upper echelons of power both in the United States and Israel. In September, he met Rappaport in Geneva and returned to Washington to hand-deliver a letter to Meese from Israeli Prime Minister Peres. The letter asked Meese for a U.S. government contact who could help Israel with the pipeline insurance.

Later, Wallach wrote Meese a "Personal and Confidential—FOR YOUR EYES ONLY" memorandum, recounting the substance of the ongoing discussions between Rappaport and Peres. His memo suggested that the Israeli Labor Party expected a quid pro quo of as much as $65 million to $70 million a year for ten years in return for its security guarantee. Specifically, Wallach wrote, "What was indicated to me, and which would be denied everywhere, is that a portion of those funds will go directly to Labor." Peres and his party leaders later would deny any knowledge of the alleged plan.

When it was eventually leaked to the press, the memo raised immediate questions about possible violations of the Foreign Corrupt Practices Act, which restricts the payment of things of value to foreign governments. Although Meese's Justice Department was charged with enforcing the act, the memo triggered no alarms when read by Meese. He dutifully contacted McFarlane, who put his staff to work on the project. The Attorney General failed to mention the secret aspect of the deal outlined in Wallach's letter.

By October, Overseas Private Investment Council officials were skeptical about the legality and propriety of the pipeline deal and decided to seek a legal opinion from the Justice Department. Wallach insisted that the request go directly to Meese; then he made sure a Meese deputy and friend, Allan Gerson, was assigned to write the opinion. Wallach was enraged to learn that OPIC officials had simultaneously requested an opinion from another office at Justice.

In mid-October, Peres came to Washington for a state visit, and Wallach was there to greet him as though he were the oldest of friends. (Actually, they had never met.) Through Marshall Breger, an assistant to President Reagan on Jewish issues, Wallach arranged for an invitation to a reception for Peres at the Israeli Embassy. At the reception, Wallach met Peres for the first time but stayed close to him, trailing him to continue an intimate conversation. The next evening, Wallach showed up at a Department of State dinner for Peres, and later he followed Peres to New York to continue their talks.

Despite his work, it soon became apparent that the insurance package was going nowhere. McFarlane's successor, John Poindexter, pulled the plug on the deal after Judge Clark warned him that it had the smell of a protection racket pushed by the Israeli Labor Party. With government interest dying, Wallach made futile attempts to find private backers.

In his communications with Rappaport, he remained upbeat, but their relationship quickly deteriorated. In November 1985, still full of hope for the success of his mission, he wrote Rappaport hoping to get a share of the pipeline profits. As he stated in his letter, in order for him to appear a successful and independent lawyer in Washington power circles, "I require an income of $1 million a year." In December, he submitted a $32,884 expense account to Rappaport, and listed the payment in his accounting records as expenses resulting from a California personal injury case. Soon afterward, the two cut off communications.

Meese was doing what he could to soothe Wallach's feelings. In late December, at Wallach's request, he contacted the White House personnel office to recommend Wallach to director Robert H. Tuttle for a diplomatic position. Wallach—the brains behind the aborted pipeline fiasco—wanted to use his refined diplomatic skills as an alternate delegate to the United Nations Human Rights Commission in Geneva, Switzerland.

Back in the Bronx, Wedtech had been hectically preparing for its second offering of common stock, scheduled for January 1986, and the president was worried. This stock offering had to go over big, or Wedtech once again was faced with financial collapse. Wedtech had banked much of its hopes for a successful offering in Chinn, who was traveling around the country making presentations to securities brokers and using his contacts to place Wedtech stock with investors.

At the same time, Rusty London was showing up in the Bronx, bug-eyed and dressed in rumpled suits. He was practically living on an airplane, jet-hopping from Hawaii to Tokyo to the South Bronx, trying to negotiate a multimillion-dollar licensing agreement for the coatings process with the Japanese Sumitomo Corporation. The Japanese were lukewarm but coming around. Although Sumitomo officials later said that London's efforts played no role in their consideration of a possible joint venture, London convinced the Wedtech officials that he was critical to the negotiations. London's plan was for Wedtech to announce a deal with Sumitomo in conjunction with its new public offering—a breakthrough guaranteed to send stock prices soaring.

Filling the void left by Wallach's other preoccupations, Chinn and London had also assumed an important role as Wedtech's intermediaries with their "good friend" in Washington on the pontoon options. Several times, they indicated to Guariglia that they had been in contact with Meese and that "everything was being taken of and don't worry about it," Guariglia later told investigators. Meese, questioned later about the Chinn–London conversations, told investigators he knew the two were involved with Wedtech but recalled no specific conversations about the company.

In his panic, Guariglia offered a proposition to his two new consultants. He told Chinn that, if he could successfully place 2 million shares of Wedtech stock, he would reward him with a $1 million bonus. Since it was more or less understood that Chinn and London were partners, the money could be split between them, he said.

Despite his president's title, Guariglia did not pull enough weight at Wedtech to make such an expensive decision unilaterally, and he might have a hard time persuading the other officers to go along. So it was agreed among the three that Guariglia would get a bonus—a $100,000 cash cut of their money—if he could successfully win board approval. It also became apparent to Guariglia in subsequent conversations that Wallach would get a $200,000 cut.

After a series of conversations, the other officers agreed to go along with the $1 million payment. Neuberger later testified that Chinn told him the money was needed for "baksheesh"—or bribe money—for individuals in Washington. In their usual attempt to cover up the payment, the officers agreed that the hefty payment would be charged as an expense related to the public offering. Under federal securities laws, the company was required to make public disclosure of fees paid for any services related to stock sales. Wedtech made no mention of the payment in its prospectus.

In early January 1986, Chinn and London flew to Switzerland on a luxury trip, which they billed to Wedtech. London left first for Zurich and was joined two days later by Chinn in Geneva, the city where Wallach was scheduled to arrive the next month as an alternate U.N. delegate. The Wedtech management would later claim in a lawsuit that during the trip the two—who were known to have access to bank accounts in Switzerland as well as Liechtenstein and the Grand Caymans—

made arrangements to secrete the $1 million they were to receive later that month from Wedtech. The $1 million also became the basis of criminal charges against them.

The stock offering was completed on January 23, with Wedtech selling 1.75 million shares for $10.125 per share. The company realized $16.6 million as its share of the proceeds. On January 29, the day before the closing, Chinn and London made another trip, which they billed to Wedtech. They took an Amtrak train to Washington where they met Wallach for a lunch with Meese at the Justice Department.

Meese had another financial matter he needed to discuss with his advisers. He wanted their help refinancing his $260,000 home mortgage so that he could take advantage of lower interest rates. Wallach intended to take up the matter with his friend, banker Jeff Cohen, but since Wallach was leaving shortly for his new U.N. job, he turned over the loan to Chinn. Grilled later about the luncheon, Meese said he could not recall if the subject of Wedtech came up.

Chinn and London made no mention of their meeting with Meese when Guariglia showed up at a New York hotel that night to hand-deliver their $1 million check, payable to IFCI. The next day, an invoice arrived at Wedtech from IFCI for $1.14 million "for services rendered in connection with the Company's registration and sale of 1,750,000 shares of common stock." The extra $140,000 was for expenses incurred by Chinn and London.

The two consultants did not forget their promise to Guariglia, the company president later testified. He said that soon after they received the payment, a limo pulled up in Guariglia's driveway. From the depths of the posh back seat, tiny Frank Chinn emerged carrying a large brown paper sack. Chinn came to the door and handed the bag over while the driver waited, according to Guariglia.

Inside, Guariglia spotted $100,000 in cash, wrapped in crisp, neat packages as he had seen only at a Las Vegas casino.

18

THE FINAL DAYS

ONCE THEY DECIDED not to kill John Mariotta—for the time being, at least—the Wedtech officers had no idea what to do with him. They returned from their 1985 winter getaway in Florida, determined to get him out of their hair. Even though it would pose immediate grounds for termination of Wedtech's 8(a) status, they had come to believe Mariotta's prompt removal, however unpleasant, was worth the risk.

On January 28, 1986, the board made one last stab at bringing Mariotta under control by drawing up a one-year employment agreement for his signature. The agreement called for Mariotta to serve as chief executive officer of the company and president of its coatings division, but made it clear Mariotta would be closely supervised by the board. Under the agreement, Mariotta would have no hiring or firing power. It also included peculiar language that Mariotta must sign a pledge of confidentiality about the company's affairs. In return for his signature, the board agreed to remain in the South Bronx "unless and until the Board of Directors of Wedtech Corp. determines, for good and justifiable economic reasons . . . that it is no longer in the best interests of Wedtech Corp. to do so."

It soon became apparent that the plan to muzzle Mariotta would not work. So on February 11, in a tense, dramatic session, the board voted to fire him, with Mariotta casting the only dissenting vote. The meeting ended with a threat that the other officers took as a pledge of vengeance. The man who had built the company from nothing, who had cultivated a work force that regarded him as the next thing to God, and who had watched a calculating California Mafia rise up to drive him systematically out, promised to destroy them all.

At the meeting's end, Mariotta walked back to his office and picked up a small statuette of Napoleon, an expensive trinket that Ehrlich, a collector of military figurines, had bought for him. Mariotta fingered the tiny statue, then handed it to Mario Moreno. "You're in charge now. Keep it," he said. Then, calmly, with no sign of the volatility that had been his undoing, he walked out the door.

The next day, a curt interoffice memorandum went up on the company bulletin board. The message read:

> At 4 P.M. Wednesday, February 11, 1986, the Board of Directors of WEDTECH CORP. unanimously elected Mr. Fred Neuberger (Co-founder of the Company) as Chairman of the Board and Chief Executive Officer of the WEDTECH CORP. and Mr. Mario E. Moreno as Vice Chairman of the Board and President of the Company's Coating Division. Mr. John Mariotta is no longer an employee of the Company. . . .

Their feeble attempt to put a presentable face on Mariotta's firing didn't wash with the company's embittered employees. Mariotta, the smiling, hand-shaking president who had listened to their troubles, lent them money, and prayed with them in the company chapel, was the only barrier standing between the employees and the treachery of the cold and greedy new regime. Within a matter of months, many of Mariotta's employee initiatives, like a free tuition program to prod dropouts to reenroll in school, fell by the wayside as part of Guariglia's cost-cutting plan. Soon, layoff notices went up, explained by Guariglia as a painful decision that "will result in a stronger and more competitive Wedtech."

One day one of Mariotta's incensed fellow evangelicals cornered Guariglia. "You have destroyed the Father and the Father's son," he screamed, equating Mariotta to a crucified Christ. Guariglia filed the comment away and recounted it later to a company consultant when he began trying to draw up a Wedtech enemies list.

In keeping with their customary practice, the Wedtech executives failed to notify the SBA of Mariotta's overthrow, deciding to let the government find out for itself. But it was hard for even the myopic SBA to shield its eyes to the tumultuous events in the board room of its favorite 8(a) company.

On February 13, 1986, *The Wall Street Journal* ran an article under the headline "Wedtech Corp. Ousts Its Founder, Mariotta, from Chief's Position." The story included the salient detail that both Mariotta and Neuberger owned 23 percent of the company's stock—a clear indication that Mariotta was not, in fact, the majority owner as continually portrayed to the SBA.

The article circulated around the SBA regional offices, which contacted the district office, and there was much discussion throughout the day about the appropriate course of action. District SBA Director Bert Hagerty dashed off a letter, which he sent by certified mail to Wedtech headquarters. It was addressed, oddly enough, to the victim of the coup, Mariotta, warning him to respond within thirty days or risk termination from the 8(a) program.

The SBA district office had already been on Wedtech's case on another subject—its obvious violation of an SBA regulation limiting it to 1,000 employees in order to receive certain contracts. Wedtech, with its plants in Israel, Michigan, and numerous sites in the South Bronx, had been growing like Topsy while still reporting to the SBA a modest work force.

In reality, the Wedtech officers had hired many of their Michigan shipbuilding workers through temporary employment services, a means of keeping the employees off the official Wedtech payroll. The services, which had been hurriedly set up by a well-connected judge and a Wedtech official, provided yet another way to skim money from the company.

Wedtech had responded to the SBA's size inquiry with outright paranoia. Moreno wrote to an SBA lawyer that the company had decided to "respectfully decline to furnish the employee count you have requested." It took months for the agency to get a simple payroll from the Carmo plant, and when it came, it was written in a Middle Eastern scrawl and virtually undecipherable.

A week after his urgent letter to Mariotta, Hagerty received a response from Moreno arguing that Wedtech's board was controlled by minorities since it included Moreno, Hispanic accountant Al Rivera, Gen. Richard Cavazos, a Hispanic American, and Franklyn Chinn, an Asian-American. Both Chinn and Cavazos had filed requests with the SBA for minority certification. Chinn, the international financier with bank accounts all over the world, sent in a lengthy financial statement to justify his status as an economically disadvantaged businessman. He placed his salary at around $40,000 and his assets at $37,000.

With Neglia no longer on hand, the SBA situation suddenly became grim. The agency had just approved $80 million in 8(a) contracts for Wedtech, but it clamped down and notified the company it would receive no more contracts until the SBA got to the bottom of the eligibility question. The decision put into immediate jeopardy the nearly completed negotiations for a $1.8 million contract Wedtech had just won from the U.S. Army.

By the middle of March, the SBA ruled that the company had far exceeded the employee limitations, and the district office was ready to begin the long process of stripping the company of its 8(a) certification—a proposition that could take months or even years by the time the company had exhausted its legal appeals.

The Wedtech officers had known it was only a matter of

time before the SBA pulled the rug from beneath them. They took comfort in the fact that, even if they lost their 8(a) status, they still would be fully eligible for options on contracts they had won through the 8(a) program, including the massive pontoon deal. Ehrlich submitted one of his inimitable legal memos to justify Wedtech's change of management. He also sent a letter to Hagerty with a blunt proposition. Wedtech, which was about to be stripped of its 8(a) status, would agree to withdraw voluntarily from the program, provided the SBA would give it one last goodie—the final Army contract.

The issue went back and forth at the SBA. Finally, the Wedtech directors, realizing they could be in for a long, difficult wrangle, held a meeting on March 27, 1986, and voted to withdraw voluntarily from the 8(a) program, which, at that point, accounted for 93 percent of the company's business. The final papers were drawn up and signed on April 8 by the SBA.

Wedtech stockholders were the last to know that the firm had ended its 8(a) participation—a decision with profound consequences on the company's stock prices. Instead, during the period while the company was planning its withdrawal, the Wedtech insiders unloaded $4.6 million in stock before its value plunged.

Not long after Wedtech made the $1 million payment to his financial consulting firm, Dr. Rusty Kent London commissioned an unusual construction project on the shores of Honolulu. London hired Yoshihiro Takishita, a Japanese antiques dealer, to transport and reconstruct piece by piece three 150-year-old farmhouses from the mountainous Gifu Prefecture of Japan. Takishita was a master in the obscure art. For this project, which he described in detail to *The Wall Street Journal,* he shipped 5,000 pieces of wood and bamboo in ten 24,000 pound containers to the waterfront parcel and brought with him a crew of seventeen Gifu craftsmen. His price was $720,000, not including the modern kitchen and baths London wanted, or the price of the shoreline lot, which cost another $300,000.

In the summer of 1986, London encountered an unexpected problem. As Squadron, Ellenoff was preparing to file that July a registration statement with the SEC for a $75 million Wedtech bond offering, the underwriters, Bear Stearns, and their counsel, Shearman & Sterling, had uncovered the $1 million payment and an invoice for another $140,000 in expenses submitted by London's consulting firm. They also found a strange letter in which London described the payment as "promotional compensation" in connection with the January 1986 stock offering.

The discovery set off instantaneous tremors among Wedtech's Wall Street advisers. It called into question the veracity of Wedtech's earlier SEC filings in January. First, there was the strong suspicion that Frank Chinn had received part of the money, and now that he was a Wedtech director, any such payments had to be disclosed in Wedtech's prospectus. Secondly, under regulations of the National Association of Security Dealers, a company could not legally pay more than 10 percent of the proceeds of a public offering to firms providing services in connection with a stock sale. Wedtech had paid its joint underwriters, Bear Stearns and Moseley, Hallgarten, $1.1 million in connection with the January offering; thus the exorbitant payment to London put Wedtech in excess of the legal limit. Finally, nowhere in the January 1986 filings was the London payment mentioned.

The problem had arisen, of course, because Guariglia had been reluctant to charge the payment as a regular operating expense. With the discovery, however, it was obvious that Wedtech had to find a way to recast the purpose of London's fee. Otherwise, Wedtech could be forced to make an offer of recision to its January stock purchasers. If the SEC found out about it, it might also cause the $75 million bond offering to come unglued.

Toward the end of June, an ad hoc committee of lawyers and Wedtech board members, supervised by Squadron, Ellenoff, was formed to get to the bottom of the payment. The committee's job was to interview all company officials with knowledge of the payment and come to a conclusion about its validity. Representing the Wedtech board on the committee were General Ehrlich, General Cavazos, and Paul Hallingby.

Back at Wedtech headquarters, the officers, Chinn, and London got together to adopt answers to give the ad hoc group. Their first impulse was to blame it on Mariotta, who, of course, was no longer around to defend himself. Moreno recalled a vague promise Mariotta had made to London one day, in which he vowed to give him $1 million if he could deliver a $50 million coatings deal with the Japanese. London had failed in that mission, but the group decided the story posed the perfect alibi. Moreno pulled out a file, threw in some additional paperwork to make it look more substantive, and said he would use the documents to substantiate London's tireless work for the coatings division.

One by one, the officers were paraded before the committee to corroborate the Mariotta story. When questioned about Chinn's possible share of the proceeds, they said they had no knowledge of such payments. Over the next few weeks, a series of letters and consulting agreements were drafted with Squadron, Ellenoff's help to restate the purpose of the $1 million payment. After three tries, the board finally came up with a letter which London signed, describing the payment as reimbursement for help on development of the coatings process and other negotiations.

Relying on the letter and with the advice of Squadron, Ellenoff and Touche Ross as backup, the special committee reported to the Bear Stearns team that London's payment was made in late 1985 by Mariotta for these services. It also said there were no indications that London had shared his fee with anyone.

On July 2, the Wedtech board met and approved a retroactive consulting agreement for London to cover the payment. Squadron, Ellenoff then filed an amendment to Wedtech's financial statements characterizing the $1 million payment as an expense to be prorated over the 1986 fiscal year. The amendment made no mention of possibility of fraud in the payment and its coverup. The actions allowed Wedtech to plow ahead no-questions-asked with its August bond sale, the last of its Wall Street offerings before the company began to self-destruct.

By the time the Wedtech officers concocted their story, the

company was hit with its first wave of grand jury subpoenas. And by the time of London's scheduled housewarming on the rugged Hawaii coastline, law enforcement and the press were rapidly closing in not only on the gang of crooks at Wedtech but on their mysterious connections to the Attorney General of the United States.

19

REPORTER'S NOTEBOOK

AT LUNCHTIME on a slow news day, I was cleaning off a desk cluttered with computer printouts and worn notebooks full of random scribbles. Breezing through them one by one, I noticed a note I had jotted to myself: "Henry Thomas, Freedom Industries." Weeks earlier, I had called Thomas, an outspoken minority Bronx businessman, after noticing his name on the list of Stanley Simon campaign contributors. The Thomas interview stuck in my mind—so much so that I had written a note to remind myself to call him again.

Thomas had detailed his contributions to Simon, explaining them as a cost of doing business in the borough. Then, in a rising fury, he had leveled a wild but alarmingly specific allegation. He said his business had been the victim of a shakedown by Bronx politicians who, when he wouldn't cooperate, robbed him of his lease on a city-owned factory site.

"When I wouldn't play ball with the politicians, they kicked my butt out of there," he told me in his colorful street talk. He rambled on about stock and someone called "the General," Susan Frank and the Department of Ports and Terminals, Mayor Koch and Hebrew National. He would give no specific names, but alluded to Stanley Friedman and Simon and seemed particularly incensed by the law firm of Biaggi & Ehrlich. He offered no details of the extortion attempt. "If you ever want a real story," he urged before hanging up to attend to more pressing business, "call me back some other time."

The note jarred my memory. I had thought about Thomas frequently, but now, with a few minutes to spare, I placed a call to his company and waited for a befuddled receptionist to track him down in the pandemonium of his new food-processing plant. Thomas needed only the slightest provocation to pick up his shakedown saga. He told me about the battle for the building at One Loop Drive, about Mayor Koch's incredible intervention in his eviction case, and about the blatant conflict of interest by the Biaggi & Ehrlich firm. He told me that Ehrlich had solicited 10 percent of his company stock and how, much to his later regret, he had backed out of the deal. As proof, Thomas offered to show me the unsigned stock transfer documents that Ehrlich had drawn up.

The trip to Thomas's factory was well worth the effort. Thomas had left the stock documents and a stack of correspondence in the care of an officer who guided me through them. In one document, I noticed the name "Wedtech." "What's this company?" I asked.

The officer told me that Wedtech was traded on the New York Stock Exchange and that it was the general belief in the Bronx that Biaggi & Ehrlich were closely involved with it. Wedtech, it seemed, led a charmed life, seizing anything it wanted, including several hundred million dollars in defense contracts and a lease on part of Thomas's old factory site at One Loop Drive.

The contrast was striking. Henry Thomas had refused to give stock to Biaggi & Ehrlich and paid the penalty. This other

South Bronx firm, Wedtech, apparently had given stock to the well-connected lawyers and reaped great benefits from the city and federal governments. An interesting premise—if I could prove it.

The next day, I cornered City Editor Arthur Browne, a bloodthirsty investigative reporter and author who'd been promoted to breathe new life into the *Daily News* metro coverage. Browne had taken on the task with a vengeance, hiring a dozen or so new reporters and turning them loose on city agencies like a pack of wolves.

Detailing my day at Freedom Industries, I showed Browne the stock agreements which Thomas refused to sign, and told him about Wedtech, the company that had apparently cashed in with the government by going a different route. An almost vacant look came over Browne's face, an expression that reporters had come to recognize as his "lost in thought" gaze. He was intrigued by the possibilities.

I told him that I intended to start the next day at the federal Securities and Exchange Commission, looking up the files on this firm I knew absolutely nothing about—the Wedtech Corp.

When a clerk handed over a thick, color-coded stack of microfiche on Wedtech, I began by looking at the most understandable documents—the ones labeled "annual reports." Written in plain language, often with beautiful color photographs and illustrations, the reports are a magazinelike chronicle of a firm's activities and achievements during the year. Ideally, they are designed to entice new investors.

Wedtech's reports told an amazing rags-to-riches story of a small South Bronx firm that had been transformed, virtually overnight, into one of the fastest-growing small businesses in America. One report included a quote from President Reagan's Waldorf Astoria speech, calling Mariotta one of the "heroes for the eighties." It was clear from a quick reading that its board of directors had changed from a list of unknowns into an impressive array of former Defense Department officials, led by a former secretary of the Air Force, Verne Orr.

Bernie Ehrlich's name showed up on the board of directors

in 1986, a sure sign of the law firm's fingerprints. In the earliest filings to the SEC, I also found listed as appendixes the stock purchase agreements for Ehrlich and Richard Biaggi. Certain now that the law firm had more than a casual interest in the company, I copied the agreements to take back to Browne.

Two things were obvious: Wedtech owed its prosperity to the Department of Defense, and the firm also depended heavily on the SBA. I was intrigued by the company's ability to stay in the 8(a) program even after its stock was publicly sold and by its obvious political connections, both in Washington and New York.

Mariotta's role with the company was also of great interest. It was clear that he had created the company, brought in a collection of savvy managers to run it, then suddenly found himself out on the street, victim of an in-house coup. I wondered if Mariotta had ever exercised any real power—or if he represented the classic "front man," a minority allowing his status to be used by others to cash in on federal favors. I jotted down his address in swank Scarsdale, determined to pay him a visit.

I took a stack of copies back to the office and called the regional office of the SBA, where I was transferred to general counsel Jack Matthews. I asked if I could come to his office to review files on Wedtech. Unlike most bureaucrats who stall for time until a formal Freedom of Information request has been filed, Matthews invited me to come right over. But he gave me fair warning: "Every paper in New York has already been here to do the same thing." Another reporter—Josh Barbanel, an excellent metro staff reporter at the *New York Times*—was hot on the Wedtech trail and had hastily canceled an appointment to dash off to New Haven, Connecticut, to cover the Stanley Friedman–Parking Violations Bureau trial. The New York *Post* also was asking questions.

My luck couldn't have been better. Because earlier reporters' FOI requests had already been processed, Matthews handed me a thick stack of SBA materials and entertained a few questions. From reading the SEC documents, I had homed in on the 1983 stock transfer agreement designed to help

Mariotta regain control of the company. I told him it was clear the agreement was only a paper transaction, that Mariotta had never in fact bought the stock or regained his 51 percent ownership of the company. Why had the SBA approved this? I asked him.

Matthews didn't dodge the question. He answered bluntly that the agreement never would have been approved if the SBA had known Mariotta intended to default on the agreement. Actually Matthews, a career government lawyer, had voiced such serious concerns about the plan in 1983 that Neglia had gone around him to find another lawyer willing to approve the sham.

Back at the office, I compared the sets of documents from two separate government agencies and found glaring discrepancies. To the SEC, where it was presenting its case to investors, Wedtech was portraying itself as a booming enterprise, raking in government contracts and rapidly diversifying its business. Mariotta and Neuberger were earning more than $300,000 a year.

To the SBA, however, where it was trying to keep its status as a minority company, Wedtech portrayed itself as a struggling, unprofitable business, trying unsuccessfully to compete with the giants of the defense industry. Mariotta was described as a disadvantaged Hispanic with meager income and holdings.

I began trying unsuccessfully to reach John Mariotta, whose telephone number was unlisted. Finally, I wrote a letter to Mariotta, requesting an interview. On a beautiful October morning, I took a train to Scarsdale and gave a cab driver Mariotta's address. His house, a long, low rancher spread over a grassy, shaded lot, was on a corner, and as we approached, I saw an unmarked car with two men inside sitting and watching the door. It pulled off as we approached.

When I rang the doorbell, a woman cracked open the door and peered around it nervously. I explained that I was a *Daily News* reporter trying to reach John Mariotta.

"He's not here," she said in a quiet voice, still ready to slam the door on a moment's notice.

"When will he be back?"

"I have no idea," she said timidly.

I asked if she would deliver the letter I had written and held out the *Daily News* envelope. She reached out, grabbed it, and slammed the door.

As the taxi pulled away, I looked in the rear-view mirror and noticed the unmarked car creeping around the corner. Clearly, the house was under surveillance by someone. I later learned that Mariotta's Wedtech colleagues were convinced by October 1986 that Mariotta was squealing his story of crime and corruption at Wedtech to the feds and possibly even to the press.

Within a week, I had written the final draft of a story based on my original premise. It painted a vivid contrast of two companies: one which had shunned a proposed Biaggi & Ehrlich stock deal and lost everything; the other, a Wedtech that had turned over stock and cashed in on federal riches. I finished the story late on a Friday, and was scheduled to leave the next week for vacation. Browne said he intended to hold the story for one week for final review by editors and run it in the next Sunday's editions.

The next week, as I was packing the car for a twelve-hour drive, the telephone rang. Browne was calling from the city desk, and he was frantic. The New York *Post,* he said, had run a Wedtech story that morning on its inside pages. The short story revealed that the Biaggi & Ehrlich law firm held Wedtech stock. But the *Post,* which had the amount of stock holdings incorrect, concluded that there was no obvious wrongdoing by Congressman Biaggi, a longtime favorite of the newspaper.

With the competition now breathing down our necks, Browne told me we had to come back with some sort of Wedtech story the next day. The weekday editions had no room for the long saga I had left with him. Besides, now that the *Post* was onto the story, we had to come back with our best possible shot.

I planted myself at the dining room table with a stack of documents and a telephone. I decided the best story I could offer was on the phony stock deal, which involved direct participation by Biaggi & Ehrlich and raised the specter of fraud. I tried without success to reach Neuberger and Moreno at Wedtech headquarters and was told that Arthur Siskind at Squadron, Ellenoff was handling all questions from the press. Over the next few hours, Siskind tried in a long telephone interview to justify the stock deal as a perfectly legal arrangement, which had passed muster with both the SBA and SEC. "If you run that story," he told me, "you will be dead wrong."

Working frantically at home to piece together a complicated story, I called Browne late that afternoon and began dictating a piece on the phony stock transaction. Editors at the racy *Daily News* did not know what to make of a story that to them seemed boring and bureaucratic. It had no blood, no guts, no sex, no cheesecake, no Mayor Koch tirades, no abused or dying animals. Managing Editor Jim Willse, a man of few words and infinite power in determining the next day's news, summed it up as he read the final version on Browne's computer screen: "We're wading through tall grass on this one."

The story ran the next day, October 15, 1986, in the weeds of the paper—page 24—under an unexciting headline, "Tainted Pact Linked to Biaggi Firm." In a few paragraphs, it summed up a stock deal that eventually became the centerpiece of a massive federal racketeering indictment:

> A Bronx firm partly owned by the son of Rep. Mario Biaggi and the elder Biaggi's former law partner was improperly approved for a program of lucrative no-bid federal contracts, the Daily News has learned.
>
> The approval helped the Wedtech Corp. blossom from a debt-ridden operation to a multi-million dollar business.
>
> The Small Business Administration approved Wedtech for the no-bid program based on representations that Richard Biaggi, Bernard Ehrlich and other company officers were transferring stock to John Mariotta, a Hispanic businessman who would hold a majority interest in the company. . . .
>
> Mariotta never took ownership of the stock, and a Daily News review of company records revealed that the transfer plan was rescinded in December.

I had made a hurried trip back to New York where, early the next morning in the din of a busy city room, I was interrupted by a telephone call from a source I used occasionally on law enforcement stories.

"Where the hell did you get that story?" he shouted into the phone. "Don't you know there's a grand jury investigation that's just begun to look into this? This could blow the whole thing."

No, I told him, I didn't know about the grand jury investigation. The story had been generated from my own research. I hung up realizing that this Wedtech thing could be bigger than I had imagined.

Later that day, a hand-delivered letter arrived in the *Daily News'* executive offices. Addressed to publisher Jim Hoge, it was signed by attorney Howard Squadron on behalf of Wedtech.

It read:

> Dear Jim,
> In the October 15, 1986 editions of *The Daily News,* a story about Wedtech Corp. appeared. The story contains many inaccuracies. The printing of these inaccuracies is particularly surprising since one of my partners, Arthur Siskind, took the time in a long telephone interview with your reporter on October 14 to clarify these facts. The suggestion that Wedtech Corp. is a failing company is false and will result in severe consequences to Wedtech. . . .
> Our client is pressing us to take legal action. On its behalf, please consider this a demand for a prompt retraction and the publishing of the correct facts in this matter.
> Sincerely,
> Howard M. Squadron

An attached press release from Wedtech Board Chairman Fred Neuberger, condemning the story as libelous, had been picked up earlier that day by the wire services.

Browne called me in for a meeting that afternoon with *News* attorney Marge Coleman, who explained that Wedtech was demanding a retraction. Was I absolutely sure of my facts? she asked. Squirming uncomfortably, I asked Browne what we should do. His response was instinctive: "Just keep going."

The next day's paper included a longer, better-displayed article under the headline: "Biaggi Link to Stox Try: Defense Firm Cried 'Shakedown.' " It began:

> A law firm tied to Bronx Rep. Mario Biaggi (D-Bronx) tried to take part ownership in a failing defense firm in return for pushing the company's cause before city and federal agencies, the Daily News has learned.
>
> But the deal fell through amid charges by the company that it was the victim of an "extortion and shakedown."
>
> The deal, detailed in documents reviewed by the Daily News, called for the Biaggi & Ehrlich law firm to get 10 percent of the stock of Freedom Industries and a $30,000-a-year retainer for representing the company before the U.S. Small Business Administration and two city agencies.
>
> The attempted stock deal came to light in a review of the activities of the Biaggi & Ehrlich firm, in which the congressman's son, Richard, and Bernard Ehrlich are partners. The firm lists the congressman as "of counsel" and pays him consulting fees and a salary. . . .
>
> A similar deal involving the law firm was previously uncovered by The News.
>
> In June, 1983, Richard Biaggi and Bernard Ehrlich were given 225,000 shares of stock in another Bronx company, The Wedtech Corp., for representing it before federal and city agencies. . . .

By Friday, October 17, we reported that SBA Inspector General Garrett Howard had begun an investigation into the *News'* charges. Then, on Sunday, we came back with a fuller version of the Henry Thomas story under the headline, " 'Extortion' Complaint Was Ignored by City." The story was the first in the series to have repercussions at City Hall with its revelation that Mayor Koch had sent a letter to the city eviction judge urging Thomas's ouster from One Loop Drive. Koch's press aide, Lee Jones, mounted a campaign in Room 9, the City Hall press room, to keep other reporters from picking up what he charged was a groundless story.

*   *   *

On Tuesday, October 21, the *Daily News* raised the possibility of conflicts of interest by Representative Biaggi in his former law firm's representation of Wedtech, its largest single client. The story revealed that Biaggi continued to draw a salary and consulting fees from the law firm, even though he professed to have divested himself of an interest in it.

From the first day the name "Wedtech" appeared in print, the *Daily News'* switchboard began lighting up with callers. Many were Wall Street brokers worried about the disastrous effects that continued bad publicity would have on Wedtech stock. There was also an avalanche of tipsters, each with a story to tell about possible wrongdoing by the company or by the Biaggi & Ehrlich law firm.

"Please for the sake of many, many individuals do what you can, now that the lid is off, to nail these criminals," suggested one detailed note signed only, "God bless you."

"You are doing one hell of a job on the Wedtech pieces," wrote another. "But you have not touched upon Peter Neglia, the former SBA regional administrator."

Out of the mass of information came a number of leads worth pursuing. One call from an anonymous tipster within the Main Hurdman accounting firm gave a detailed account of Wedtech's audit coverup by former accountants Tony Guariglia and Richard Bluestine. The tipster said the audit had uncovered millions of dollars in phony invoices submitted by Wedtech to federal defense agencies.

The influx of tips was so overwhelming that, in a meeting with Browne, we decided to bring in two other reporters, Kevin McCoy and Jerry Capeci, to help pursue various leads. By that time, I had received a phone call from a Wedtech insider, a former company employee who wished to remain anonymous, suggesting that the *News* had only touched the tip of the iceberg by revealing the Biaggi connection.

"Biaggi's not the only one," he said bluntly. "Lyn Nofziger got stock, and Ed Meese may have gotten money, too."

He spelled out the fascinating story of the Army engine contract and Wedtech's efforts to buy influence by hiring the biggest guns in Washington. He told me about Dickey Dyer,

Verne Orr, and James Jenkins. But his best information was about E. Robert Wallach, who he knew had pushed the company to Meese.

A few days later, the tipster came in with a briefcase of documents substantiating much of what he had said. He said later he felt compelled to do so after reading a short article in the *Daily News* on October 23.

The article was about a lawsuit filed the previous day in Manhattan Supreme Court against the *Daily News* by the Wedtech Corporation. It named as parties in the suit Marilyn W. Thompson, publisher Hoge, editor F. Gilman Spencer, and managing editor Willse. The suit claimed I had written about the company "with actual malice and with willful intent to injure and damage plaintiff and its good name and reputation and to impute to plaintiff misconduct, incapacity and general impropriety which would interfere with its ability to maintain and solicit business." The suit also charged that I had "acted in a grossly irresponsible manner without due consideration for the standards of information gathering and dissemination ordinarily followed by responsible parties."

Attorney Coleman had thrown the legal papers on my desk along with the news that Wedtech appeared to be seeking damages of $1 billion.

"Don't worry," she said. "The *News* is insured for $999 million."

The tall, patrician Spencer, born and bred on Philadelphia's Main Line, stood over me, nervously dragging on a cigarette. "You're onto something," he said. "Just keep going."

THE FEDS MOVE IN

STEVE COSSU was a labor investigator who specialized in the paper trail, the time-consuming business of building criminal cases out of seemingly disconnected documents. He could, for example, take a stack of routine office correspondence and, with enough painstaking research, turn an innocuous-looking business letter into grounds for a federal mail-fraud indictment. Quiet and unassuming, with a round choirboy's face and thick, closely cropped brown hair, he had an encyclopedic mind that could search out significant details like a radar sweeper.

A devout Catholic and devoted father of three sons, Cossu had wanted to be a priest as a child but grew up instead to become a detective. He had spent fifteen years delving into one of the dirtiest businesses around—the New York water-

front. As a detective for the Commission on the New York
Harbor, he had earned a modest salary and even lower prestige, but he had accumulated a massive amount of information
about mobsters and union bosses of interest to federal
prosecutors. In October 1985, he got a chance to make better
use of his talents when he was hired as one of the 100 federal
agents assigned to the Office of Labor Racketeering, an investigative arm of the U.S. Labor Department. OLR, a distant
second-cousin of the FBI, was charged with a frustratingly
narrow mandate of investigating and prosecuting violations of
federal labor laws. Yet even when it developed major cases,
the all-powerful FBI was apt to step in and take credit. Cossu
worked out of the Southern District of New York, under
crime-busting U.S. Attorney Rudolph Giuliani, a dogged
prosecutor appointed by President Reagan in 1983 and billed
by an admiring New York press as a latter-day Elliot Ness.

Cossu had been working for months on a highly sensitive
case involving the Wedtech Corporation when one night he
received an urgent message from one of his secret contacts
within the Department of Defense: The New York *Daily News*
was preparing to break a story, the informant said, and he
wanted Cossu to know that he was not the reporter's source
for it. Oh, no, Cossu said to himself. He had been dreading
the moment when the press discovered the scandal he had
spent the better part of the year trying to break open. Cossu
turned to his partner, Mike Raggi, a Defense Department
investigator who had begun working with him a few months
earlier. "We're sitting on a time bomb," he predicted.

Cossu had been on the trail since early 1986 when he and
a partner were interviewing a confidential informant, a Bronx
businessman who knew a lot about the activities of Biaggi &
Ehrlich. Cossu was snooping into the firm's activities with a
number of city unions, which had chosen Biaggi & Ehrlich to
deliver prepaid legal services to their members. He was leaving one interview when the informant offered, in passing,
"There's a company called Wedtech that you should look into.
I don't know why, but it does what it wants, when it wants."
He said the company was somehow tied in with Biaggi &
Ehrlich too.

Tips offered so casually are often lost in the blur of events, but this one intrigued Cossu, who had heard of Wedtech before. He remembered seeing an article in the *Wall Street Journal,* reporting that the firm's board of directors had ousted its minority founder. A few weeks later, he breezed over to the SEC's records room and pulled the file on the company. At first, he had the name of the company wrong, searching futilely under the name "Webtech." Finally, he found a stack of microfiche encompassing three years of the company's SEC filings.

Through experience, Cossu knew just what to look at first: the firm's initial prospectus, the strict liability statement in which the company was required to air all its dirty laundry. Combing through the pages, he was startled by a number of "red flags" that leaped out from the pages, begging further investigation.

Why was a minority company borrowing money in a smelly transaction with a Netherlands Antilles company? he asked himself. Who was Richard Bluestine? Why had Wedtech lent him nearly a million dollars, then fired him after nine months? He pulled out pen and paper and began scribbling information that, a while later, in his office, he would assimilate into neatly organized charts.

At the top of one page, he wrote "Property 977–989 East 149th St. Bronx," the address of the Wedtech pontoon plant. Although the language in the prospectus seemed deliberately obscure, he saw how the property had been leased with a purchase option by the New York State Urban Development Corporation to PDJ Simone Realty Corporation.

Then, he saw how Simone had created a new leasing company, PJ Associates, to lease the building to Wedtech. But the fascinating part of the puzzle was the disclosure of a group called Jofre Associates set up by Wedtech officers Mariotta, Neuberger, Moreno, Shorten, Guariglia, and Bluestine. It appeared that Jofre had paid Simone $999,950 for an interest in PJ Associates, which entitled them to a one-third cut of the lease. He also saw that the officers initially expected to spend $2.8 million on building renovations, but eventually reported expenditures of nearly $10 million. Another alarm went off; from his training, Cossu knew that padded construction costs were a sign of potential illegality.

He uncovered the agreements to transfer stock to Bernie Ehrlich and Richard Biaggi in exchange for their valuable contributions to the company. Then, he saw documents that the two had signed to transfer 59,000 shares each to Mariotta, as part of a huge stock package assembled to help Mariotta regain control of the company.

Intrigued, Cossu pulled out another sheet of paper. He drew a flow chart with Mariotta at the center, receiving bundles of stock from Neuberger, Moreno, Shorten, Guariglia, and, in a separate deal, from Ehrlich and Richard Biaggi. He noted that Mariotta did not have to pay for the stock up front. Neither the phoniness of the agreement nor its potential impact was lost on Cossu. Later, he would say it was obvious from Day One that the stock transaction was a sham. He wrote in his notes:

"If payment does not take place Wedtech has received an extra 2 years of SBA contracts since Dec. 1983—In excess of $80,000,000 has been received."

In disclosures about the distribution of insider stock, he noticed curious wording, revealing that the company had distributed 259,000 shares of stock to "four individuals and one partnership." The names of the owners were not disclosed. It would take months for him to discover that this was Wedtech's method of disclosing its stock gifts to Nofziger & Bragg, Bob Wallach, Ceil Lewis, Bernard Ehrlich, and Richard Biaggi.

After a few hours poring through documents, Cossu was both elated and disturbed. He saw the photo of Ronald Reagan on the opening page of an annual report, and the growing clout of the company's board of directors with Verne Orr, the former Air Force secretary, and Richard Cavazos, the retired four-star general. In one afternoon, he had compiled enough questions and leads to keep him busy for months. But one question haunted him.

"Why is this hitting only me?" he muttered to himself. "This stuff should have been picked up a long time ago."

*   *   *

Cossu had made another notation in his notebook: The over-whelming majority of Wedtech's business was through no-bid contracts from the Department of Defense.

He placed a call to the Defense Criminal Investigative Service to ask if its agents had any background on Wedtech. Curiously enough, about a week earlier Raggi had resurrected several complaints about the company that had been filed with the office nearly a year before. Two separate allegations had come into the office, one charging that Wedtech got special treatment from the New York office of the Defense Contract Administrative Services Management Area, another charging that a high-ranking DCASMA official may have gotten Wed-tech stock. The charges had been assigned to an agent who had recently resigned from DCIS, leaving behind his unfinished work.

Investigators from separate federal agencies are often reluc-tant to share information, partly out of fear of blowing a developing case but largely because of territorial instincts. It was with initial trepidation that Cossu and Raggi agreed to meet, but they soon found their personalities meshed well. They had never met, but coincidentally, they had grown up only a few blocks apart in Greenwich Village and used to hang out at the same neighborhood youth center. Raggi had begun his career as an FBI clerk, then spent four years putting to-gether sex crimes cases for the Brooklyn district attorney's office. His dream was to prosecute white-collar crimes, hope-fully from within the elite ranks of the FBI. But after a brief stint in the U.S. Department of Commerce inspector general's office, he had landed an investigative job with DCIS, an office charged with rooting out waste, fraud, and mismanagement in the huge Department of Defense. He found the detailed work well-suited to his talents.

When the two agents got together to share information, pieces began to fit together. Both of them walked away con-vinced that they had the beginnings of a case of corporate fraud plus some potential low-level bribery cases against at least two Department of Defense employees. Both were intrigued by the role played by Bernie Ehrlich. Cossu, however, could not see the "hook" that would allow him to continue work on the case, since there was no obvious labor angle. He decided to back off and let Raggi handle the case.

Raggi's next step was to share their information with Benito Romano, the head of the Public Corruption Unit in Giuliani's office. Romano, who headed a team of six anticorruption prosecutors, could give the go-ahead for further investigation by a grand jury. His office was in the midst of the explosive and draining Parking Violations Bureau corruption investigation, which would lead to the prosecution that autumn of Bronx Democratic boss Stanley Friedman. The Friedman case was such a seminal event in the city's history that Giuliani had decided to try it himself.

Romano agreed to meet with Raggi and also called in Assistant U.S. Attorney Mary Shannon, a young spitfire, who had helped develop the PVB case and was free for another assignment. She was known in the office—and on the streets—as a tough but fair prosecutor and a good-hearted woman, whose simple acts of human kindness toward the accused were often appreciated by those she put in jail. Shannon, a Las Vegas native who earned her law degree at New York University law school, was an incurable trial junkie. She had developed an enviable talent for cross-examination while working for two years with her mentor, Nicholas Kasanoff, a noted Manhattan defense lawyer.

Romano and Shannon were interested in what they heard, but hardly overwhelmed. They thought they had the makings of a few possible indictments against paper pushers in the Department of Defense. But the signs of involvement by Ehrlich and the possible path to Mario Biaggi, which Cossu had developed, were tantalizing. Romano decided to bring Cossu back onto the case.

Cossu and Raggi began plotting strategy. Cossu's recommendation was that they proceed with a risky tactic. "We've got to shake the trees at the top, and see where it filters down," Cossu told Raggi. They sat down with top officials of DCASMA to ask why Ehrlich and Wedtech were receiving such special treatment, and immediately hit a nerve. Employees who had endured Ehrlich's arrogance came out of the woodwork to tell what they knew.

Slowly but surely, the case began growing in scope, with clear indications of corporate fraud. Raggi had pulled together lists of subcontractors used by Wedtech and the particulars of the Army engine deal. The Defense Contract Audit Agency had also discovered an apparently phony invoice in a routine check of Wedtech's progress-payment requests.

There is nothing investigators like less than to find themselves stepping on one another's toes. In June, Shannon learned that Bronx District Attorney Mario Merola also was investigating Wedtech and had already served a broad subpoena on the company for its records. Merola's staff had stumbled across Wedtech while investigating Stanley Simon's President's Club. Wedtech had treated the state subpoena with disdain, turning over nothing more than a few of its annual reports.

Giuliani's office was already operating under a cross-designation agreement with Merola, in which they agreed to share resources and grand jury materials, a procedure that had worked well in probing cable TV and towing contracts in the Bronx. A dozen assistant DAs had been cross-designated as special assistant U.S. attorneys after extensive background checks by the FBI, but only one, Ted Planzos, assumed a major role on the Wedtech team.

In July, the federal investigators had enough information to execute their first grand jury subpoenas—one for the records of Wedtech, another for the records of the Biaggi & Ehrlich law firm. They were broad, "everything but the kitchen sink" subpoenas, intended to develop a clear-cut case of corporate fraud and flesh out Biaggi's involvement.

The documents were slow in coming. Biaggi & Ehrlich stalled for time. Cossu decided to drive to Wedtech's headquarters to begin reviewing documents. He thought it was important to look the officers square in the eye and make his presence known. He took with him a quiet paralegal, Donna Merris. Cossu made it clear to the Wedtech crew that he was playing tough. As Moreno would later tell Cossu, the officers knew they were doomed when they first sighted Cossu. "Steve," he said in his rhythmic cadence, "you had fire in your eyes."

By August, Cossu and Raggi suspected there was a network of secret Wedtech stockholders, who were deliberately kept out of the public eye because of their political connections. They put together a list of probable Wedtech stockholders for Shannon's review. In the middle was the name of Lyn Nofziger. Cossu had discovered that Nofziger's public relations firm had been earning monthly retainer payments from Wedtech, and he had strong indications that Nofziger had gotten stock in the company. But Cossu did not catch the significance of Wedtech's having hired Nofziger within weeks after he left the White House. Shannon, who only glanced at Cossu's memo, knew that Nofziger had been Reagan's campaign manager but did not realize he had also worked in the White House.

When the *Daily News* began breaking stories almost every day in late October, Cossu and Raggi picked up their pace. The early stories focused squarely on possible corruption in the Small Business Administration. In addition to the phony stock deal, the *News* also revealed that Peter Neglia, the former SBA regional administrator who approved the deal, went to work for the Biaggi & Ehrlich law firm after leaving government.

The stories left the feds to play catch-up, for Cossu and Raggi had not yet subpoenaed the SBA's records. They went to the SBA inspector general's office only to discover a new complication—the intrusion of yet another local prosecutor, Manhattan District Attorney Robert Morgenthau. Morgenthau, they were told, had already subpoenaed the records as soon as the *Daily News* stories appeared. There was no love lost between Morgenthau and Giuliani, who had openly sparred over jurisdiction in the Parking Violations Bureau scandal. Morgenthau's frauds chief, John Moscow, had uncovered the fingerprints of Wedtech and Ehrlich in his investigation of corruption within the state National Guard and had begun interviewing witnesses with intimate knowledge of Wedtech's political connections. Morgenthau's staff believed the grandstanding Giuliani, with obvious ambitions for higher office, had dragged his feet in developing the Wedtech case out of fear of its political ramifications. When the *Daily News* reported that the SBA inspector general had started a probe of the phony stock transfer, Moscow, a brash young prosecutor not used to treading lightly in sensitive areas, slapped a subpoena on the federal agency for all of its Wedtech records.

The theory that Giuliani had political interests to protect was fueled on October 26, when the *Daily News* ran a story entitled "S. Bronx Firm's D.C. Connection," suggesting the first connection to Giuliani's boss, Attorney General Meese. The story, which Kevin McCoy and I prepared, revealed that Wedtech had hired a number of influential figures with high-level Washington contacts, including Nofziger; James Aspin, the brother of Rep. Les Aspin, then a member, later chairman, of the House Armed Services Committee; and Verne Orr.

It also revealed for the first time that E. Robert Wallach, a United Nations delegate who was chief counsel to Meese during his confirmation hearings for Attorney General, held stock in Wedtech. Wallach, whose comments from a telephone interview were included in the story, told me at the time that he had been given 3,500 shares of stock in Wedtech as partial payment for his services. Later, when questioned about the accuracy of his figures, he revealed that his stock gift was more like 31,250 shares. He said he just couldn't remember the specifics. Wallach's actual stock gift was 45,000 shares, 1 percent of the company's stock.

Nothing did more to speed up the federal case, however, than a phone call I made to Dennison Young, Giuliani's right-hand man, seeking comment on a story the *Daily News* was preparing on Lyn Nofziger's Wedtech involvement. The story was to reveal that prosecutors had been told that Nofziger got $1 million worth of stock in return for his services. As was his custom, Young played coy, trying to get as much information as possible while giving away nothing.

When we hung up the phone, Young called Shannon. No one fully realized that the low-level corruption case kicking around the office for months had a potentially explosive White

House connection. Shannon, stumbling for an explanation, took out her frustrations with a phone call to Cossu.

"If I were to ask you who in the administration is involved in this case, who would you say?" she asked.

"Lyn Nofziger," Cossu replied.

"Get your ass down here!" Shannon shouted brusquely into the receiver.

Up to that point, Cossu and Shannon had worked well together, although at a comfortable distance, each doing his own thing. In the privacy of Shannon's office, Cossu told her that for several months she'd had a piece of paper on her desk listing Lyn Nofziger as a likely holder of Wedtech stock. In the future, he said, "You should at least have enough respect for my work to read what I'm giving you." The two would later remember the moment as a kind of marriage, sealing a bond of understanding that was never again called into question.

The *Daily News* broke the story of the Nofziger stock deal on November 2 under the headline "Probers Told of $1M Stox for Nofziger." The story included the first reports of the involvement of Nofziger's White House office in promoting the company. It also included excerpts of Wedtech memos to Nofziger—the first White House documents revealed by the press—which had been funneled to me by a confidential source. And it included extended comments from Wallach, who had returned my phone calls, in which I had sought clarification of his stock holdings.

As the story noted:

> Last week, Wallach told The News he held 3,500 shares. But this week he said he received substantially more—approximately 31,250 shares—for legal services and has sold most of it. He said Wedtech "wanted the best" and used stock to pay top consultants, a practice which he said is customary.
>
> Wallach declined to discuss his law work but said he didn't represent Wedtech on contractual matters or push its cause to the White House or Meese.

My story was followed on November 4 by a blockbuster in the *New York Times.* The paper had had in its possession a curious letter on Nofziger–Bragg stationery written to White House Deputy Counselor James Jenkins. Suddenly, the letter's significance became apparent, and reporter Josh Barbanel pulled it together into a major piece that, for the first time, suggested a possible violation of law in Nofziger's lobbying efforts. It noted that Nofziger had written Jenkins four months after leaving the White House in a possible violation of the federal Ethics in Government Act, which prohibits former high-level administration figures from lobbying their old agencies for one year. Nofziger would later be convicted on ethics charges. But after a long, grueling legal battle that went to the U.S. Supreme Court, he saw the conviction overturned.

While the Nofziger–White House angle clearly added dimension to the case, Giuliani's staff was certain that if criminal allegations surfaced against Nofziger, the Watergate-era Independent Counsel Act would come into play. Nofziger would be investigated and possibly prosecuted, not by Giuliani, but by a special prosecutor appointed by a three-judge panel in Washington. Under the law, designed to ensure that there would be no executive-level interference in the judicial process, the Justice Department's only role was to conduct a threshold investigation to determine if criminal charges were warranted. If so, Attorney General Meese would have to recommend to the court appointment of an independent counsel.

For a while, this knowledge left the investigators in a kind of twilight zone, confused on how to proceed. If they even suspected that the independent counsel statute could come into play—which they did in early November—they were precluded by law from using grand jury subpoenas, conferring immunity or plea bargaining in investigating the charges. Even more disturbing was the suggestion, at that time aired only by the *Daily News,* that Meese was directly linked to one of the principal characters in the Wedtech drama.

As I had written on November 5, Meese was reviewing the appointment of a special prosecutor for Nofziger's Wedtech involvement amid growing indications of his own ties to the firm:

The Daily News learned Wedtech sought to get help from Meese and his White House office as part of a high-powered 1982 effort to win the contract to supply the Army with small horsepower engines. Meese then held the White House post of counselor to the President. . . .

Documents obtained by The News and interviews with former company officials show that by June 1982, Wedtech believed its problems getting the contract had been communicated directly to Meese in the White House. . . .

Determined to go as far as they could without overstepping their bounds, Giuliani's office requested all the White House records related to the Wedtech Corporation. Shannon ventured another step. She placed a phone call to Wallach and asked him to come in voluntarily for an interview. Wallach showed up on November 9 with his lawyer, Seymour Glanzer.

The interview went on for the better part of the day but gave no inkling of major Wedtech involvement by Meese. In his soothing voice, Wallach told the investigators—as he had told the *Daily News* a few weeks earlier—that he never lobbied Meese or anyone at the White House on behalf of Wedtech but had provided legal advice to the company.

By mid-December, the federal team received word from the White House that its records were ready for review. By that point, they still had no idea of the extent of Meese's involvement. They were informed that there was a large volume of documents, stacked in dusty boxes in a room in the Old Executive Office Building. Under the White House's elaborate records-keeping system, each document was computerized, numbered, and boxed, which made it difficult to retrieve a single piece of paper. It would take days before the documents could be processed, copied, and shipped to New York.

In the interest of time, with the Christmas holidays rapidly approaching, Giuliani's team decided to stage a frontal assault on the gigantic task. Shannon, Romano, and a few investigators went down to see how far they could get in a day. Cossu stayed behind to handle interviews and other business in development of the New York case. That afternoon, Cossu received a panicked phone call from Shannon. "Get your ass down here," said Shannon, surrounded by stacks of paper that climbed the walls. "Nobody knows what they're looking for."

Cossu and Merris went down the next morning. They checked in with the guards at the security desk, then walked through the dark, hollow halls of the gargantuan building, and finally found the small room where the bleary-eyed Shannon and her team were sorting through boxes.

In time, however, the pieces began to fall together. They began to discover the trail of correspondence and memos from Nofziger to Dole to Jenkins and Meese. Clearly, the Attorney General's involvement was much broader than any of them had expected, documented by a clear paper trail that underscored the need for further investigation. With each new discovery, the search took on more purpose and energy.

In the hall, they could hear from time to time the heavy footsteps of a guard, pacing back and forth. The room was as hushed as a library, their communications done in whispers. "You would see something on paper and you'd think, 'This is it. I've found it.' And you'd want to jump up and scream, but you couldn't," Cossu recalled.

Cossu went back to work with renewed vigor. He had left Washington with the clairvoyant sense that the Wedtech case was going to make history, and that he would be a part of it.

21

CHAOS
AT HEADQUARTERS

THE LAST WEEKS OF OCTOBER were a time of anger and
anguish at Wedtech corporate headquarters. The most successful Ponzi scheme in history was toppling like a chain of
dominoes, setting off Wedtech's longstanding paranoia, for it
was clear that the stories—based increasingly on leaked corporate and government documents—were originating from their
growing camp of enemies.

Guariglia and Shorten, trying to figure out who was behind
the *Daily News* attacks, zeroed in at first on Mariotta. They
could not forget his parting threat that he would destroy them
all. They debated their suspects over and over until, finally,
the *Daily News* ran a photograph of Mariotta. It showed him
gesturing wildly to President Reagan and Vice President Bush
at the White House conference on urban enterprise zones—it

249

had been Mariotta's favorite photo. Now, they had no doubt who was out to do them in.

The Wedtech officers held a series of panicked conferences, trying to map out a public relations strategy. They believed Squadron could take care of the New York *Post* through a phone call to his client, publisher Rupert Murdoch. The *Daily News* was another matter, however. The newspaper's first story alleging a Wedtech stock scam was quickly followed by an editorial in *Barron's,* condemning abuses of the 8(a) program. The *Barron's* article in turn touched off sparks on Wall Street, and for the first time, stockbrokers and investors began jamming the Wedtech switchboard, demanding more details.

The *New York Times'* Barbanel had jumped into the story, exposing James Jenkins' continuing role with the company and Wedtech's retention of Mitchell, Mitchell & Mitchell. At the *Daily News'* offices, Howard Squadron's threat of a lawsuit had done nothing to lessen the newspaper's interest. The paper had published stories under my byline on the George Bush– Dickey Dyer connection and the roles played by former White House aides Pier Talenti, Wayne Valis, and Henry Zuniga. Kevin McCoy, a dogged *News* investigative reporter, was digging into Wedtech's buildings acquisitions and its Washington and state National Guard connections, and Jerry Capeci, the *News* organized crime and former federal courts reporter, was pursuing a tip on the Main Hurdman invoice fraud coverup.

The articles were having dramatic repercussions. Wedtech was in the midst of acquiring another subsidiary in a $51 million cash purchase, but the negative publicity was jeopardizing the negotiations. Wedtech's banks were calling, raising fears that its overextended lines of credit would be cut off. The Navy, already disgusted with Wedtech's dismal performance on the pontoon contract, was threatening to pull the plug. And on Capitol Hill, the Senate Subcommittee on Oversight of Government Management, chaired by Michigan Sen. Carl Levin, began an investigation into Wedtech's favorable treatment from federal agencies.

But the effects were most dramatic on the prestigious New York Stock Exchange, where Wedtech was trying to raise $75 million through a bond sale. Stock prices were plunging, from a high of $6.2 on October 15, the day of the first *Daily News* article, to a high of $3.2 when the Nofziger revelations appeared. Soon, a share of Wedtech stock could be bought for less than the price of a subway token.

Out of the chaos, Wallach emerged to help Wedtech define a defensive posture. He was scheduled to leave with Meese for a week-long trip to Frankfurt on October 25, so he had to work quickly. He assured the Wedtech crew the firm was too big, too smooth, too connected to be beaten down by the muckraking New York City press. The officers later testified that he also offered the most comforting words imaginable—that no matter how serious Wedtech's problems seemed, they would not go to jail. They took comfort in knowing that Meese was at the helm of the Justice Department.

By the previous July, the Wedtech officers had been awash in subpoenas from the U.S. attorneys' offices in the Southern and Eastern Districts of New York and Baltimore, and from the Bronx and Manhattan district attorneys' offices. Wallach had advised Wedtech at that time to retain a criminal lawyer, and had recommended respected Manhattan attorney Steve Kaufman. Kaufman who was close to Manhattan DA Morgenthau—he told them in an aside—whose frauds bureau was then hot on their trail.

But except for Wallach, the officers had kept their mounting legal difficulties secret from their other attorneys, even from their corporate lawyers at Squadron, Ellenoff. Wallach and Squadron had had a major falling out, which Squadron later attributed to his refusal to give Wallach a larger cut of the firm's legal fees.

Largely at Wallach's urging, the officers plunged ahead with the *Daily News* lawsuit. The *News* at that point was the only paper writing about Wallach's links to Ed Meese. The go-ahead decision was made in a meeting at Squadron, Ellenoff, where both Siskind and Squadron expressed reservations about taking on the *Daily News*. Squadron later said that he told the group that, as a lawyer for the Murdoch empire, he had reservations against libel suits in general. But Wallach was insistent and the Wedtech officers said that, if Squadron, Ellen-off refused to represent them, they would find another law firm.

Squadron was also incensed to discover that subpoenas had been floating around Wedtech for months without the firm's knowledge and that the officers had retained Kaufman at Wallach's recommendation. In one tense conference call, Squadron told Wedtech board members that Wallach was giving them bad advice.

Following the meeting to plan the lawsuit, Wallach arranged to meet at the Grand Hyatt with John Kehoe, Wedtech's savvy investor relations representative. Since the scandal broke, Kehoe and his staff had been working overtime fielding phone calls from Wall Street and from reporters. Kehoe had joined Wedtech at the recommendation of some of his most trusted contacts on Wall Street. He was impressed by Guariglia's intelligence and by the company's ambitious plans, and when the news stories began breaking, he was assured by Guariglia and Shorten that the revelations were totally unfounded. In dealing with the media, he had simply responded to each new allegation by quoting from Wedtech's "Bible"—its bulky filings with the SEC. Kehoe's integrity was such that he could not fathom the notion that the SEC filings were a litany of lies.

The meeting with Wallach was the first time Kehoe realized the extent of Wedtech's legal problems. Calmly Wallach told Kehoe that Kaufman would be handling criminal allegations against the company and serving separately as counsel to Ehrlich. Wallach's friend John Kotelly, of the Washington firm Dickstein, Shapiro, would be handling the Maryland investigation, the *Daily News* suit, and the Defense Department's probe of progress payments. (Kehoe knew nothing about the progress payment matter, but did not ask questions.) Wallach also said that he would serve as "coordinating counsel" to make certain that all lines of defense meshed properly.

Wallach wanted Kehoe to put a certain spin on Wedtech's problems. It should be made clear, he said, that the press had misread the facts and, in doing so, jeopardized hundreds of minority jobs. Law enforcement matters should be referred to as "inquiries" rather than investigations. No suggestion of criminality should be allowed.

Kehoe went back to his office troubled. For two years, he had worked closely with Squadron, Ellenoff, and he trusted the firm. Now with a field of lawyers handling separate matters, the possibilities for conflict and confusion were rampant. He went to see Howard Squadron, threatening to resign from the account, unless Squadron, Ellenoff resumed its role as Wedtech's chief legal firm. Squadron agreed to push the point.

But the Wedtech officers by that time had already decided that, if it came down to a showdown between Howard Squadron and Bob Wallach, they would side with Wallach. They firmly believed that Wallach, through his connection to Meese, was their only hope of salvation.

Around that time, Wallach finally returned my numerous unanswered telephone calls. His voice was as pleasant and unruffled as usual. "This will probably be the last time I talk to you," he said pensively. He would probably be facing me soon in court as a lawyer for Wedtech in its lawsuit against me and the *Daily News.*

At 595 Gerard Avenue, a reassuring notice under Guariglia's signature went up on the company bulletin board:

> Most of you have seen some of the recent articles in the newspapers about Wedtech. These articles imply that this Company had engaged in questionable conduct in order to obtain government contracts. As the President of Wedtech, I want to assure you that these articles are factually inaccurate and misleading. Wedtech has done nothing wrong. . . .
>
> We have no doubt that the results of the investigations will prove that it is the News, not Wedtech, that is guilty of questionable conduct. . . .

Around the middle of October, when the newspapers unearthed the first hints of the Wedtech scandal, Eileen Neuberger began making increasingly desperate phone calls from her Sutton Place home. Her speech slurred, she called others in the Wedtech clan to report her fears that Fred was going to kill her. Eileen, who had a long history of psychiatric problems, had hired a lawyer that fall to file for divorce against her womanizing husband. But she told anyone who would listen that Fred was going to get rid of her.

The Wedtech crew knew all about Eileen. A year earlier, tormented by visions and voices, she had spent several weeks in the psychiatric ward of Mount Sinai Hospital—a hospital bill Neuberger later neglected to pay. That same year, on July 4, she threw herself in the East River, resisting a force that told her to murder their two adopted children, then one and two years old. When police fished her out of the river, her purse was filled with credit cards under an alias, Mary O'Connor.

She was hospitalized again in January 1986 for an overdose of barbiturates, and six months later she tried to kill herself again. By the fall of 1986, her paranoia had become so severe that she fired her South American nannies and left her children unattended while she roamed the streets at 4 A.M. She began showing up at the 19th Precinct station house nearly every day to complain of robberies, attacks, or suspicious followers.

Police were called to her home on October 17 and again on October 23 to investigate complaints that Fred had assaulted her. Fred explained her bruises as a fall down the stairs resulting from an unhealthy combination of alcohol and prescription drugs. But one worker at the 149th Street plant heard Fred boast that he was going to have his wife taken care of. The entire company, of course, knew the tragic story of Helen Neuberger's suicide and could not help linking the two.

On November 11, 1986, Neuberger reported Eileen missing, but the police almost disregarded his complaint because of Eileen's weeks of pestering the station house. She had left on November 9, leaving behind her clothes, money, and jewelry. According to Fred, she placed a call in the middle of the night to their housekeeper in an effort to speak to their children. He hired a highly decorated former police detective, private eye Bo Dietl, to try to find her, but the trail led nowhere.

The mystery of Eileen Neuberger's disappearance—so close to the outbreak of the Wedtech scandal—caught the imagination of New Yorkers. At the Wedtech plant, the rumor circulated that her body was entombed in a floating pontoon boat. One anonymous caller suggested to me that she could have been buried in Mario Moreno's underground pool during suspicious excavations at his home that lasted into the night.

Assistant Manhattan DA John Moscow, investigating the disappearance, reopened the Helen Neuberger case for possible clues. But he could go nowhere without locating Eileen's corpse. Federal prosecutors dismissed the idea that Neuberger could have murdered Eileen. They said that, although he was cold and amoral in his business affairs, his personality warmed around his family. In debriefings, he would break down in tears when he talked about Helen's tragic death. They came to consider Eileen a probable suicide victim.

In the early days of November 1986, Wedtech's officials steadfastly adopted Wallach's rationale that the company was the victim of a racist press out for sensational headlines. But the tide turned dramatically on November 9, when the *Daily News* ran an article under Jerry Capeci's byline that included an astounding admission. Through attorney Arthur Siskind, the company admitted on paper that over the course of years it had routinely submitted phony invoices to the Department of Defense to secure up to $6 million in progress payments. Siskind justified the act as a normal business procedure done with the knowledge and approval of the DOD and the SBA.

The story was a testament to Capeci's street-wise reportorial skills. He had been pursuing the tip that had come my way from an anonymous Main Hurdman employee about Guariglia's and Bluestine's roles in covering up a huge invoice fraud at Wedtech. The tip had been specific but anonymous, little help to a reporter needing substantiation. Quick calls to the defense agencies involved produced nothing at all. Main Hurdman's lawyer admitted there had been an invoice problem, but provided only the barest details.

Early on, however, Capeci contacted Siskind and John Kehoe, seeking comment on the as-yet-unproven allegation. Capeci told them he had information that Wedtech had sub-

mitted $6 million in false invoices to the federal government.
Using an old reporter's tactic, he told them he had confirmed
the gist of the story with Main Hurdman and intended to write
a story based on the accounting firm's comments for Sunday's
publications.

Kehoe, who had been wrestling with his own doubts about
Wedtech, was disturbed by Capeci's phone call and the speci-
ficity of the charge. He had been repeatedly assured by the
officers and Wallach that Wedtech had done nothing wrong.
He told Capeci to give him a few days, and he would provide
a response to the charge.

Kehoe reached Guariglia in London, where he was trying
to raise money, and the two of them hooked up with Larry
Shorten on a lengthy conference call. Guariglia was adamant
that the company had done nothing illegal. As the former
Main Hurdman auditor assigned to the Wedtech account, he
insisted that he had been the "good guy," discovering the
wrongdoing and following the proper course of action in
reporting it to his firm and to the government.

Piece by piece, Guariglia began reconstructing the story of
Wedtech's suspicious 1982 audit. Kehoe listened, sorting out
in his mind disturbing inconsistencies. Moreno, the purported
villain in the invoice fraud, had obviously suffered little for his
transgressions; he had been promoted to vice chairman of the
board. The Defense Department requirement that every
progress payment be audited had never been disclosed in the
company's SEC reports. Kehoe considered the omission a
withholding of material information to which shareholders
were entitled.

Kehoe drafted a letter, which went through the expanding
chain of Wedtech advisers for review, first to Kaufman, then
Guariglia, then to Howard Squadron. It ended on the desk of
Siskind, who read it, edited it, and had the final version hand-
delivered to Capeci. It read:

November 7, 1986

Dear Mr. Capeci:
   We have been advised that you are preparing a news
story centered around an allegation of a $6 million fraud

against the U.S. Government during the period 1981–1982 by Wedtech Corp. (then operating under its former name, Welbilt Electronic Die Corporation), relating to progress payments billed for work on certain Small Business Administration contracts for the Department of Defense.

The following are the facts in that situation.

Main Hurdman was engaged in 1982 to conduct an audit of Wedtech Corp. beginning with the balance sheet and income statements for the periods ended December 31, 1981 and 1982.

Anthony Guariglia, currently president and chief operating officer of Wedtech Corp., was the Main Hurdman manager on that audit and was assigned that responsibility because of his extensive experience with defense contracting audit work.

In the course of the audit, Main Hurdman encountered difficulties in reconciling certain progress payments received by the Company to accounts payable to various vendors for materials purchased . . .

Mr. Guariglia, upon discovering the invoice fabrication, immediately presented his findings to Main Hurdman's engagement partner, National Standards Department, the National Accounting and Auditing Office and the firm's outside legal counsel and recommended that Main Hurdman disengage from the audit. A meeting was then convened between Wedtech management and Main Hurdman's National Office where Wedtech was advised of the auditor's findings and their intent to disengage.

While invoices had been fabricated to support progress payments, the amounts of those invoices were consistent with the amounts subsequently billed to, and paid by, the company. The company was under a fixed price contract with the SBA. Not only had there been no increase in the cost of the product billed to the U.S. Government but, had there been such an increase in cost, it would have had to be borne by Wedtech under the terms of the contract. . . . The action by Wedtech had been taken out of a simple need for capital to finance the project.

In order to continue the audit engagement, Main Hurdman made certain demands. They were: that there be 100% examination of every transaction and 100% confirmation of all transactions; and that the company institute certain financial controls; and that there be full disclosure to the SBA and other appropriate governmental agencies, primarily the Defense Contract Audit Agency. Even after compliance with these parameters, Main Hurdman gave the company no assurances that it would render a clean opinion. Wedtech Corp. agreed to the demands and Main Hurdman went forward with the audit uncovering no further irregularities. . . .

One final point: we are advised by Main Hurdman's counsel that, because the engagement partner and manager of that audit subsequently joined Wedtech Corp. and the latter, as noted, now serves as president of the company, the 1984 audit performed by Main Hurdman was significantly expanded beyond regular auditing procedures and no irregularities in that or the prior audits were involved.

While we can only speculate as to the DAILY NEWS' sources on these matters, we hope it is apparent to you that the motive behind the information you are receiving is destructive and creates jeopardy for the company's employees and shareholders. We doubt whether other defense contractors, many times the size of Wedtech, could withstand such close scrutiny of their financial dealings with the Government.

I am available to discuss any material questions you may have in this matter.

Very truly yours,
Arthur Siskind

When the letter came across Capeci's desk, he and City Editor Arthur Browne could not believe what they had in their hands. After weeks of adamant denials, backed by a massive libel suit, Wedtech was admitting that it had, in fact, committed potentially illegal acts. Even more astounding, the admission had come in the form of a carefully crafted written statement on the letterhead of one of the city's eminent law firms. Neither of the veteran newsmen had ever seen such a thing. In its arrogance and confusion, Wedtech and its supporters clearly thought they could admit to crimes openly and justify their actions with a glib "so what" attitude.

Capeci and Browne worked until midnight that Friday, reducing the convoluted letter to its simplest form. Under the headline "Wedtech Admits Forging Bill for 6M Cash Advance," it told the story of Wedtech's incestuous relationship with the Main Hurdman auditors and their rationalizations of flagrant violations of law. It began:

> The Wedtech Corp. submitted "fabricated" bills to the federal government, enabling the firm to prematurely collect $6 million on its defense contracts, the company's lawyer has acknowledged.
>
> After questions were raised by the Daily News, Wedtech's lawyer, Arthur Siskind, confirmed that the Bronx defense contracting company gave forged invoices to the Small Business Administration in 1981 and 1982 in an effort to ease financial problems the company was then facing.
>
> At the time, Wedtech held a number of Small Business Administration contracts to manufacture equipment for the Army. The invoices—bearing the names of Wedtech suppliers—were printed up and submitted to the administration as evidence that the government owed the company money for costs it ran up in the manufacturing process.

The Capeci story was a major turning point in the development of the federal case. For the first time, the prosecutors had a written admission of potential criminality and a powerful bargaining tool in bringing the Wedtech officials to the table as cooperators. As it turned out, a thorough investigation of the fraudulent invoices showed that the company had secured $4.7 million, rather than the $6 million they admitted to, through the scam.

For Kehoe, the story was the final straw. He believed that, if he stayed on, he would be a party to the Wedtech fraud. Kehoe had never before walked out on a client, especially one with the backing of some of the most prestigious firms on Wall Street. There also was a pure business consideration, since Wedtech owed him $40,000, which he risked never collecting if he dropped the firm as a client. Nevertheless, Kehoe typed a letter of resignation, sent it by messenger to the Wedtech headquarters, then dropped in later when the Wedtech officers showed up for a meeting at Squadron, Ellenoff. There he told Tony Guariglia to his face why he was resigning.

When Kehoe walked out, he became a pariah in the eyes of Wedtech and its staunch supporters. It was clear that in the view of Squadron, Ellenoff, Bear Stearns, and the other respected firms that had banded together behind the company, Wedtech's problems were manageable, and the vicious press would be quickly put in its place.

In late October and early November, the officers later testified, Bob Wallach assured them that he was keeping his friend Ed Meese fully briefed and obtaining information from him on the status of the criminal investigation. They were heartened by the news.

Wallach's pipeline of information about the probes seemed astoundingly good. Through him, they learned of likely charges and possible plea bargains. Guariglia testified that he, Wallach, Moreno, and Neuberger met several times for briefings over dinner at La Guardia Airport when Wallach flew in from Washington. At one session, he said, Wallach ended with the encouraging words, "Hang tough. I spoke with Ed Meese, and we're trying to get this investigation quashed." Meese would later deny any knowledge of such conversations and of any effort to quash the probe.

By early December, the officers had vested all their hopes in Wallach. Their legal and business affairs had reached the breaking point. Squadron, who had never regained control of the company's disjointed legal affairs, made good on his threat and resigned from the Wedtech account. At Wallach's insistence, they signed up Dickstein, Shapiro as their new corporate counsel and tendered a check for $500,000. They also wrote a $95,000 check to Wallach as a referral fee.

In a meeting at Dickstein, Shapiro's New York offices, Moreno and Guariglia finally approached Wallach with a desperation offer. They believed they had already paid off Meese indirectly by subsidizing Wallach while he was serving as Meese's unpaid lawyer. Now, they would each give

Wallach $100,000 if he would persuade Meese to stop the federal investigation and keep them out of jail.

Although Wallach later denied the conversation ever took place, Guariglia said Wallach told him: "I'm very appreciative of the offer. It's a nice amount of money. And if I succeed, I will take the $100,000."

Throughout late October and November, the months of Wedtech's mounting legal troubles, Meese's office logs show Wallach meeting or talking with Meese regularly. The substance of those meetings is not known, but they occurred while Shannon and the Giuliani team in New York were in regular contact with the Justice Department's Criminal Division on the development of their case. Although the federal probers had no reason to believe Meese was channeling information to Wallach, their meetings made the probers most uncomfortable.

By then, the department was moving inevitably toward the appointment of a special prosecutor in the Nofziger matter, and Meese was taking steps to remove himself from the criminal investigation of his old friend. But in a lapse of judgment that later brought him under severe criticism, Meese still had not recused himself from the Wedtech case as a whole. A recusal would have served as a formal step to ensure that he played no role in the department's handling of the matter.

As fear finally took hold of the embattled Wedtech officers, they had decided, one by one, that if things became too hot, they would simply leave the country, living off the stolen riches they had stashed in foreign bank accounts.

Guariglia had obtained a phony passport and was under considerable pressure to flee. As he began making plans, Guariglia said he talked with Wallach about extradition policies of various foreign countries. Wallach claimed to have helped Marc Rich, the orchestrator of a legendary IRS tax swindle, to avoid extradition by setting up residency in Spain. As Guariglia later explained the conversation, Wallach promised he "would get back to me and outline those areas that were safe harbors. He also told me that I should be very cautious of the fugitive laws and that if I was ever caught it meant mandatory jail."

Moreno, meanwhile, was taking his own steps to flee. He considered fleeing to his native Colombia but dropped the idea when Larry Shorten began making arrangements for him to get a phony Swedish passport for $20,000. He also set up a number of foreign bank accounts, containing over $400,000, to provide his living expenses. For months after they signed cooperation agreements, Moreno and the others conveniently neglected to tell prosecutors they were living off stolen money while cooperating with the government.

While the Wedtech officers scurried to hide their money abroad, the company that had made them all rich was rapidly plunging toward bankruptcy. The Defense Department, finally pressed into action, cut off the vital progress payments. Wedtech's banks, scared by the bad publicity, closed its credit lines. On November 12, the first of a series of Wedtech stockholders filed suit against the company, charging fraudulent filings with the SEC. Two days later, the company announced it expected to post a "substantial and material" third-quarter loss, blaming the decrease partly on recent news reports.

From Washington, Biaggi was watching with great concern as the company's financial affairs deteriorated, precipitating the rapid devaluation of his secretly held stock. He called Moreno every morning for an update. This 7 A.M. call became such a part of Moreno's routine that he told Caridad he could throw away his alarm clock.

Biaggi pressed the officers to do whatever they could to obtain additional financing and offered them several possibilities. The company had been negotiating with the Chrysler Credit Corporation in the hopes of securing a $25 million loan. When the process reached a stalemate, the officers testified, Biaggi approached Bill Fugazy, owner of a Manhattan limousine service, for an introduction to Lee Iacocca, the president of Chrysler Motor Corporation. Later, Biaggi placed a call to Iacocca and received slight encouragement.

In October 1986, again using Biaggi as their contact, the Wedtech officers turned to Carmine D'Angelo, a longtime Queens Teamsters leader, for a loan from the Teamsters Pension and Welfare Fund. D'Angelo arranged for Wedtech to talk to Jackie Presser, the Teamsters' international president, at the union's headquarters in Washington. Afraid of flying, D'Angelo took a train to Washington and met Ehrlich and Moreno for their brief morning audience with Presser. Frantically, Moreno and Ehrlich explained to Presser that Wedtech was on the cusp of bankruptcy and that its failures would put hundreds of people out of work, most of them minorities.

Presser, the overseer of 1.6 million union members, looked unimpressed. "Do you know how many members I represent?" he retorted. Presser told them there was no way the union could bail out Wedtech.

By early December, with no hope in sight, another set of lawyers entered the Wedtech picture, the Manhattan firm of Pollner, Mezan, Stolzberg, Berger & Glass. Fred Neuberger had retained Martin Pollner as his individual counsel earlier that fall. The chain-smoking Pollner had built a career in government law, serving as assistant U.S. attorney, deputy assistant secretary of the Treasury, and director of law enforcement for the Internal Revenue Service and the Secret Service.

Around the first of December, the Wedtech officers approached Pollner about representing the troubled company in its mounting civil litigation. Pollner called Mary Shannon in an effort to scope out the progress of the federal case. She outlined for the first time the grim dimensions of Wedtech's legal problems. Yes, she told him, there was going to be an indictment of Wedtech's officers, and it was going to be soon. Her investigators had uncovered the FHJ account, knew it had been used as a slush fund by the corporate officers, and were aware of the long-running Department of Defense billing fraud. They had discovered payoffs to government officials. She anticipated a prosecution both of the company and the individual officers, seeking a broad-based forfeiture of corporate and personal assets. The only way to save the company itself from indictment and seizure would be for the officers to plead guilty and agree to cooperate with the government.

There was a bit of bluff in Shannon's presentation. Although Cossu and the other investigators were aware of the FHJ account, at that point they had no idea of its magnitude or that it had been used to fund payoffs and bribes to a host of government officials. The feds were still coming to terms with one of the basic puzzles of the Wedtech case. They could not understand how the officers of a publicly traded firm represented by responsible auditors and lawyers could skim millions of dollars off the top and get away with it for so long.

To Pollner, Wedtech's imminent collapse was a tragedy for the city, which stood to lose hundreds of desperately needed minority jobs in its most depressed borough. His first concern was to save the company. Pollner clung to the hope that Wedtech could be rejuvenated and its public investors saved if the company embarked on an orderly Chapter 11 bankruptcy followed by a series of lawsuits to reclaim damages and stolen funds. He passed on word to the officers—and to Wedtech's other legal counsel—that the firm had no other course but to file for bankruptcy.

On December 10, the Dickstein, Shapiro law firm, after a conference in its Washington office, decided to back away from its representation of Wedtech. The retainer checks written two days earlier to the firm were abruptly returned. Guariglia, Moreno, Shorten, and Neuberger decided that day to follow Pollner's advice and file for protection under the federal bankruptcy laws.

That same day, Guariglia said he got a panicked call from Wallach, who fully realized that the end was near. "Just take it easy, don't do anything," Guariglia remembered Wallach warning him.

The officers, however, were fed up with Wallach's advice. They piled into a cab and made a beeline for Martin Pollner's office on Lexington Avenue.

The next day, December 11, Wallach placed a call to Pollner and told Pollner it was important that he be involved in Wedtech's legal representation. He also showed up at a New York hotel suite, where the Attorney General had arrived after an official visit to London. At around 10 A.M., Meese's press secretary, Terry Eastland, was closeted with Meese preparing him for a luncheon meeting with the editorial board of NBC News. Eastland was perturbed when Wallach knocked on the door. He had only thirty minutes to prepare Meese for the NBC appearance, which was to include an after-lunch question-and-answer session. In the midst of this, Wallach wanted a private audience with Meese, and led the Attorney General out of Eastland's hearing range.

For the next twenty-five or thirty minutes, the two old friends engaged in an intense conversation. It took so much time that Meese had to rush to NBC's studios and walk in completely cold. But when questioned later about this meeting, Meese testified he could not remember the details of the conversation but it was "entirely possible, actually probable" that the two might have discussed the deteriorating affairs of Wedtech.

With the Christmas holidays, the bankrupt company abruptly shut down its Navy pontoon plant, laying off hundreds of workers. Six days later, Wedtech Vice President Matt Harrison abruptly posted a notice alerting the remaining workers that the company was shutting down all its operations. "We hope this will be a temporary situation," the memo said.

The public bankruptcy notice came in the form of a December 15 press release from Tony Guariglia. It read:

> Anthony Guariglia, president of the Wedtech Corp., (NYSE) stated today that the company had filed for protection pursuant to the reorganization provisions of Chapter 11 in the U.S. Bankruptcy Court for the Southern District of New York. The decision to file under Chapter 11 was made by Wedtech's board of directors in order to permit the company time to develop a plan of reorganization, and to preserve assets of the company pending the submission of the plan of reorganization for approval by the court and the company's creditors. . . .

The more than 1,000 employees affected by the notice—the downtrodden workers of the South Bronx who had built their own dreams upon the grand vision of John Mariotta—found themselves facing a penniless Christmas and a bleak future. After weeks of clinging to their management's adamant professions of innocence, the workers lined up at the factory gates in stunned silence.

In their frustration and betrayal, they lashed out at anyone who would listen. "Merry Christmas. We hope you are satisfied," jeered one anonymous caller who reached me at the *Daily News.*

Steve Cossu, who was continuing his review of Wedtech's records, emerged from the plant door and found himself facing a line of angry, laid-off workers. Many were holding crying children in their arms, wrapped in blankets against the cold New York winter. They stared at Cossu as if he were the enemy. "Merry Christmas," they said bitterly as Cossu moved through the throng.

For the first time, the human dimensions of Cossu's months of investigation came home to him. As he climbed into his comfortable car, the weary investigator found himself fighting back tears.

22

BLIND JUSTICE

MARY SHANNON TOOK a disturbing report back to her boss, Rudy Giuliani. The federal team had finished its Christmas mission at the Old Executive Office Building, and they had found Ed Meese's fingerprints everywhere. The evidence posed a delicate problem for the Giuliani team, which was reporting its findings to Meese's Justice Department. Meese had backed away from the department's investigation of Nofziger, but he still had not signed a statement formally recusing himself from the Wedtech matter as a whole. Thus, he could easily learn that the department's investigation of Nofziger was rapidly closing in on his friend, Bob Wallach, and on himself.

There was no love lost between Meese and Giuliani. Meese, who saw his own ethics troubles as the creation of a biased press, frequently had made disparaging remarks about Giuliani's headline-grabbing investigations, according to his associates. He could not understand why the press showed so little interest in many of his staged media events while lapping up Giuliani's pronouncements.

Giuliani had little respect for Meese's ability and could not identify with a public official who constantly found himself under ethical attack. In December 1986, Meese had shown up with Wallach at a New York lawyers' cocktail party, one month after Wallach had been in Giuliani's offices undergoing an intensive interview. On the basis of press accounts alone, Wallach was clearly under suspicion in the case. No one in Giuliani's squad had any inkling that Wallach, only weeks earlier, had allegedly promised the Wedtech officers that he could keep them informed of the Giuliani investigation and save them from going to jail.

On November 4, *Daily News* Justice Department reporter Joe Volz called Meese's office for comment on the Attorney General's involvement in the Wedtech engine contract. The *News* planned to run a story under my byline the next day, giving the first hints of Meese's Wedtech involvement.

The official response from Deputy Press Secretary Pat Korten was that the Attorney General had no recollection of discussing Wedtech with his friend, Bob Wallach. Meese's White House office, Volz was told, fielded hundreds of calls from businesses with grievances about the federal government.

By mid-November, Meese quietly backed away from any involvement in the Nofziger investigation by signing the recusal statement, and turned all decisions over to Deputy Attorney General Arnold Burns, a staunch Meese loyalist. Burns considered Meese an intelligent, thoughtful man and a keeper of "copious, well-structured, magnificent notes," he later told me. He had such a quick mind that months after hearing a fact, "he could pull it right back on the screen."

A larger recusal would have taken Meese out of the Wedtech case altogether, triggering alarms at the Justice Department to ensure that he had no access to internal memos, FBI reports, or other documents involving the Wedtech case. Routinely, a U.S. attorney had to notify and seek permission from Washington for racketeering prosecutions, lawyer subpoenas, and immunity requests. Under Meese, Giuliani and other U.S. attorneys also had been required to notify the Justice Department in advance of any subpoenas or indictments of members of Congress.

Giuliani's team could not understand why, as an ethical safeguard if nothing more, Meese did not make a blanket written recusal in the Wedtech matter. But Meese later defended his actions, saying he played no role in the Wedtech case once Nofziger's involvement surfaced. Nonetheless, since he had assumed the Attorney General's job, Meese had exhibited a poor record on recusals, a matter of some concern to his subordinates. In addition to the Wedtech matter, Meese also had participated in Justice Department discussions of an antitrust action involving a number of regional telephone companies in which he held stock.

On January 7, 1987, Justice requested the U.S. Court of Appeals to appoint an independent counsel in the Nofziger case. The department had concluded that Nofziger probably had violated the law by writing a letter to his old White House colleague, Jim Jenkins, seeking a "letter of intent" from the Army to the Welbilt Corporation.

By that time, another behemoth crisis—the Iran-Contra scandal—had erupted within the Reagan administration, requiring Meese's almost undivided attention. He excluded the Justice Department's criminal division and public integrity section from participation and stopped bringing note-takers to record interviews with key officials. He failed to take steps to prevent the destruction of important documents by Oliver North and National Security Adviser John Poindexter, and at a November 25, 1986, news conference he made factually inaccurate, misleading statements about his inquiry. The probe of the secret arms sales was so bungled, in fact, that a year later Meese would be accused by a special congressional Iran-Contra committee of poorly serving President Reagan as his top legal adviser.

In December, with the Iran-Contra scandal still preoccupying him, Meese held another press conference, and Volz, shouting a question over the clamor of a crowded briefing room, took the opportunity to put Meese publicly on the spot about his Wedtech connection. Meese told Volz that, yes, he seemed to have some memory of Wedtech. It seemed to him that the company was an outstanding minority firm located somewhere in the South Bronx.

During the last days of December and early January, Martin Pollner and his associate, John Lang, spent the better part of their evenings trying to talk sense to the Wedtech executives. The lawyers' only hope of saving Wedtech from seizure under the federal racketeering statutes was to force the resignations of the top company officials, then bring them to Giuliani's bargaining table.

Their task was made somewhat easier when Guariglia spotted a revealing note on Lang's desk from a telephone conversation he had had with Mary Shannon: the initials "FHJ." Guariglia turned dead white. If the Wedtech probers knew about FHJ, then clearly, all of them were doomed.

During these weeks of intense discussions, Pollner had developed a certain rapport with Guariglia, who was clearly the intellectual leader of the Wedtech group. Over a long dinner, Pollner and Lang first broached the subject of Guariglia's cooperating with the government. Instead of rejecting the idea, Guariglia seemed almost anxious to talk.

He began in a hypothetical way about Wedtech's Washington connections, but Pollner cut him off. These were matters for Guariglia's criminal lawyer, not Wedtech's new corporate counsel. At the meeting's end, Guariglia agreed to think about cooperating with the government and to sound out the others.

Guariglia clearly knew who was clean and who was dirty, and he and Pollner developed an elliptical screening method as the lawyer began trying to reorganize the company's fractured management. Pollner would mention a name; Guariglia would either nod or shake his head. In this way the Pollner firm moved quickly to secure the resignations of board members Ehrlich and Chinn, while convincing retired Gen. Richard Cavazos that he should head the reorganized Wedtech. Cavazos had been little more than a figurehead, whose important name Wedtech could use to open doors.

Guariglia talked with Moreno and Shorten, and Pollner conferred with Shannon. On January 2, the officers met Pollner again, this time in the company of Neuberger. Slowly, the officers began to realize their only chance of saving themselves from extended time in prison was to take their saga of political corruption to federal prosecutors. Pollner set up each of them with experienced criminal lawyers—Guariglia with Norman Ostrow, Neuberger with Kal Gallop, Moreno with Arthur Christy, and Shorten with Karl Savryn.

Anxieties ran high as the Wedtech officers, through their attorneys, began tentative talks with the U.S. attorney's office. Soon word leaked out that the officers were about to flip, a potentially devastating prospect to the many ensnared in Wedtech's web. Guariglia, convinced that his cooperation with the government would put his life in danger, was especially anxious.

Guariglia testified that, one day, after investigators were reported in the press to be exploring possible payoffs to Teamster leaders, he took a call at Pollner's office from John Tartaglia, Pat Simone's attorney.

"Do you know what you're doing?" Guariglia remembered Tartaglia saying.

"Yes."

"Do you know you could get hurt?"

"Yes," Guariglia said.

Guariglia also testified that he did not know if the communication was intended to be a threat on his life, but he speeded up his plans to leave the country if things got really bad.

With pressure mounting, Shannon informed the officers' attorneys that Giuliani was prepared to indict on Monday, January 26, 1987. The lawyers urged a delay of several days, but the federal prosecutors were insistent that the deal be made that weekend or they would go forward with the indictment. On Friday, January 23, the lawyers trooped in to see

Howard Wilson, Giuliani's criminal division chief. They wanted to cut a "global" deal, as Wilson called it, in which they would agree to plead guilty once, on the condition that they would face no further charges from the various state and federal jurisdictions. The attorneys talked in guarded tones, without naming names, but they suggested that the cases would involve three sitting congressmen, as well as various high-ranking current and former federal officials. "How far do you think it could go?" one of the Giuliani team asked.

Neuberger's lawyer, Kal Gallop, a quiet man not given to exaggeration, answered bluntly, "All the way to the White House."

In Wilson's mind, the meeting brought into focus for the first time the dimensions of the Wedtech case. He had been among the skeptics in the office, questioning whether Shannon and her investigators would ever prove large-scale public corruption. But that statement cracked it open for him.

The federal position was clear—a so-called "three, two and one deal." They agreed to accept pleas from Neuberger and Moreno on three counts—two of conspiracy and one of mail fraud—with possible jail terms of up to fifteen years. Guariglia must plead to two conspiracy counts and Shorten to one. They were to report on Monday the twenty-sixth, to begin spelling out their misdeeds and naming names.

In personality and potential value to investigators, the four officers were strikingly different. Neuberger was condescending, suffering from what one prosecutor dubbed "oversmartness." Shorten was a witness whose only concern seemed to be to cast blame on someone else. Guariglia had an accountant's mind that could remember every document, every detail, every dollar. Moreno gave an oral history in so much flowery prose that prosecutors continually had to interrupt him to push for relevant facts.

As the questioning began that Monday, the federal team divided their inquiries into various subjects, based on the proffers made by the cooperators' attorneys and their own knowledge of Wedtech's misdeeds. The Wedtech officials were asked about Biaggi, Borough President Simon, the De-

partment of Defense, Congressman Garcia, and Peter Neglia
of the SBA. Shannon, operating under what she perceived to
be firm instructions from the Justice Department, had warned
the federal team to steer clear of any areas involving the White
House.

At one point, Moreno's attorney, Arthur Christy, said his
client was prepared to offer "information" about Attorney
General Meese and his friend and lawyer, Wallach. The very
mention of Meese's name set off jitters among the Giuliani
team. They understood, from confidential discussions with
their superiors in Washington, that they were to avoid any
allegations of criminality involving the Attorney General,
since any such material would naturally fall under the realm
of an independent counsel.

As a result, for several months no one investigated possible
misconduct by the Attorney General in the Wedtech affair.
Later, when reporters questioned the slow start of a Meese–
Wedtech investigation, the Justice Department denied ever
having issued such instructions to the Giuliani team. Shannon,
in retrospect, would regret not having plunged into early
questioning about Meese's involvement.

Meanwhile, top officials at the Justice Department were
growing increasingly concerned by reports out of Giuliani's
office: The Wedtech case would almost certainly ensnare Wallach. Meese, of course, still had not signed a formal recusal.
On January 29, 1987, three days after the four cooperators
began laying out their litany of crimes, Meese accompanied
Wallach to his installation to the Human Rights Commission
delegation.

It was perhaps Meese's greatest gift to Wallach, affording
him the stature and rank he had sorely wanted. Meese had not
only pushed Wallach for the post but recommended to the
White House that Wallach be approved for higher rank as a
United Nations ambassador, a $70,500-a-year position. Secre-
tary of State George Shultz had approved the rank in November, and President Reagan gave his approval on December 4.
The promotion was never formalized, however, after Wallach's name surfaced as a target of the Wedtech probe.

In early February, Wallach proudly began his six weeks of
service in Geneva, far removed from the all-day debriefings
taking place in Giuliani's office. As he wrapped up his negotiations and prepared to head home, Wallach left a grateful
message to Meese: "I owe it all to you."

While Bob Wallach was in Geneva, the three-judge federal
panel in Washington announced the appointment of an independent counsel in the Lyn Nofziger matter. The court's selection was a prominent Washington trial lawyer, James McKay.
McKay, then sixty-nine, was a respected antitrust lawyer,
known as fair-minded, thorough and a gentleman. He was so
kind-hearted that after he convicted Nofziger, he told reporters how sorry it made him to have done so.

Upon his appointment, McKay said he hoped to complete
his task in three or four months. But events in New York
would slow things down. In a sealed proceeding on January
30, the Wedtech cooperators pleaded guilty before Federal
District Judge Charles E. Stewart. Under the terms of the
agreement, Neuberger, Moreno, and Guariglia pleaded to
one count of conspiracy in connection with various frauds
against the Wedtech Corporation and one count of conspiracy
to bribe public officials. Neuberger and Moreno each also
pleaded to a mail fraud charge. Shorten pleaded to only one
conspiracy count.

Their indictment, as described by Stewart, charged that the
cooperators had "engaged in a conspiracy to give things of
value to federal officials, to influence their official acts and to
induce them to omit to perform certain acts, in violation of
their duty. . . ." They were charged with making false claims
on progress-payment applications in an amount in excess of $5
million, with defrauding the SBA through false representa-
tions about Wedtech's minority ownership, and with conducting a fraud upon the purchasers of Wedtech securities. The
indictment spelled out the existence of the FHJ account and
charged each officer with diverting at least $500,000 from
Wedtech funds. Each count carried a possible five-year prison
term and $250,000 fine.

After entering their pleas, the officers continued laying out

Wedtech's criminal history to federal prosecutors in sessions that stretched on for days—an elaborate soap opera of crime. U.S. Attorney Breckenridge Willcox in Baltimore needed the cooperators for his developing case against the nephews of Parren Mitchell. McKay would need days with the executives to piece together Wedtech's Washington involvement.

In New York, the Giuliani team also divided up its work, delicately treading around areas that could come into conflict with McKay. From the major crimes unit, Harvard Law School graduate Baruch Weiss probed the mounting charges against Wallach. Celia Barenholtz was assigned the Mario Biaggi and SBA angles. Victor Pohorelsky was given the Teamster bribery charges. Shannon continued development of the case against Stanley Simon and opened a probe of Robert Garcia.

Again, the Justice Department was being kept apprised of the developments as investigators moved ever more closely to Meese's doorstep. He himself considered it nothing out of the ordinary when, shortly after 7 P.M. on a February evening, he was routinely notified of the issuance of subpoenas in the case against Congressman Biaggi and two others in the Wedtech matter. The contact did nothing to limit his association with Wallach, whom he spoke to in Geneva a few days later.

In the middle of March, the Wedtech cooperators began telling federal investigators the story of the California Mafia, centering on Wallach and the confidantes he brought in to run the firm. Much of the story involved the little-known financial adviser named Franklyn Chinn, who had touted himself as a money manager for important government officials in Washington, including Edwin Meese III. Once again, the federal probers were startled and disturbed by the Attorney General's Wedtech entanglements.

The cooperators said they had paid large sums of money to Chinn and his friend, Rusty London—amounts that they were told would be split with Wallach under secret arrangements. Although the officers divulged many intimate details of Wedtech's dealings with Wallach—including the payment of fees which they believed were indirectly financing Meese's legal representation—investigators did not learn until weeks later that the Wedtech officials had tried to use Meese, through a payoff to Wallach, to keep out of jail. Giuliani's team did not hear about this until April 1987, and McKay not until late that summer.

The Chinn revelations once again pressed home the conflicts posed by Meese's failure to sign a formal recusal statement. In conversations with Giuliani, Shannon was insistent that Meese should have absolutely nothing to do with the Wedtech investigation and that it must be put in writing before any further information could be channeled to Justice.

Finally, in late March, Giuliani placed a call to Bill Weld in the criminal division at Justice. He told Weld that the Wedtech investigation had uncovered substantial evidence of possible crimes involving Wallach and Chinn, all swirling directly around the Attorney General. He wanted a formal, written recusal from Meese as soon as possible, or all contact with Washington on the Wedtech investigation would cease.

Weld reached out by telephone for Burns and told him that Giuliani had uncovered another Meese link in the case through Chinn and London. The allegations "rocked me and socked me," Burns later told me. It was now imperative that the Attorney General, who had proved he would not do so on his own, be made to see the necessity of removing himself from the probe and distancing himself from his closest friend. Burns' conviction was underscored when the FBI sent an urgent message to Washington to signal another major development in the case—the discovery that Chinn had received possibly fraudulent money from Wedtech at the same time that he was managing Meese's money account.

Weld told Meese that Wallach was in "deep yogurt," a subtle way of warning Meese, but Burns decided to be more direct. On April 8, he went in to meet privately with Meese and in guarded terms warned him that there was a serious problem involving Wallach and Wedtech. "As your friend, I'm advising you to distance yourself from him," Burns remembered telling Meese.

The discussion succeeded in convincing Meese that he should sign a recusal statement that same day, removing himself from the Wedtech investigation. But a few weeks later, on or about May 1, Meese shared information with Burns that almost floored him. Kenneth Cribb, longtime counselor to the Attorney General, was returning to the White House to be Reagan's domestic policy adviser, and Meese had offered the vacated job to Wallach. The offer was still outstanding.

Burns struggled to remain impassive—keep a "poker face," as he later described it—but he realized that none of his warnings had even fazed the Attorney General.

Slowly but surely, Meese's memory of Wedtech began improving as the pressure picked up in the month of April 1987, but there still were inexplicable lapses into forgetfulness. In a press conference on April 6, he finally conceded under increasingly heated questioning that, yes, he had interceded on Wedtech's behalf while serving as counselor to the President: "Deputies in my office did make sure the Wedtech people did get a fair hearing." He also acknowledged getting a "half a dozen" memos from Wallach, his first recollections of the voluminous correspondence.

Around the same time, Meese's press secretary, Terry Eastland, took an upsetting telephone call from Dennis Bell, a new reporter in the Washington bureau of the Long Island-based *Newsday.* Bell had received a tip to look into Meese's relationship with Frank Chinn, who also had some sort of connection to Wedtech. Bell spent several days piecing together details of Meese's "limited blind partnership" with the firm.

Bell called Eastland and, as Eastland recalled, asked, "Terry, does the name Frank Chinn register with you?"

Eastland promised to get back to him, but as he hung up the phone, he thought to himself, Oh, no! He remembered having had a strange gnawing feeling in the pit of his stomach when he first noticed the limited blind partnership during a casual review of Meese's financial disclosures. He had asked an agency ethics officer for an explanation but was told there was no further information about the relationship between Meese and Chinn. With Bell's phone call, Eastland thought to himself, Oh, gosh, here it comes.

Eastland called Bell the next day, and the reporter sensed

a note of resignation in the caller's voice. As Bell said: "It was more or less like, 'You got us!' "

Bell's story ran on April 16 under the headline "Meese Associate Was on Wedtech Board." It began:

> A financial associate of U.S. Attorney General Edwin Meese III sat on the board of directors of Wedtech Corp. . . .
>
> According to documents obtained by Newsday, in May 1985 Meese invested between $50,000 and $100,000 with Financial Management International Inc., a financial consulting firm headed by W. Franklyn Chinn, 44, of San Francisco. Chinn sat on the Wedtech board from August, 1985, until early February of this year. Through a spokesman, Meese said yesterday that he was not aware of Chinn's Wedtech connections. . . .

The story set off a new round of Wedtech inquiries. Reporters from all over the country left for San Francisco to search for details about Chinn. As I prepared for a California trip, I reached out once again to Wallach. He told me he had just returned from Geneva. "I've been trying to say nothing about Wedtech," he said, but assured me the Chinn–Meese connection was "very innocent." Since he had brought Meese and Chinn together, Wallach said, he felt totally responsible for the embarrassment it was causing Meese.

Wallach closed the conversation by suggesting several of his favorite restaurants that I might want to try while I was in San Francisco.

While the news media pursued the Chinn connection, Weld paid another visit to Meese's office, this time in the company of Jeff Jamar, supervisor of the FBI's white-collar-crime section. This time, Weld came not as a helpful subordinate, but to inform the Attorney General that the FBI wanted to interview him about Wallach and Chinn.

Meese agreed to talk with the FBI, and on April 17, two agents arrived to question him. Meese's memory was fuzzy, particularly on job discussions he had had with Wallach. As one agent wrote in his notes, "Meese advised that Wallach was not considered for a position in the Department of Justice, although he and Wallach did talk about taking a position. This discussion occurred in January or February of 1985. No specifics . . ."

Four days later, Meese contacted one of the FBI agents. He wanted to set the record straight. Yes, he had talked with Wallach about several Justice Department jobs. Once, a year earlier, he had asked Wallach to serve on a Justice Department advisory committee, a job Wallach rejected because of other commitments. Then, as the agent wrote in his notes:

"Meese advised that approximately two weeks ago, Wallach was asked to serve as counsel on the personal staff of the Attorney General. . . . Meese did not advise as to whether a decision had yet been made."

23

ALICE
IN WONDERLAND

BILL WELD, one of Boston's toughest federal prosecutors, had come to Washington at Meese's invitation in 1986, vowing to make white-collar crime a top priority of the Justice Department's Criminal Division. Suddenly, in the spring of 1987, he found himself in the difficult position of investigating his own boss. If the Criminal Division found enough evidence of possible wrongdoing, it would forward a request to the court for an independent counsel to continue the probe.

Weld had in front of him the 302—the FBI report of the April 17 interview—as well as continuing communications from Giuliani's office. He was increasingly disturbed by what he saw. To his mind, Meese's involvement with Wallach posed a serious conflict with an executive order, in effect since 1965, which said federal employees must avoid any action which might "result in or create the appearance of using public office for private gain," either for themselves, friends, or family.

Weld also came to a professional conclusion that Meese's conduct could run afoul of the federal gratuity law. The statute provided a two-year term in jail for anyone who "directly or indirectly gives, offers or promises anything of value to any public official for or because of any official act performed or to be performed by such public official." It also forbade public officials to receive anything of value in return for "any official act performed or to be performed by such official."

As he looked at the mounting body of evidence about the symbiotic relationship between Meese and Wallach, Weld was hard-pressed to interpret the long list of favors as simple acts of friendship. It was obvious that Wallach had publicly advertised his friendship as a lure to attract clients; then, as Weld later testified, he had "sent Mr. Meese . . . a fairly steady stream of memoranda recommending action on a wide variety of issues, supplemented by telephone calls, personal meetings." Welbilt and its stalled engine contract were specifically brought to Meese's attention, followed by a series of actions by Meese and his deputies. Meese also was instrumental in helping Wedtech in 1983 with respect to the EDA subordination matter. To Weld, the bottom line was clear: Wallach had earned more than $1.3 million for his services to Wedtech.

In the weeks following the revelations of Meese's relationship with Frank Chinn, Weld came to another conclusion: Meese might not be aware of intimate details of Wallach's financial arrangements with Wedtech, but he knew that Wallach was "making money off his performance for the Wedtech company, and his performance consisted, in large measure, of official acts that Mr. Meese was doing for him."

By early May, Weld and Burns had reached the conclusion, on the basis of evidence before them, that the Justice Department must turn over the allegations against Meese to Independent Counsel McKay for further investigation. McKay's office, already knee-deep in Wedtech, could simply expand its probe to include Meese.

McKay was already under pressure from Senate Judiciary Committee Chairman Joseph Biden and House Judiciary Committee Chairman Peter Rodino to undertake a Meese inquiry as an outgrowth of his Nofziger investigation. In a joint letter sent on April 29, the two Democratic chairmen noted Meese's assistance to Wedtech, his investments with a company known to have Wedtech ties, and his failure to recuse himself "from two criminal investigations of Wedtech" being conducted in New York and Maryland. McKay had written the congressmen on May 5 that he would assume the job if asked to by the Justice Department.

On May 10, Burns, Weld, and Charles J. "Chuck" Cooper, head of the Justice Department's Office of Legal Counsel, informed Meese, as a courtesy, of the imminent referral to McKay. Meese was incredulous. Convinced that there was nothing improper in his relationship with Wallach, he could not believe his subordinates would put such stock in totally specious charges coming from admitted felons in New York. Burns, however, could not erase the memory of Meese dropping the bombshell that Wallach was still under consideration for the counselor's job. As Burns later described the atmosphere of those days, "It was a world of Alice in Wonderland. . . . A world in which up was down and down was up . . . rain was sunshine and sunshine was rain. . . ."

Months later, Meese would criticize Burns and Weld for thoroughly bungling the preliminary investigation of his conduct. But, like Weld, Burns had also reached the inevitable conclusion that Meese's relationship with Wallach crossed the bounds of the law. "Mr. Wallach was benefitting to the tune of over a million dollars from his relationship with the Attorney General . . ." he told the Senate. "He was actually out marketing that relationship." The notion that he and Weld, as an act of loyalty to Meese, should sweep the allegations under the carpet was unthinkable.

The next morning, May 11, with a deep sense of regret, Burns forwarded the official notification to McKay requesting that he take over the Meese probe. The letter spelled out McKay's mandate, which was to determine whether federal conflict of interest statutes or any other provision of federal law were violated by Meese's dealings with Wedtech from 1981 to the present. It also asked him to examine possible criminality in Meese's dealings with Lyn Nofziger, E. Robert Wallach, W. Franklyn Chinn, and Financial Management International Inc. He wrote:

> In fairness to Mr. Meese, I should state that the reports we have received concerning Mr. Meese's relationships with Wedtech-associated individuals and entities are only fragmentary and do not show that Mr. Meese ever received any compensation from Welbilt/Wedtech, nor that he ever invested in the securities of Welbilt/Wedtech.

By that time, Meese had retained the excellent Washington law firm of Miller, Cassidy, Larroca & Lewin to represent him in the criminal inquiries. His principal lawyers, Nathan Lewin and James E. Rocap, represented Meese with aggressive tactics and brilliant damage control. On the same morning that Burns sent McKay the referral letter, Meese's lawyers forwarded another letter to McKay in which the Attorney General asked him to undertake an independent investigation of his conduct in the Wedtech matter. The move allowed Meese, whose hand had been forced, to take credit for initiating the probe.

By the spring of 1987, the reverberations of the Wedtech scandal were being felt up and down the East Coast. In Baltimore on April 2, a federal grand jury indicted Clarence and Michael Mitchell. In New York, the city's political structure was shaken to its roots. The first to fall was Stanley Simon, indicted on tax-evasion and extortion charges in the Wedtech case. Giuliani, convinced that Simon presented the simplest case for prosecution, had served up the indictment early to ease the public clamor while his assistants worked toward development of a larger racketeering case.

Simon began an uninspired resignation by inserting his foot

in his mouth, an old Simon tradition. Intending to profess his innocence, Simon proclaimed, "I am guilty," then quickly stammered and backpedaled.

Throughout the spring, press reports signaled the imminent indictment of Biaggi, and it was believed for some time that Garcia would be included in the original racketeering case. But prosecutors ran into major delays developing the Garcia angle, so he was not indicted until November 1988.

There was debate about the scope and dimension of the Wedtech racketeering indictment. The case was to be built around a central theory—that Wedtech had been turned into a vehicle for the payment of bribes to public officials. It would focus on the phony stock transfer—used by Wedtech as a means to hang on to its 8(a) status—and detail a series of extortions and bribes. Originally, Giuliani and Bronx DA Merola contemplated naming as many as fifteen public officials, ranging from low-level agency bureaucrats to important congressmen, but as the indictment drew closer, prosecutors decided they must keep the case to a manageable dimension. In racketeering cases, prosecutors must prove that all defendants were involved in the same basic conspiratorial setting, and with a large and diverse cast of defendants, that becomes extremely difficult. The prosecution could lose the jury with too many interconnecting paper trails.

Eventually they decided to limit the case to Biaggi and others considered central to the Wedtech fraud: Simon, Ehrlich, Richard Biaggi, Peter Neglia, and Mariotta—the only major Wedtech official who had failed to cut a deal with the prosecutors. Mariotta clung to his view of himself as an innocent victim of the scandal.

Many others were listed as unindicted coconspirators in a letter drawn up by prosecutors and presented to the judge. Among the latter was Arthur Siskind, who had crafted the paperwork for the stock transfer. Siskind contended he had no prior knowledge of the fraudulent intent of the deal.

The trial team was to be led by Howard Wilson, Giuliani's Criminal Division chief, backed up by Shannon and Ed Little, a respected assistant with extensive experience in racketeering prosecution.

On June 3, a fifty-eight-count indictment was handed up, charging bribery, payoffs of money and stock, tax fraud, perjury, and the illegal spending of at least $5.5 million in Wedtech funds. Giuliani told a crowded press conference, "It's fair to say that this does not in any way end the investigation of the matters arising out of Wedtech." He noted that the defendants faced up to forty years in prison and fines up to $8.9 million.

In July, McKay indicted Nofziger for illegal lobbying in violation of the Ethics in Government Act, making him the first former administration official to be charged under the law. (Later that year Nofziger's friend, Mike Deaver, would be convicted in connection with his activities as a private lobbyist, but Deaver was charged with perjury rather than with a violation of the ethics law.) Nofziger's indictment cited specific infractions in his lobbying on behalf of three clients—Wedtech, Fairchild Industries, and the Marine Engineers Beneficial Association—all within a year of leaving the White House. The Wedtech count involved Nofziger's lobbying of Meese and Jenkins in an effort to speed up the award of the Army engine contract.

The linchpin of the ethics law was that McKay must prove that the matters on which Nofziger lobbied were of "direct and substantial" interest to the White House, and Nofziger's attorneys argued that it was laughable to think the White House was devoting major energy to the Wedtech matter. Nofziger himself made it clear he considered himself innocent of the charges and would fight the indictment to the end.

Nofziger's business partner, Mark Bragg, was charged with one count of aiding and abetting Nofziger's illegal lobbying. The case against Bragg was so weak and fraught with problems that he was eventually acquitted. Meese, who was not charged in the case, was later criticized by the Justice Department for allowing Nofziger to lobby his office.

It was obvious by the fall of 1987—when Meese was again called before a grand jury—that most of the criminal cases arising out of the Wedtech matter would not name Meese but instead would attempt to portray him as a knowing participant in the schemes.

That fact became even more obvious in December 1987 when Giuliani announced an eighteen-count indictment of Wallach, Chinn, and London on racketeering, fraud, and conspiracy charges. It charged that Wallach "sought to influence Edwin Meese and other government officials on behalf of Wedtech, primarily in connection with Wedtech's efforts to obtain government contracts." It also mentioned Wallach's efforts to secure from Wedtech prepayment for legal services at a time when he anticipated employment at the Justice Department.

Giuliani refused to discuss Meese's entanglement in the case. Meese, through his lawyers, predicted he would be cleared in the investigation of his own conduct then under way.

Jim McKay's probe, which started with a narrow focus of Meese's involvement with Wedtech, expanded in all directions as he began to unravel the complex, intertwined business and personal relationships of the Attorney General and Wallach. He could scarcely conclude one area of inquiry before another strong suggestion of impropriety surfaced in the press or at the Justice Department, which was forwarding any findings related to Meese from the Giuliani probe to McKay.

McKay began by pursuing the question of whether Meese had received a gratuity in return for his official acts on Wedtech's behalf. An exhaustive review of Meese's financial records from 1981 to 1986 revealed that his account with Frank Chinn earned $30,943 from an original investment of $54,581—a 56.6 percent return.

The probe met immediate obstacles, particularly in the tight-lipped silence of Wallach, Chinn, and London, who invoked their Fifth Amendment rights. Wallach offered limited unsworn testimony but refused to answer any questions about Wedtech or his personal financial affairs.

The Chinn angle opened a can of worms—shady investment practices in locations halfway around the globe. Investigators discovered that Chinn maintained a so-called Meese account in Hong Kong, which he used for the purpose of trading in the gold market, plus some mysterious offshore bank accounts. Investigators flew to the West Coast in November with a search warrant for Chinn's San Francisco offices, while a simultaneous search was under way in Hong Kong.

In July 1987, McKay's office uncovered still another matter requiring inquiry—Wallach and Meese's involvement with the Aqaba pipeline. The questions heightened when McKay discovered that Wallach made $150,000 from the deal, which was wired directly to Frank Chinn. A check with the IRS revealed that Wallach had not reported the payment as income. He did not do so until he was asked to produce his financial records for review.

The pipeline inquiry encountered other roadblocks, including the Top Secret classification that the Justice Department had attached to Wallach's memos to Meese. It took an action of a White House interagency panel to declassify the relevant documents. McKay was dealt another major blow in mid-March 1988 when Rappaport withdrew from a cooperation agreement and declined to testify about his dealings with Wallach.

There was also the matter of the telephone stock. In their routine review of Meese's financial disclosures, the Justice Department's ethics officials uncovered evidence that Meese failed to divest himself of seventeen shares of stock in each of seven regional Bell Telephone companies, as he had told the Senate he would do immediately after becoming Attorney General. This was significant because the Justice Department, under the terms of a court settlement in the AT&T antitrust suit, maintained considerable sway in the operations of the seven companies.

Furthermore, the department concluded that Meese had participated in Justice Department decisions related to the regional companies while still technically holding their stock. He had met with agency antitrust officials to discuss the regional companies and had communicated with other government agencies regarding the firms. He also had communicated directly with officials of the regional Bell firms and other telecommunications officials. Moreover, his friend Wallach had twice given him written advice on telecommunications matters during the period when Wallach was associated with the Dickstein, Shapiro firm, which was retained by the seven regional phone companies. McKay set out to determine if Meese had violated conflict-of-interest statutes.

In mid-February, McKay learned of Wallach's involvement in Ursula Meese's job hunt. He began calling grand jury witnesses to determine whether there was a link between the renewal of the Justice Department lease and the Benders' financing of Mrs. Meese's $40,000-a-year job. His probe was again hampered by Wallach's refusal to testify.

As the investigation swerved in all directions, McKay tried to accommodate the concerns of Meese's crack legal team, which argued that the independent counsel should quickly put to rest each charge against the Attorney General that proved to be unfounded. In an extraordinary attempt to be fair, McKay bowed to those wishes on several occasions. His conduct would raise eyebrows among experienced criminal prosecutors.

While his grand jury was still sitting, McKay issued several public status reports on his investigation—a practice virtually unheard of in criminal prosecutions. In January 1988, he took another highly unusual step. The courtly prosecutor paid a courtesy visit to the White House to brief Chief of Staff Howard Baker and White House Counsel A. B. Culvahouse on his probe into the Iraqi pipeline matter. But President Reagan made it clear he had no intention of throwing his trusted adviser to the lions.

As McKay's investigation dragged on, graffiti began springing up on the streets of Washington, on street corner lightposts and bridge overpasses: "Meese Is a Pig." The slogan caught on so quickly that entrepreneurs slapped it onto $12 T-shirts that became a hot fashion item in the nation's capital. At the Justice building itself, signs were even more direct: "Resign," "Sleazy." Security guards set out to find the perpetrators, but to no avail.

Arnold Burns was disturbed by reports filtering back to his office of Justice Department workers being upbraided on the streets about their association with Meese's agency. Department morale was sinking with each new development in the McKay investigation. His own was not much better.

The long-running probe caught him "between a rock and a hard place," he later told the Senate Judiciary Committee. He was disturbed by the Iraqi pipeline development and by Meese's failure to shed the regional telephone stock. Furthermore, Burns believed the department's functioning was seriously hampered by the problems at the top. Meese, because of his own legal problems, increasingly had to recuse himself from important Justice Department cases.

What bothered Burns the most, however, was Meese's total oblivion to ethical considerations in his relationship with Wallach: "Mr. Meese continued to support Mr. Wallach and to defend Mr. Wallach in the press, in testimony before the Congress, and in public. This continued after Mr. Wallach was indicted by Mr. Meese's Department of Justice."

Weld made a blunter assessment, based on his years of prosecutorial experience. He concluded, as he explained to the Senate, that the situation "constituted the use of Mr. Meese's public office for the private gain of Mr. Wallach." On his review of the facts, he said, he would indict Meese.

Separately and then as a team, Burns and Weld decided that they could no longer continue to work for Meese. They presented their letters of resignation to Meese together on the morning of March 29, 1988.

They went into Meese's office just before the regular morning staff meeting. Startled by the displeasure of his two aides, Meese once again steadfastly professed his innocence. But Weld gave a frank analysis of the legal infractions posed by his relationship with Wallach in the Wedtech and Iraqi pipeline matters. "Ed, I don't gainsay that there are other reasons why you might have wanted to push these two projects—redeem the campaign pledge in the South Bronx, save our cities, peace in the Middle East—that is not the question, though."

The question, he later told the Senate Judiciary Committee, was whether Meese took official actions that he knew would redound to the financial benefit of his friend. Moreover, the favors went both ways. Wallach represented Meese for free before the Senate and forgave $65,000 in legal fees for the Stein investigation. Wallach introduced the Meeses to a financial adviser who could make a 20 percent profit for them. Weld also pointed out to Meese, he said, the problems with Wallach's solicitation from the Benders. One mention of Ursula Meese's need for a job, and Wallach is "all over this family in the real estate business . . . trying to get them to support this job for Mrs. Meese."

Weld listened to Meese's explanation—that his help for Wallach was simply based on longtime friendship—but in his mind it didn't wash. "My conclusion was, there were simply too many official acts performed by Mr. Meese for Mr. Wallach and too many financial benefits conferred by Mr. Wallach on Mr. Meese."

The resignations of the two top officials sent tremors through the Justice Department. They were followed immediately by the resignations of Burns' top aides, Randy Levine and Boykin Rose, and Weld's aides, Mark Robinson and Jane Serene.

In mid-April, Burns and Weld, who had been in touch with Howard Baker while they were making their decisions, were summoned to the White House to explain to Reagan and Bush the reasons for their resignations. Baker and Culvahouse sat in on the forty-minute meeting, a grim airing of unpleasant facts that had all the impact of smoke blowing into a blustery wind.

Weld laid out what was later described as a "hypothetical indictment" of Meese. "Here are the facts," he later recalled saying. "I think it's afoul of Executive Order 11222, and I think it's over the line of the gratuity statute."

The President seemed to him distressed by what occurred, and likewise the Vice President was "very florid and upset." Bush turned to Burns and asked for a report on morale in the department and whether other resignations were likely to follow. The news was not encouraging. Burns etched a picture of a department badly demoralized.

As the meeting drew to a close, Burns and Weld believed they had told the President, in the frankest terms they could muster, about the problems posed by Meese's criminal investigation. But a few days later, Reagan—hounded by reporters

on his way into the White House—finally made his first remarks on this meeting.

"Should Meese resign?" a reporter asked.

"No," shouted the President.

"Has he offered to?"

"No."

Reagan was then asked how he thought the Justice Department was functioning.

"Just fine," came the reply.

24

"MEESE IS A SLEAZE"

JIM MCKAY RESPONDED to the furor of the Burns and Weld resignations by issuing a press release on April 1, essentially clearing Ed Meese of criminal charges in the pipeline and so-called Baby Bell matters. His investigation had not been completed at the time. In fact, his staff was still taking depositions. But McKay was alarmed by the rising clamor for Meese's resignation, which had turned into an incessant drumbeat on Capitol Hill. Bill Weld might have seen reason to indict Meese on violations of federal gratuity laws—a conviction so strong he aired it to the President. McKay clearly did not.

Meese reacted to the heightened pressure with bungling and bravado. He conducted a hurried job search and announced his replacements for top department jobs before concluding standard FBI background checks. His choice for Burns slot was a prominent St. Louis lawyer named John Shepherd, but Shepherd hurriedly withdrew his name after a television station in St. Louis aired allegations of sexual misconduct.

Meese abruptly fired Terry Eastland, his chief spokesman and a popular figure, for not defending him aggressively enough. Meese was especially angered by a report that he had used the Attorney General's stationery to send out 30,000 invitations to a conference in Japan sponsored by a profit-making group which had recently picked up Ursula Meese's expenses for a trip to China. Meese replaced Eastland with a more agreeable mouthpiece, Patrick Korten, the unrelenting office bulldog.

As the turbulent spring ended, the Attorney General was widely cast as the enduring embarrassment of the Reagan administration. His caricature in a variety of compromising situations had become a favorite subject for editorial cartoonists. But Meese seemed determined to stay on. He told Capitol Hill conservatives that a resignation would be an admission of guilt. Reagan backed him, calling the allegations empty charges.

Meese banked all his hopes for vindication on the stalled release of the McKay report, despite early indications that the document would be highly critical. For Meese and his allies, the bottom line was that Meese would not be indicted. It seemed to escape their notice that, in a crowded New York courtroom, Meese was already on trial.

When the Wedtech racketeering trial began in March 1988, Meese's presence so pervaded the courtroom of U.S. District Court Judge Constance Baker Motley that he could have been sitting at the defense table alongside the seven indictees. By then, McKay had already won the later-overturned conviction against Nofziger on illegal lobbying charges. Meese, called as a witness in the case, demonstrated such a clouded memory on the stand that he had to invent a dozen or so ways to phrase his stock response, "I don't recall." The defiant Nofziger compared his conviction—and subsequent ninety-day jail sentence—to punishment for an offense akin to "running a stop sign."

The defendants charged in the voluminous racketeering indictment in New York, topped by Bronx political heavyweight Biaggi, opened their case with a united strategy. In order to prove they were of little real value to the company, they would point the finger at the real powers behind Wedtech. They would use what came to be known as the Meese defense—homing in on his extraordinary involvement with the South Bronx defense firm and the huge payments funneled to Wallach. Their plan would challenge the Giuliani team's ability to keep the cumbersome case narrowly focused—a difficult proposition since the New York prosecutors had concluded that Meese's involvement with Wedtech was indeed an indictable offense.

Criminal chief Howard Wilson kicked off the case by tracing Wedtech's history of favors, its meteoric rise, and the important and interconnecting roles played by the seven men on trial—Biaggi, his son Richard, John Mariotta, Bernie Ehrlich, Stanley Simon, Peter Neglia, and his alleged bagman, Ron Betso. He began with a simple statement of facts:

> This is a case about corruption and greed and the sale of public office. It's a case about public officials who used their office to help themselves. It's a case about public officials who want to get paid twice: once by the government, the people who pay them to do their job, and once by someone else. . . .
>
> This case involves the rise of a little company in the Bronx, Wedtech. It was a very small company in the South Bronx. It was started in 1965 by John Mariotta, who is the defendant there. By 1978, before Wedtech had met any of the people that are on trial here, it was still a small company. It had grown. It had 50 employees, about a million and a half dollars worth of sales each year.
>
> Seven years later, this . . . was a large public company. . . . Ninety percent of its business came from the government. It had a thousand employees. . . . It had $117 million worth of revenues, . . . and was the biggest single employer in the Bronx.

The company symbolized the success story of a government program that was designed to help minorities. . . . But this case tells a tragic story, because that great success was achieved through corruption, through lies, paying off public officials, the key executives of the company stealing, stealing from the company.

The public officials that are on trial here . . . all treated this company as a gold mine, each was going to take some gold. Some took a lot of gold, some took a little. But they all took.

Biaggi's attorney, James LaRossa, approached the case with a totally different point of view. LaRossa had often been the lawyer of choice among machine politicians in trouble, and over the years, had counted among his clients Brooklyn union bosses and even mob bosses. LaRossa had an aggressive, sometimes surly courtroom manner that often bordered on intimidation. Questioning a witness in a deep, gravelly voice, he would lean on the lectern, his lips protruding and jaw bulging as he glared at the witness over wire-framed spectacles and bushy eyebrows.

LaRossa began his opening argument by telling the jury he would present "the truth as to what happened to this company called Wedtech in the Bronx. . . . You are going to hear about four dishonest people who met a group of individuals who began to run this country."

He went on:

I am going to talk to you about the President's chief of staff at the time, Ed Meese, now the Attorney General of the United States; Jim Jenkins, former counsel to the President; Nofziger, the assistant to the President; Wallach, a lawyer from San Francisco who worked for Ed Meese, who assisted Ed Meese and who was, in Ed Meese's words, his best friend.

I am going to tell you about how this company, Wedtech corrupted an entire administration. . . . Ronald Reagan . . . the President while Mario Biaggi was a Democratic congressman from the Bronx without the power to award any of these contracts. That is what this case is to be about in its broadest brush.

We are going to show you how these four people—Mario
Moreno, Fred Neuberger, Anthony Guariglia and Larry
Shorten—lied, stole, plundered and raped this country, stole
from you and I, American citizens, stole from the shareholders
who were suckered into buying the stock; stole, lied and
cheated every government agency they operated with, and in
addition to all of those things, stole from each other. . . .

In 1982 or late 1981, they meet a lawyer, a lawyer from San
Francisco, whose name is e. robert wallach. . . . Who is e.
robert wallach? e. robert wallach is a California lawyer. . . .

One, Lyn Nofziger becomes a representative of Wedtech.
Who is Lyn Nofziger, you say? He was the political adviser and
counsel to the President. Two, Jim Jenkins becomes a spokesman for Wedtech. Who is he? Same thing, right out of the
White House. A man by the name of Mark Bragg becomes a
spokesman. And two other people, a financial adviser by the
name of Franklyn Chinn and a man by the name of London.
Who are they? Close to Wallach. They run Ed Meese's blind
trust account. . . .

You will find that through this group the Secretary of the
Navy, John Lehman, was put at the table, the acting secretary
. . . Everett Pyatt, was put at the table, the head of the Small
Business Administration for the entire United States, whose
name was Sanders, was put at the table; and that Ed Meese,
the then chief of staff for the President [sic], the man who
ran the domestic policies of the United States, through his
people, said, "The President wants these contracts to go to
Wedtech." . . .

As he thundered to a conclusion, LaRossa went on to mention the officers' belief that they could pay Wallach to fix the
investigation—an effort, he said, to buy the Attorney General
of the United States.

Over the next five and a half months, LaRossa and the other
defense lawyers—Dominic Amorosa for Richard Biaggi,
Peter Driscoll for Ehrlich, Maurice Nessen for Simon, Kevin
McGovern for Neglia, and Alan Kaufman for Betso—set out
to prove the California Mafia's control of Wedtech's corrupt
affairs. Their clients were faced with mounds of documentary
evidence backed by the devastating accusations of the four

cooperators, Moreno, Guariglia, Neuberger, and Shorten, whose testimony was carefully corroborated by a stream of accountants, lawyers, and other less culpable Wedtech officers called by the prosecution.

But in cross-examinations, the defense lawyers hammered away at the Meese connection. They fought for—and lost—the right to call Meese himself as a defense witness, along with Jenkins and Terry Good, a White House documents custodian. Wilson protested, telling Motley the request by Amorosa was "in reality an attempt to cause a mini-trial on the issue of the guilt of the Attorney General of the United States of various Wedtech-related crimes."

Nevertheless, the defense lawyers thrust Meese into the picture as often as they could, eliciting testimony about his involvement in the Army engine deal and Wedtech's belief that he was also responsible for the crucial Navy contract, about using Meese to fix the Wedtech case, about his phone call to Malcolm Baldrige, about his introductions to the Wedtech officers and Mrs. Meese's warm, familial greetings.

Giuliani's team realized to its dismay that the unrelenting Meese defense was swaying the jury. Ed Little complained repeatedly to Motley about the tactic, arguing that the defense was trying to impugn the integrity of the federal prosecution of the Democratic congressman Biaggi. In the minds of the jury, Meese was the prosecution's "boss."

As the long trial drew to a close, the prosecutors were confident they had made their case against the defendants, but the Meese defense still posed a threat to the case because of the defense efforts to portray prosecutors as "minions" of an unscrupulous Attorney General.

Little prepared his summation with care, wading through the voluminous trial record and the stacks of evidence. He wanted to choose his words precisely, so as to not understate the seriousness of Meese's Wedtech involvement and yet to detach the present trial from the Attorney General's lack of ethics.

On a Sunday afternoon, Little went to talk with Giuliani about his dilemma: He intended to make the candid argument that, while Meese's hands might be dirtied by Wedtech, that did not excuse the corrupt intent and workings of Biaggi and the other men on trial.

Little wanted to use a specific and carefully chosen word in describing Meese—the term "sleaze." To Little, the word was a step removed from "crook" and did not necessarily imply criminality. But it certainly conveyed the slipshod ethics and judgmental errors he believed were demonstrated by the record of the trial.

Giuliani pondered the term for a moment, then looked up at Little and nodded. "Go right ahead," Little remembered him saying.

Little began his summation at 9 A.M. on July 20, a painstaking regurgitation of five months' worth of facts that would take two days to complete. He plodded through the stock agreement, the political contributions, the congressional letters and hotel and expense bills. Off and on, he brushed by the White House connection, hardly dismissing it, but suggesting it was only a piece of a broader conspiracy grounded in the actions of the seven defendants. After concluding the first day's remarks by calling Biaggi "a thug in a congressman's suit," Little waited until almost the end of the second day to address the Meese defense. When he did, reporters on the front row of the packed courtroom began scribbling furiously, confident of the next day's headlines. As Little said:

> There is only one way out for Congressman Biaggi and his son, Richard Biaggi, and this is a defense which his lawyers have pounded away with from the very beginning of this case. They opened up on this. Mr. LaRossa told you that he is going to tell you about Ed Meese. He was going to tell you about Ronald Reagan and the White House . . . the Wallach case, the Jenkins case, the Nofziger case, the Meese case. All this other detail which is fundamentally irrelevant to this case.
>
> These people aren't being tried for what Meese did or Jenkins did or Nofziger did or any other of those people. This is a distraction. . . .
>
> Because what's the defense here? You are going to hear this one, and it's very clear. "The Wedtech officers would not have bought Congressman Biaggi. . . . They already bought Ed Meese." Well, this is ridiculous. . . .

There are two short answers to this Meese defense: First is, Meese was a sleaze. The second is, Meese was a sleaze, too. Also. In addition to these people. Because what these people did well was to sell influence in New York City and to sell influence in Congress. . . . And what Jenkins did and what Wallach did and what they did together. . . . But whatever they did with Meese was wrong, but that was done separately in the Executive branch. . . .

When reports of Little's remarks filtered out to the Justice Department in Washington, Korten, the new press spokesman, said the department would take appropriate action. Little's name was promptly forwarded to the department's Public Integrity Section for possible disciplinary action, but the office said it saw no basis for it.

In a press conference on other matters, Meese was asked about the remark and said it was his understanding Little's remark was unauthorized by Giuliani. But Giuliani leaped to Little's defense. Later that day, Giuliani said by telephone that Meese's comments were "highly unfair to Little. [Little's] remarks were fully supported by the record in the case. . . ."

Meese stole some of the thunder of Little's remarks by suddenly announcing on July 5, before a televised Sacramento press conference, that he was resigning from office sometime the next month. The announcement came thirty minutes after Meese placed an afternoon phone call to Reagan to tell him the news. Meese proudly proclaimed himself "vindicated" by the McKay report, not yet publicly released. "I am confident that when the public is able to hear both sides of the story . . . it will be clear to all that I have acted lawfully and properly."

Reagan lauded Meese as a "darned good Attorney General," and his spokesman, Marlin Fitzwater, told the press the next day that Reagan believed Meese's service as Attorney General "has distinguished the office and himself." Others in the White House breathed a quiet sigh of relief. Reports indicated a deep underground effort within the Cabinet to pressure Meese's resignation, principally because of fears that his tarnished image would rub off on the upcoming George Bush campaign. Bush, who had ducked public comment on the Meese issue, responded to his resignation by delicately distancing himself from the Attorney General: "Ed did the right thing, and I wish him well."

The public release of the sealed McKay report was anti-climactic but again underscored McKay's dubious prosecutorial mettle. The thick report from the long investigation was a staggering chronicle of the favors, gifts, and gratuities exchanged between the Attorney General and his best friend. McKay conceded that his investigation was, in some cases, incomplete because of a lack of critical testimony. But he said he found no evidence to prosecute Meese for violations of federal gratuities laws. Unlike Weld, who saw friendship as no excuse for crossing ethical restraints imposed by the law, McKay portrayed the actions of Meese and Wallach as the excusable give-and-take of longtime bosom buddies.

McKay conceded that Meese had probably committed two felonies and a misdemeanor by willfully filing a false income tax return, failing to pay his taxes on time, and violating a criminal conflict-of-interest law in connection with his holdings of the telephone stocks. But he still declined to prosecute the charges, because "there is no evidence that Mr. Meese [violated the law] from motivation for personal gain. . . ."

In some circles, McKay's exhaustive report raised many questions. Had Meese, simply because of his prominence, benefited from a lower standard of justice than that applied to private citizens? The tax matter, uncovered through a review of Meese's personal finances, involved his failure in 1985 to declare capital gains from securities sold by Franklyn Chinn. Meese failed to give his accountant John McKean the necessary documentation to calculate the tax, so the two of them decided to file the return with no mention of the securities sales. They said their intention was simply to file an amended return later. But the return was not amended until February 1988, while Meese was under investigation.

In the Baby Bell matter, McKay found that Meese had, in fact, held legal title to regional telephone company stock while participating in Justice Department discussions relative to the seven companies. At one point, Meese endorsed the department's position, urging that the companies be allowed to branch into new areas of business. But McKay chose to accept Meese's explanation that he mistakenly thought he had turned over legal title of the stocks to Chinn.

In a series of press conferences on the day of the report's release, Meese and his skilled lawyers with great indignation lambasted McKay for the unfairness of labeling Meese a probable felon. Meese pinned the blame on the "gang of crooks" in New York who had filled prosecutors' ears with groundless accusations about his role in the Wedtech debacle.

The gentlemanly McKay was caught between Meese's outrage and the hostile questioning of the press, which grilled him repeatedly on his decision not to prosecute. McKay said he had decided that the average citizen would not be prosecuted for similar charges.

In a final act of housecleaning, McKay sent over a copy of his report to the Justice Department's Office of Professional Responsibility for further scrutiny of ethics issues.

Meanwhile, in New York, the testimony of the "gang of crooks" that once counted Meese as their chief ally successfully convicted six of the seven defendants in the Wedtech racketeering trial. The little-known Ronald Betso was acquitted on all charges.

Hardly anyone noticed in early 1989—long after George Bush's resounding presidential victory and Meese's departure—when the Justice Department's Office of Professional Responsibility finally released its thin report on Meese's conduct.

The Justice Department, then under former Pennsylvania Gov. Dick Thornburgh, found that its former leader had engaged in a pattern of questionable ethics, circumvented numerous White House and departmental policies, and should have been severely disciplined by President Reagan for his entanglement in the Wedtech affair.

THE CAGED BEAST

WHEN THE TIME CAME for Mario Moreno to go to prison, he approached it as he had every other challenge in his life— with studiousness and contemplation. He read voraciously anything he could find on the federal prison system, determined to proceed intelligently. Soon, he was the instant expert, able to pontificate at length on nuances of prison regulations. It was the sort of natural curiosity that had served Moreno well in his early career on Wall Street and later at Wedtech, where he could authoritatively deal with engine parts, pontoon production, government loans and contracts while simultaneously wining and dining Arab princes and reputed Bronx mobsters.

But in his unending quest for superficial knowledge, sometimes Moreno's judgment suffered from a glaring lack of common sense—a fatal flaw that seemed contagious in the upper ranks of Wedtech management. He had read somewhere that he would be allowed five books in his cell. Deadly serious, he began compiling his master list—five carefully chosen works of literature that would see him through weeks of solitude. It was months before it dawned on him that, although he could have only five books in his cell at one time, the volumes could be regularly exchanged at the prison library for new ones.

By the spring of 1989, Moreno had spent more than a year traipsing across the country from one federal courthouse to another telling his tale of corporate gluttony and the voracious greed of public officials. Though his own honesty and integrity had been attacked from every conceivable angle, he had delivered to the government one solid victory after another in the courts. More than any of his fellow cooperators, he had convinced juries of the criminal intent of the Mitchells, Nofziger, Biaggi, the Teamster leaders, and the others. Now, from a holding tank in the Metropolitan Correctional Center, he waited to go on the stand again to testify against Meese's friends, Wallach, Chinn, and London, who would all be convicted eventually on federal charges. Moreno also was biding time until his own date with destiny—his sentencing and ultimate moment of shame before Judge Charles Stewart.

His friends now were the federal prosecutors, who spent days upon end picking his brain for details. They had developed not only a genuine affection for Moreno but also a certain admiration, since, in his penitence, he had never once tried to mislead them or understate his own criminal involvement. Steve Cossu, his reputation enhanced by his fine performance in the Wedtech case, had been promoted to special agent in charge of the active New York labor racketeering office, while his Defense Department counterpart, Mike Raggi, had moved on to a big promotion in Syracuse. Donna Merris, the soft-spoken paralegal, had passed the bar and was named a special assistant U.S. attorney to help try Robert Garcia, who also was convicted, along with his wife, Jane Lee.

Two of Moreno's favorites, red-haired, spirited Mary Shannon and her trial partner, Ed Little, had fallen in love during the long, unromantic evenings preparing the Wedtech rack-

eteering case. They were married on the first anniversary of
the opening of the Biaggi trial.

The cane-carrying Biaggi had been carted off to federal
prison in Fort Worth, Texas, to begin serving time on his first
federal conviction, his appeal still pending on an eight-year
prison sentence imposed in the Wedtech case. Biaggi had
wept in Judge Motley's courtroom, begging for mercy for his
convicted son, Richard, and sobbing that he had "died a little
bit every day" since his conviction and his August 5, 1988,
resignation from the House. "I have served some 50 years in
public life, serving people . . . happily. I fed off them. They
nourished me. They nurtured me. They inspired me. I loved
to be loved, and I loved to love them," he tearfully described
to Motley. With his prison sentence, he joined an exclusive
club of fourteen congressmen who had served prison terms
since 1949.

When the time came for him to surrender, Biaggi appealed
for more time so he could be by the bedside of his sick wife,
the loyal woman whom he had publicly humiliated by carous-
ing in Florida with his shapely, redheaded mistress. Not so
well publicized was the fact that Marie Biaggi had filed for a
legal separation only weeks before.

Mariotta, until the end proclaiming his innocence, began
serving time at Allenwood, where he struck up a fast friendship with his partner in scandal, Stanley Simon. The two would
often be seen strolling the prison grounds together, remem-
bering, no doubt, better days gone by. Simon spent his free
time offering legal help to inmates, Mariotta polishing his
English for the day he would once again mesmerize heads of
state.

Lyn Nofziger, after disdainfully calling his ethics conviction
the equivalent of a traffic violation, succeeded nearly a year
and a half later in having his conviction overturned by a U.S.
Court of Appeals panel. The two Reagan administration appointees on the panel found a problem with the language of
the 1978 ethics law. In their long opinion, the judges claimed
the law was flawed in its careless use of the term "knowingly."
The dissenter on the panel, a Carter appointee, said his colleagues "labored mightily to find an ambiguity" in the law

which did not exist. McKay appealed the decision to the Supreme Court, but Nofziger prevailed. At the Bush White House, the President, Secretary of State Jim Baker, and Chief of Staff John Sununu praised the appeals rulings—which, in effect, struck down the first test of a government lobbying ban.

Ed Meese rebounded better than any of them from the ugly specter of Wedtech. While his friend Wallach fought off prosecutors in New York, Meese was lecturing friendly conservative audiences at the right-wing think tank, The Heritage Foundation. In many quarters, however, Meese's name would be etched in history as a synonym for "sleaze."

In Congress in 1989, the wounded Republican Party responded with a string of righteous attacks on prominent Democrats, arguing that Meese was not the only one to engage in questionable ethical conduct. The Democratic Speaker of the House, Jim Wright, resigned in disgrace after charges were leveled against him before a new get-tough House Ethics Committee. House Democratic Whip Tony Coelho quit, too, after reports surfaced about his involvement in questionable junk bond deals.

The reform movement even swept once again through the SBA. Severely chastised by Sen. Carl Levin's oversight subcommittee for allowing Wedtech to rape and pillage the 8(a) program, Congress went through its third attempt in a decade to tighten program rules, passing the Minority Business Development Reform Act. The new law required competition for most federal contracts awarded by the SBA and set up new procedures for weaning companies from dependency on the agency. It also established new, tougher criminal penalties to prevent a repeat of the Wedtech affair.

In New York, the bankrupt Wedtech Corporation had been reduced to a small office in midtown Manhattan that served basically as a repository of company files needed for the stream of pending civil and criminal litigation. A brief attempt to revive the company in early 1987 had fallen flat after Joe Felter, the overwhelmed new president, found a looted treasury, undecipherable books, and an avalanche of irresolvable management problems.

Of all the conspirators, Moreno seemed the best hope for

rehabilitation as he stood before Judge Stewart to hear his sentence. He had voluntarily surrendered in November 1988, ready to begin doing his time. By April, when Moreno appeared for sentencing, Ed Little came with him, carrying letters from eight other prosecutors, Senator Levin, and Independent Counsel McKay attesting to Moreno's extraordinary cooperation with the government.

"I have to begin by saying there is no doubt that Mr. Moreno did commit a number of very serious crimes including bribery, mail fraud, tax crimes, and related things of that nature in connection with the Wedtech debacle," Little began.

"However, after the investigation uncovered some of this criminal activity, Mr. Moreno and the three other cooperators voluntarily entered into a cooperation agreement with the government, and they succeeded in uncovering probably the largest corruption case in the past ten years, which involved congressmen, which implicated the Attorney General of the United States, and a whole host of other figures. Without Mr. Moreno's cooperation, that case could never have been made. . . .

"Mr. Moreno from the beginning exhibited an unusual degree of remorse and what appeared to be . . . a sincere belief that the only way that he could in effect make up for his criminal activity was to assist the government in uncovering everything."

Then, as usual in the sentencing process, Stewart offered Moreno the chance to speak for himself. Moreno did so haltingly at first, building to a lyrical cadence as he delivered the part-speech, part-poetry he had rehearsed over and over in his head for months.

"When I started at Wedtech over ten years ago," Moreno said, "I did it because I had a dream. I thought that I was going to be able to help in the repair of all those buildings in the South Bronx, and I had a very good job in Wall Street. I left all of that because I sincerely believed that my contribution was going to be meaningful.

"We started, we sacrificed ourselves. There was no greed at that time. We thought that things could be done in a normal business-wise way. We tried to get a major contract, a so-called engine contract that had been widely reported in the press. And when we approached the Army, people at the Army indicated to us that the South Bronx was a no-man's land, that we were not entitled or we were not capable of producing minor things, much less a sophisticated engine.

"We continued and continued trying to do it in the normal way until we saw that it could not be done in that format. . . . We learned to bribe, and we bribed. And then there was a time when the company almost went bankrupt because of all these expenses that we were incurring because of the bribes and because of a lot of other necessary things. . . . We had to make a decision for the company whether to let the company go bankrupt, and 200 employees, which we had at the time, lose their jobs, or the only other alternative was to falsify some invoices so that the government would give us some advance payments for contracts that we were performing. . . .

"Then came a stage when the company decided that in order to solve a lot of our financial problems, we would become a public company, and we misled the public, we filed false statements with the Securities and Exchange Commission. We also misled a lot of other public agencies . . . and I regret that we did it, and I'm remorseful for it. . . .

"We knew that the South Bronx was one of the most dilapidated places in the United States. We wanted to make a contribution. We gave hope to a lot of people there. The hope, because of the false foundations, came down. We destroyed that hope. I regret it and I am remorseful for it. . . .

"I can only say this, and I emphasize it to your Honor, that whatever sentence you place upon me, I will accept it with respect and I will have no anger."

Stewart looked sternly at Moreno, studying his face. "Deciding an appropriate sentence in your case has been extremely difficult," he said. "You engaged, as you know better than I do, in some very serious misconduct. On the other hand, you have cooperated with the government in an unusual and complete manner. You seem truly repentant."

He sentenced Moreno to eighteen months in jail, with credit for time served, and 300 hours of community service, which Moreno promised to serve by aiding the homeless. But when word of the light sentence hit the streets, many of those snared in the Wedtech scandal—largely as a consequence of Moreno's allegations and testimony—railed at the unfairness of it all. To them, the sweet-talking Moreno was the ultimate corrupter, dangling the irresistible bait of easy money before hungry eyes.

As Moreno returned to jail, there was really no way to tell when the Wedtech trail would finally sputter to an end. More than two years after the scandal broke, the newspapers were still unearthing questionable Wedtech connections. Resolution of the stack of civil suits pending against the company and its greedy officers would take years, as would the hunt for squandered Wedtech money.

The Wedtech mysteries lingered, buried in shredded files and safe deposit boxes, and behind the sealed lips of men like Wallach who, true to his word, accepted total blame for Meese's Wedtech involvement and never once turned on his "good friend" in the White House.

They remained harbored under secret passwords stored in Wedtech computers, like the expensive Wang system that ended up as a contribution to an unsuspecting New York City charity. An employee with a yen for computers told me in 1989 that he was baffled when he pulled the donated system from a dusty corner, hooked it up and soon found himself immersed in the top-secret files of Deborah Scott, Moreno's confidential secretary. The worker, who knew Wedtech only as a buzz word for corruption, spent weeks trying to break her secret codes. He never realized federal investigators had gone through the same tedious process before landing on the master code word: "Coitus."

Some of the mysteries would never be solved; others merely awaited discovery by private eyes, state or federal probers or determined reporters capable of unearthing final shreds of evidence. It would remain to be seen whether all the stolen dollars would ever be found, or whether somewhere in the remains of the government-financed empire that was Wedtech, the corpse of frail Eileen Neuberger lies buried under the rubble of broken dreams.

NOTES

From mid-1986 until 1989, the author, working as a reporter for the New York *Daily News,* covered the Wedtech story on virtually a full-time basis. During this period, she interviewed more than 300 sources and reviewed hundreds of thousands of pages of documents filed in the criminal, civil, and bankruptcy courts of New York, Washington, Baltimore, Michigan, Texas, and San Francisco. In her reporting, she drew heavily from the files of the U.S. Securities and Exchange Commission, Small Business Administration, Economic Development Administration, and other city, state, and federal agencies which dealt with the Wedtech Corp. In early 1988, she covered the Lyn Nofziger trial as a New York *Daily News* reporter, then was assigned to daily coverage of the U.S. Justice Department and the demise of Attorney General Edwin Meese. She also covered some portions of the federal racketeering trial of Bob Wallach in 1989.

The following abbreviations have been used in these notes:

MCKAY: Report of Independent Counsel James McKay in re Edwin Meese III, July 5, 1988.

STEIN: Report of Independent Counsel Jacob A. Stein Concerning Edwin Meese III, September 20, 1984.

LEVIN: Wedtech: A Review of Federal Procurement Decisions, A Report Prepared by the Subcommittee on Oversight of Government Management, Committee on Governmental Affairs, United States Senate, chaired by Sen. Carl Levin (D-Michigan), May 1988.

HEARING RECORD: Transcript of Hearings Before the Subcommittee on Oversight of Government Management, Committee on Governmental Affairs, United States Senate, September 29–30, 1987.

WALLACH SENATE INTERVIEW: Transcript of a lengthy interview of E. Robert Wallach by the Subcommittee on Oversight of Government Management, Committee on Governmental Affairs, United States Senate, conducted on June 29, 1987.

BIAGGI TRIAL: Transcript of *United States of America* v. *Stanley Simon, Mario Biaggi, Peter Neglia, John Mariotta, Bernard Ehrlich, Richard Biaggi, and Ronald Betso,* United States District Court, Southern District of New York. The trial ran from March 11, 1988, through August 4, 1988.

WALLACH TRIAL: Transcript of *United States of America* v. *E. Robert Wallach, Wayne Franklyn Chinn, and Rusty Kent London,* United States District Court, Southern District of New York. The trial ran from April 17, 1989, through August 8, 1989.

MITCHELL TRIAL: Transcript of *United States of America* v. *Clarence M. Mitchell III and Michael B. Mitchell,* United States District Court for the District of Maryland. The trial ran from October 26, 1987, to November 7, 1987.

STOLFI TRIAL: Transcript of *United States of America* v. *Richard Stolfi and Frank Casalino,* United States District Court, Southern District of New York. The trial ran from September 26, 1988, to October 18, 1988.

NOFZIGER TRIAL: Transcript of *United States of America* v. *Franklyn C. Nofziger and Mark A. Bragg,* United States District Court for the District of Columbia. The trial ran from January 4, 1988, to February 11, 1988.

1 The Gang That Couldn't Shoot Straight

1 "I'm going . . . son of a bitch.": Neuberger testimony, Biaggi trial. The Wedtech cooperators also testified about their murder discussions in the Stolfi and Wallach trials.
2 For a few thousand dollars . . . assassinate Mariotta.: Ibid.

3   "Fred, I'm not sure . . . dealing with Boy Scouts.": Moreno testi-
     mony, Biaggi trial.
4-5   "I understand . . . in that thing at all.": Moreno testimony, Stolfi
     trial.
5   Neuberger called . . . the murder scheme.: Ibid.
5   "She's no more . . . resign immediately.": Moreno testimony,
     Biaggi trial.
5   "We have no choice . . . get rid of him.": Neuberger testimony,
     Biaggi trial.
6   "getting impossible . . . something about it.": Ibid.
6   "It's very dangerous . . . that kind of information.": Moreno testi-
     mony, Stolfi trial.

2   Rough Beginnings

8   "You want your money . . . you schmuck.": Interview by author
     with former Wedtech board member who witnessed the event
     and asked for anonymity, June 1989.
10-11 "Do you mind . . . talking about?": Mariotta testimony, Biaggi trial.
11   "ownership of your company . . . in the 8(a) program.": Letter from
     Walter Leavitt to John Mariotta, September 25, 1975.
12   "pushed . . . ": Mariotta testimony, Biaggi trial.
12   "damn good education . . . ": Ibid.
13   "All I know is . . . girlfriend.": Ibid.
14   "I needed . . . Puerto Rican.": Ibid.
15   "Hundreds of people . . . my way home.": Letter to Federal Judge
     Charles Stewart from Neuberger, read at his sentencing.
15   "The route was . . . lasted for weeks.": Ibid.
16   "the dope pusher . . . in the middle.": Mariotta testimony, Biaggi
     trial.
16   "as soon as you mention . . . forget it.": Ibid.
17   "wigged out of her mind.": Ibid.
17   "by reason of . . . of the corporation.": Wedtech board minutes,
     April 18, 1975.

3   A Thug in a Congressman's Suit

20   "Your successfulness . . . contact me.": Biaggi letter to Welbilt,
     February 6, 1978.
20   "How would you like . . . Biaggi?": Neuberger testimony, Biaggi
     trial.
20   "Christmas gifts . . .": Ibid.
21   "a lot of good . . . politically.": Moreno testimony, Biaggi trial.
22   "his influence . . . help us.": Neuberger testimony, Biaggi trial.
22   "thug in a congressman's suit.": Assistant U.S. Attorney Ed Little
     in closing arguments, Biaggi trial.

26 "good soldier . . . he was told.": Strahle in 1989 telephone interview with author.

28 "General Ehrlich . . . ": As described in interviews with numerous Ehrlich associates and federal officials who dealt with him.

30 "make him inclined to help . . .": Neuberger testimony, Biaggi trial.

32 "Devil's disciple . . . bossism.": The *Village Voice,* October 8, 1980.

34 "hysterical laughter . . .": Levin Report, p. 20.

35 "Al, I have the Welbilt . . . that we have.": Moreno testimony, Biaggi trial.

35-36 "[The] South Bronx . . . stigmata.": Mariotta letter to Army Secretary John Marsh, April 14, 1981.

36 "cheap Jew . . .": Moreno testimony, Biaggi trial.

36 "like the cop . . . corner bookie.": Neuberger testimony, Biaggi trial.

36 "This thing . . . $5 million.": Mariotta testimony, Biaggi trial.

36 "What are you . . . crazy promises for?": Neuberger testimony, Biaggi trial.

37 "Who are they? . . . the congressman seriously.": Moreno testimony, Biaggi trial.

4 Private Eyes

42-43 "Graduate of University of California . . . to present.": Wallach résumé presented by Bechtel to Israeli Prime Minister Shimon Peres, as cited in McKay Report, p. 698.

43 "low-profile . . . foreign affairs.": Wallach letter to Meese, October 26, 1985, as cited in McKay Report, p. 539.

44 "I couldn't understand . . . executive branch energy.": Eastland in 1988 interview with author.

45 "an emotional tie . . . anything.": Ibid.

46 "The plant outside . . . military bases.": Wallach Senate Interview.

46 "good friend . . .": Term used by Wallach in referring to Meese in repeated communications with Wedtech officials.

47 "appropriate person . . . on your behalf.": Wallach letter to Wedtech, April 24, 1981.

47-48 "an absolute perfect . . . great American dream.": Wallach memo to Herbert Ellingwood, May 11, 1981.

48 "a direct interview . . . a real find.": Wallach letter to Meese, May 11, 1981.

48 "look into . . . ": McKay Report, p. 147.

48 "Bob Wallach . . . Ed Meese.": Ibid.

49 "general recollection . . . by the Army.": Meese grand jury testimony as cited in McKay Report, p. 143.

5 The Nofziger Connection

51   "I thought it was . . . cracking the bureaucracy.": Dyer in 1989
      telephone interview with author.

51   "misbehaving . . . Reagan–Bush administration.": Dyer letter to
      Army Secretary Marsh, August 12, 1981.

51   "good for America.": Dyer in 1989 telephone interview with au-
      thor.

51   "I said to them . . . something else.' ": Ibid.

52   "Mr. Dyer . . . greed.": Ibid.

53   "Write this down . . . has the clap.": Nofziger quoted in the Wash-
      ington *Post,* April 12, 1981.

54   "Decay . . . London after the Blitz.": *The New York Times,* August
      6, 1980.

54   "You ain't going . . . get elected.": Ibid.

55   "The President . . . done good, too.": The Washington *Post,* April
      12, 1981.

55   "Nofziger clearance . . .": The Washington *Post,* June 25, 1981.

57   "a matter affecting . . . (Aug. 5, 1980).": Wayne Valis letter to
      Army Secretary Marsh, Sept. 4, 1981.

57   "audit, audit, audit.": Levin Report, p. 27.

57   "These people . . . are no good.": Ibid., p. 28.

57   "broad detail . . . after five years.": Rollins testimony, Nofziger
      trial.

58   "a modest . . . link with us.": Sanchez memo to Lyn Nofziger,
      March 1981.

58   "I hope we can get . . . I will try.": Nofziger letter to Sanchez,
      October 13, 1981.

58   "getting hit over the head . . .": Stohlman as cited in Levin Report,
      p. 29.

58-59 "I've had experience . . . contract.": Keenan, as described in Wal-
      lach memo to Meese, October 7, 1981.

59   "Pier Talenti has . . . this Administration.": Sanchez letter to Nof-
      ziger, November 9, 1981.

59   "put away . . . a couple of years. . . . ": Ed Rollins quoted in the
      Washington *Post,* October 27, 1985.

60   "looked at each other . . . raised our eyebrows.": Templeman in
      1989 interview with author.

60   "Give them a fair . . . a year old.": Final draft of Levin Report, p.
      34.

60   "Lyn's last week . . . get this contract.": Wallach memo to Meese,
      January 19, 1982.

6 Pressure from Above

63-64 "It is likely . . . apparently very high.": Levin Report, p. 35.

64   "letting us know . . . reasonable negotiations.": Ibid.

64   "I think they . . . to do that.": Ibid., p. 40.
64   "listen carefully . . . very great here.": Nofziger letter to Meese, April 8, 1982.
65   "Key Participants . . . as Keenan himself.": Wallach memo to Meese, January 21, 1982.
65   "he is the key . . . defeat it.": Ibid.
65   "fair hearing . . .": Meese testimony, Nofziger trial.
66   "political decision . . .": Letter from Sen. Robert Kasten to Deputy Secretary of Defense Carlucci, August 24, 1982.
67   "For us to make . . . as a whole.": Letter from Turnbull to Juanita Watts, March 19, 1982.
67   "do what we could do . . .": Templeman in 1989 interview with author.
67   He testified later . . . White House interest.: Wedtech Hearing Record, Part 1, p. 29.
68   "Ed Meese has asked . . . SBA's recommendations.": Jenkins letter to Sanders, April 22, 1982.
68   "understood the importance . . . the administration.": Levin Report, p. 40.
69   "no member of the White House staff . . . other communications.": Memorandum from Fred Fielding, counsel to the President, July 13, 1981.
69   "Lyn Nofsiger [sic] . . . type of thing?": McKay Report, p. 170.
69   "Strongly recommend . . . be taken.": Ibid.
69   "he [Fuller] wasn't my boss . . . tell me not to.": Levin Report, p. 38.
70   "like he had been dragged . . . on a leash.": Moreno testimony, Nofziger trial.
70   "We realized . . . all the way.": Ibid.
71   "all possible efforts . . .": August 11, 1982, telex from Jay Sculley to TSARCOM, cited in Levin Report, p. 44.
72   "$28 million SBA Award . . . Creates Jobs.": Wedtech press release, October 4, 1982.
72   "one of . . . America's best investments . . .": Ibid.
72   "remarkable effort . . .": Ibid.
72   "They really put . . . at cost.": Ibid.
73   "Though you cannot . . . this project.": Jenkins note to Meese, as noted in McKay Report, p. 178.
73   "our silent partner, God.": Mariotta letter to Reagan, October 27, 1982.
73   "In his office . . . most intently.": Transcript of October 5, 1982, radio broadcast, CBS News.

7 Corporate Craziness

75   "feeding the beast . . .": Term used by Mario Moreno in discussions with federal prosecutors, as related to author in interviews with

Prosecutors Ed Little and Mary Shannon, and federal agent Steve Cossu.

76 "The bank is . . . given in cash.": Moreno testimony, Biaggi trial.
76 "John, the situation . . . other solution.": Ibid.
77 "his" bank: As described by the Wedtech cooperators in testimony at Biaggi trial.
78 "John, I am . . . something for you there.": Moreno testimony, Biaggi trial.
79 "Mario needs . . . this morning.": Ibid.
81 "Surely, you're not going . . . into this thing.": Ibid.
84 "accordance with . . . come to our attention.": Agreement between Wedtech and KMG Main Hurdman.
85 "Every job . . . fuck it up.": Moreno testimony, Biaggi trial.
86 "You continue . . . bottomless pit.": Ibid.
87 "major problem . . .": Ibid.
87 "Mr. Ehrlich has . . . against Welbilt.": Letter to KMG Main Hurdman.
89 " 'running' the St. Louis . . . old contacts.": Wallach memo to Meese, April 2, 1983.
90 "an atmosphere of professionalism . . .": Wallach Senate Interview.
90 "This struggling . . . representing Wedtech.": Ibid.
91 "This firm . . . go public.": Moreno testimony, Biaggi trial.
91 "Congressman . . . to reach you.": Ibid.
91 "Why did you . . . happen anymore.": Ibid.
92 "privileged to move . . . this lifestyle.": Wallach letter to Welbilt, May 19, 1983.
92 "Once again . . . social contribution.": Ibid.
92 "You can accomplish . . . the General.": Ibid.

8 The Five Percent Solution

95 "Where is Fred . . . bastard Jew?": Moreno testimony, Biaggi trial.
96 "Bernie . . . because of us.": Ibid.
96 "Congressman . . . lot of expenses.": Ibid.
96 "You're crazy . . . without anything.": Ibid.
97 "totally outrageous . . .": Neuberger testimony, Biaggi trial.
97 "You should be happy with that.": Ibid.
97 "We have done . . . spending with you.": Moreno testimony, Biaggi trial.
97 "That's all you're going to get.": Ibid.
97 "Fred, I already . . . at this time.": Ibid.
97 "John has convinced . . . the agreement.": Ibid.
98 "What else do you want?": Ibid.
98 "I have made . . . destroy it.": Ibid.
98 "Look what . . . it's blackmail.": Ibid.
98 "no way he would . . . board of directors.": Guariglia testimony, Biaggi trial.

100 "Any communication . . . interference.": Fielding memo to Fuller, June 8, 1983, cited in McKay Report, p. 20.

9 Crisis in Washington

101 "every Tom, Dick and Harry . . .": Moreno, cited in McKay Report, p. 205.

102 "get into the White House . . .": Ibid., p. 206.

105 "significant funds . . . credibility.": Wallach in December 1, 1983, letter to Moreno, cited in McKay Report, p. 546.

106 "it's quite important.": Wallach telephone message to Meese, cited in McKay Report, p. 209.

106 "get the loan . . . can't be made.": Irving Margulies to deputy general counsel Robert Brumley, cited in McKay Report, p. 211.

108 "will no longer . . . 8(a) program.": Wedtech preliminary prospectus, July 1983, p. 4.

108 "have to deal . . . SBA anymore.": Moreno testimony, Biaggi trial.

108 "may no longer be qualified . . .": Wedtech prospectus, August 1983, p. 4.

109 "a mistake . . . number of people.": Wallach Senate Interview.

10 The Phony Stock Deal

112 "Pete, I need to talk . . . people are crazy.": Moreno testimony, Biaggi trial.

114 "The Board concluded . . . such purpose.": Wedtech board minutes, October 31, 1983.

115 "Every time . . . going along.": Moreno testimony, Biaggi trial.

116 "Legislative history . . . 8(a) program.": Wedtech memo to SBA, December 12, 1983.

117 "My examination . . . 8(a) program.": Neglia letter to SBA Associate Administrator Henry Wilfong, January 5, 1984.

11 "The Fix Is On"

118 "Big Man . . .": Ramirez in 1989 interview with author.

119-20 "How can we . . . the money in cash.": Ibid.

120 "most important mole we could install . . .": Moreno testimony, Wallach trial.

120 "Good . . . use it.": Guariglia testimony, Biaggi trial.

122 "In my view . . . federal government.": Moreno in affidavit given to United States Senate investigators, September 28, 1987.

123 "not to make waves . . .": Levin Report, p. 135.

123 "the fix . . . that contract.": Ibid.

125 "He denied . . . at the time.": Govan in 1989 telephone interview with author.

126 "cook the books . . .": Guariglia testimony, Biaggi and Wallach trials, also cited in McKay Report, p. 218.

126 "tokenism . . .": Moreno testimony, Wallach trial.

127 "Everything's . . . taken care of.": Ibid.

127 "had changed . . . entire contract.": Ibid.

127 "I'm very happy . . . did it.": Ibid.

128 "We were asked . . . be done.": De Vicq in 1989 interview with author; De Vicq also gives this account in Levin Report.

128 "The trouble . . . nautical experience.": Admiral Tom Hughes in Levin Report, p. 80.

128 "Mr. Medley . . . Justice Department.": Moreno testimony, Wallach trial.

129 "Contractor . . . by Wedtech.": Levin Report, p. 238.

130 "we could . . . construction side.": Guariglia testimony, Biaggi trial.

130 "Why didn't you . . . did there!": Moreno testimony, Biaggi trial.

130 "That S.O.B. . . . I own him.": Guariglia testimony, Biaggi trial.

131 "Tell Mr. Nofziger . . . tell him this.": Moreno testimony, Biaggi trial.

12 Simple Simon

133 "At the time . . . terrible state.": Simon testimony, Biaggi trial.

133 "working for a candidate . . . nothing to say.": From a column in the New York *Daily News* by Ken Auletta, June 17, 1979.

135 "we could build . . . Stanley Simon.": Koch to Ferrick commission, April 1989.

136 "person who . . . to be cultivated.": Moreno testimony, Biaggi trial.

136 "I don't want . . . over here.": Moreno testimony, Biaggi trial.

136 "That guy . . . employees.": Ibid.

138 "The best . . . $50,000.": Neuberger testimony, Biaggi trial.

139 "Don't talk to her . . . Bernie Ehrlich.": Ibid.

141 "extortion and shakedown . . .": Thomas in letter to Ports Commissioner Susan Frank, July 1984.

141 "local politicians . . . 'play ball.' ": Ibid.

142 "to be without merit.": Frank response to Thomas, July 1984.

142 "move his ass.": Moreno testimony, Biaggi trial.

13 Buying Justice

145 "make government secrecy . . . the wealthy few." Washington *Post,* January 24, 1984.

147 "While Meese allowed . . . in history.": Washington *Post,* March 2, 1984.

148 "the one with the halo around his head.": Stein Report, p. 110.

148 "The facts . . . whatsoever, Senator!": Washington *Post,* March 3, 1984.

149 "put the client at ease.": Garment in 1989 telephone interview with author.

151 "Americans are . . . renewal.": *The New York Times,* March 7, 1984.

151 "The Republican victory . . . in 1984.": Presidential papers of Ronald Reagan, March 6, 1984, pp. 311–14.

151 "real plus in the Senate . . .": Ibid.

152 "Real progress . . . for the eighties.": Ibid.

152 "major East Coast clients . . .": Wallach letter to Mariotta, March 2, 1984.

153 "wish list . . . one could have.": Wallach memo to Meese, March 7, 1984.

154 "that I was . . . remain with them.": Wallach Senate interview.

155 "I want to thank you . . . to the company.": Moreno testimony, Wallach trial.

156 "Commencing with my retention . . . private practice.": Wallach affidavit, filed with the U.S. Circuit Court of Appeals for the District of Columbia, December 14, 1984, as cited in McKay Report, pp. 238–39.

156 "major assist . . . activities there.": Wallach memo to Meese, February 27, 1985.

156-57 "More and more . . . and experience.": Wallach memo to Meese, May 1, 1985.

157 "There were a number . . . severely curtailed.": Meese grand jury testimony, as cited in McKay Report, p. 255.

157 "a piece of furniture . . .": Eastland in 1988 interview with author.

14 Four More Years

161 "You'd be sitting . . . deal with you.": Albany businessman Harry Apkarian in 1989 interview with author and New York *Daily News* reporter Kevin McCoy.

170 "sales speech . . .": De Vicq in 1989 interview with author.

170 "an R2D2 . . . five records.": Ibid.

170 "ally structure . . . gently indicated.": Wallach memo to Wedtech, November 12, 1984.

171 "we would have to do other things.": Moreno testimony, Wallach trial.

172 "license to steal . . .": Wedtech Hearing Record, Part 2, p. 23.

172 "What are you willing to do?": Moreno testimony, Wallach trial. Moreno also gave a version of this event in an affidavit with Senate investigators, September 28, 1987.

173 "riding too hard . . .": Levin Report, p. 173.

174 "What are . . . offering you.": De Vicq in 1989 interview with author. De Vicq also gives an account in Wedtech Hearing Record, Part 2, p. 15.

175 "with some urgency . . .": Wallach cited in McKay Report, p. 483.

177 "Are you on time . . . the Wedtech clan.": Moreno testimony, Wallach trial. Guariglia also testified to the Ursula Meese incident in Biaggi trial.

15 The Last in Line.

178 "Why did . . . strangers?": As related by Moreno in interviews with Wedtech prosecutors.

181 "who seemed . . . his community.": The *Village Voice,* March 24, 1987.

182 "humane legislator . . . constituents.": From a Citizens Union brochure, obtained from files of the New York *Daily News.*

182 "My claim to fame . . . together.": Ibid.

186 "Sign the papers or . . . have any peace.": Hahn statement as reported in the Washington *Post,* June 5, 1987.

187 "pray for us . . .": Interviews by author in 1987 with members of Cortese's congregation.

16 The Baltimore–Washington Connection

196 "What's this going on . . . this particular company.": Parren Mitchell testimony, Mitchell trial.

196 "Hey, Parren . . . presidential award.": Ibid.

196-97 "Look, I am sorry . . . flagship company.": Ibid.

197 "If the Small Business Administration . . . the company.": Ibid.

197 "very strong . . . questions.": Moreno testimony, Mitchell trial.

198 "Is that Parren Mitchell from Baltimore?": Strum testimony, Mitchell trial.

198 "Most definitely . . .": Ibid.

199 "get rid of the problem . . .": Ibid.

199-200 "to get Parren Mitchell . . . I don't recall.": Ibid.

201 "serious, serious problem . . .": Ibid.

201 "Michael Mitchell said . . . to be made.": Ibid.

202 "the real agreement . . . covered.": Moreno testimony, Mitchell trial.

202 "window dressing . . . for the fee.": Strum testimony, Mitchell trial.

203 "many, many millions . . . going good.": Ibid.

17 The Slicks Move In

208 "One of these days . . .": Moreno testimony, Biaggi trial.
208 "Listen carefully . . . this company.": Wallach letter to Wedtech, April 22, 1985, as cited in McKay Report, p. 263.
211 "I suspect . . . in this country.": Wallach letter to his daughters, as cited in McKay Report, p. 685.
212 "What was indicated . . . to Labor.": Wallach memo to Meese, September 25, 1985.
214 "I require . . . $1 million a year.": Wallach letter to Rappaport, November 27, 1985, as cited in McKay Report, p. 812.
215 "everything . . . about it.": Guariglia grand jury testimony, as cited in McKay Report, p. 274.
215 "baksheesh . . .": Neuberger testimony, Biaggi trial. Also cited in McKay Report, p. 272.

18 The Final Days

218 "unless and until . . . to do so.": Mariotta employment agreement, January 28, 1986.
218 "You're in . . . Keep it.": Interview with former Wedtech board member, who asked not to be named, June 1989.
218 "At 4 P.M. . . . of the Company.": Wedtech internal memo, February 12, 1986.
219 "will result . . . Wedtech.": Wedtech internal memo, July 1986.
219 "You have destroyed . . . Father's son.": Several interviews by author with Jack Kehoe, 1988, 1989.
219 "Wedtech Corp. . . . Chief's Position.": *The Wall Street Journal,* February 13, 1986.
220 "respectfully decline . . . requested.": Moreno letter to SBA, March 1986.
222 "promotional compensation . . .": London invoice to Wedtech, paid January 29, 1986.

19 Reporter's Notebook.

226 "When I wouldn't play ball . . . some other time.": Thomas in 1986 telephone interview with author.
226 "What's this company?": From the author's 1986 conversation with a Freedom vice president.
228 "Every paper . . . same thing.": SBA regional counsel Jack Matthews in 1986 conversation with author.
229 He answered bluntly . . . default on the agreement.: Ibid.
229-30 "He's not here . . . no idea.": Conversation with an unidentified woman in 1986 at Mariotta's home.

231 "If you run that story . . . dead wrong.": From a 1986 telephone
     interview with Arthur Siskind.
231 "We're wading . . . on this one.": New York *Daily News* Managing
     Editor James Willse, as related by newsroom observers.
231 "A Bronx firm . . . in December.": The New York *Daily News,*
     October 15, 1986.
232 "Where the hell . . . the whole thing.": From 1986 telephone conver-
     sation with a source who asked not to be named.
232 "Dear Jim . . . in this matter.": Letter from Wedtech attorney Howard
     Squadron to New York *Daily News* publisher James Hoge, October
     15, 1986.
232 Was I absolutely sure of my facts?: Attorney Marge Coleman in
     meeting with author and New York *Daily News* City Editor Arthur
     Browne, October 15, 1986.
233 "Just keep going.": Browne in meeting with author, October 15,
     1986.
233 "A law firm . . . city agencies.": New York *Daily News,* October 16,
     1986.
233 " 'Extortion' Complaint Was Ignored by City.": New York *Daily
     News,* October 19, 1986.
234 "Please . . . God bless you.": Anonymous letter to author, October
     1986.
234 "You are doing . . . regional administrator.": Anonymous letter to
     author, October 1986.
234 "Biaggi's not . . . money, too.": From a 1986 telephone conversation
     between author and a former Wedtech official who asked not to be
     identified.
235 "with actual malice . . . responsible parties.": Lawsuit filed by Wed-
     tech Corp. against the New York *Daily News,* Supreme Court of the
     State of New York, October 22, 1986.
235 "Don't worry . . . $999 million.": From a 1986 conversation between
     author and attorney Marge Coleman.
235 "You're onto . . . keep going.": From a 1986 conversation between
     author and F. Gilman Spencer.

20 The Feds Move In

237 Oh, no . . . time bomb.": Cossu, as related in numerous interviews
     with author 1988, 1989.
237 "There's a company . . . when it wants.": Ibid.
238 "Property 977 . . . Bronx.": From written notes of Cossu, provided
     to author.
239 "If payment . . . been received.": Ibid.
239 "four individuals and one partnership . . .": Wedtech prospectus,
     August 1983.

239   "Why is this . . . long time ago.": Cossu, as related in numerous interviews with author.

241   "We've got . . . filters down.": From 1989 interviews with Cossu and Mike Raggi.

243   "Steve, . . . in your eyes.": From 1989 interviews with Cossu.

244   "S. Bronx Firm's D.C. Connection.": New York *Daily News,* October 26, 1986.

245   "If I were . . . ass down here!": As related by Cossu and Shannon in numerous interviews with author.

245   "You should . . . giving you.": Ibid.

245   "Last week . . . White House or Meese.": New York *Daily News,* November 2, 1986.

247   "The Daily News . . . White House.": New York *Daily News,* November 5, 1986.

247-48   "Get your ass . . . looking for.": From 1989 interviews with Cossu and Shannon.

248   "You would see . . . but you couldn't.": Cossu in numerous interviews with author.

21 Chaos at Headquarters

252-53   Calmly, Wallach told Kehoe . . . criminality should be allowed.: From a 1989 telephone interview with Kehoe.

253   "This will probably . . . to you.": From a 1986 telephone conversation with Wallach.

253   "Most of you . . . questionable conduct.": Wedtech internal memo, October 1986.

254   That same year . . . in the East River.: From an account given by Shannon during Biaggi trial and in interviews with author.

255   At the Wedtech . . . pontoon boat.: From numerous interviews with police and Wedtech personnel at the time of Eileen Neuberger's disappearance in late 1986.

256   As the former Main Hurdman . . . "good guy.": From 1989 interview with Kehoe.

256-58   "Dear Mr. Capeci . . . in this matter.": Siskind letter to Capeci, November 7, 1986.

259   "Wedtech Admits . . . Cash Advance.": New York *Daily News,* November 9, 1986.

259   "The Wedtech Corp. . . . manufacturing process.": Ibid.

260   "Hang tough . . . quashed.": Guariglia testimony, Biaggi trial.

261   "I'm very appreciative . . . the $100,000.": Ibid.

261   "would get back . . . mandatory jail.": Ibid.

262   He called Moreno . . . his alarm clock.: Moreno testimony, Biaggi trial.

263   "Do you know . . . represent?": From 1989 interview with participant who asked not to be identified.

264   "Just take it . . . anything.": Guariglia testimony, as related in McKay Report, p. 280.

265   "entirely possible, actually probable . . .": Meese grand jury testimony, as related in McKay Report, p. 282.

265   "We hope . . . temporary situation.": Wedtech internal memo, December 1986.

265   "Anthony Guariglia . . . creditors.": Press release, December 15, 1986.

266   "Merry Christmas . . . satisfied.": Anonymous phone call to author at New York *Daily News.*

22   Blind Justice

268   "copious, well-structured . . . back on the screen.": From 1988 interview with Arnold Burns.

271   "Do you know . . . Yes.": Guariglia testimony, Biaggi trial.

272   "How far . . . White House.": From 1989 interviews with Mary Shannon and Howard Wilson.

272   "three, two and one deal.": From 1989 interviews with Mary Shannon.

272   "oversmartness . . .": Ibid.

274   "I owe it all to you.": Justice Department log of Meese-Wallach contacts, January 1981 to April 1987.

274   "engaged in . . . of their duty.": Indictment of four cooperators as cited in court proceeding, January 30, 1987.

276   "rocked me and socked me": From 1988 interview with Arnold Burns.

276   "deep yogurt . . .": Ibid; Burns also uses this term in testimony to the Senate Judiciary Committee, July 28, 1988.

276   "As your friend . . . from him.": Ibid.

277   "poker face . . .": Ibid. Also McKay Report, p. 257.

277   "Deputies . . . a fair hearing.": Meese press conference, April 6, 1987.

277   "Terry, does the name . . . with you?": From 1988 interview with Terry Eastland.

277   Oh, no!: Ibid.

277   Oh gosh, here it comes!: Ibid.

278   "It was . . . 'You got us.' ": From 1989 interview with Dennis Bell.

278   "A financial associate . . . Wedtech connections.": *Newsday,* April 16, 1987.

278   "I've been trying . . . very innocent.": From 1987 telephone conversation with Wallach.

278-79   "Meese advised . . . no specifics.": McKay Report, p. 255.

279   "Meese advised . . . been made.": Ibid., p. 256.

23 Alice in Wonderland

281 "result in . . . private gain.": Executive order cited by Weld in testimony to the Senate Judiciary Committee, July 26, 1988.

281 "directly . . . such official.": Federal gratuity statute cited by Weld in testimony to the Senate Judiciary Committee, July 26, 1988.

281 "sent Mr. Meese . . . personal meetings.": Weld testimony to the Senate Judiciary Committee, July 26, 1988.

281 "making money . . . doing for him.": Ibid.

282 "from two criminal investigations of Wedtech . . .": Letter from Rep. Peter Rodino and Sen. Joseph Biden to Independent Counsel James McKay, April 29, 1987.

282 "It was a world of Alice . . . sunshine was rain.": Arnold Burns in testimony to the Senate Judiciary Committee, July 26, 1988.

282 "Mr. Wallach was . . . relationship.": Ibid.

283 "In fairness . . . Wedtech.": Burns's letter to Independent Counsel James McKay, May 11, 1987.

284 "I am guilty.": Simon in March 11, 1987, press conference covered by author.

285 "It's fair to say . . . Wedtech.": Giuliani press conference, June 4, 1987.

286 "sought to influence . . . government contracts.": Indictment of E. Robert Wallach, December 22, 1987.

289 "between a rock and a hard place . . .": Burns's testimony, Senate Judiciary Committee, July 26, 1988.

289 "Mr. Meese continued . . . Department of Justice.": Ibid.

289 "constituted the use . . . Mr. Wallach.": Weld before the Senate Judiciary Committee, July 26, 1988.

289 "Ed, I don't gainsay . . . not the question though.": Ibid.

290 "all over this family . . . Mrs. Meese.": Ibid.

290 "My conclusion was . . . Mr. Meese.": Ibid.

290 "hypothetical indictment . . .": Ibid.

290 "Here are . . . gratuity statute.": Ibid.

290 The President seemed . . . "florid and upset.": Ibid.

291 "Should Meese . . . Just fine.": Associated Press report, April 22, 1988.

24 "Meese Is A Sleaze":

293 "I don't recall.": Meese testimony, Nofziger trial.

294 "running a stop sign . . .": Nofziger in remarks to reporters, February 11, 1988.

294 Meese defense . . .: From 1988 and 1989 interviews with federal prosecutors Mary Shannon, Ed Little.

294-95 "This is a case . . . they all took.": Prosecutor Howard Wilson, opening statement, Biaggi trial.

295 "The truth . . . run this country.": Defense attorney James LaRossa, opening statement, Biaggi trial.

295-96 "I am going to . . . go to Wedtech.' ": Ibid.

297 "in reality an attempt . . . crimes.": Wilson in Biaggi trial.

297 The prosecution's "boss": From 1989 interviews with Ed Little.

298 "Go right ahead.": Ibid.

298 "a thug in a congressman's suit . . .": Little in Biaggi trial.

298-99 "There is only one way . . . Executive branch.": Ibid.

299 "highly unfair . . . in the case.": From Giuliani's 1988 telephone interview with author.

299 "I am confident . . . properly.": Meese press conference, July 5, 1988.

299 "darned good Attorney General . . .": Associated Press dispatch, July 7, 1988.

299 "has distinguished . . . and himself.": Fitzwater press conference, July 8, 1988.

300 "Ed . . . wish him well.": Bush quoted in press reports, July 8, 1988.

300 "there is no evidence . . . personal gain.": McKay Report, p. 51.

301 "gang of crooks . . .": Associated Press dispatch, July 7, 1988.

25 The Caged Beast

304 "died a little bit . . . to love them.": Biaggi at sentencing hearing, as quoted in the Washington *Post,* November 19, 1988.

304 "labored mightily to find an ambiguity . . .": Judge Harry T. Edwards, as quoted in the Washington *Post,* June 28, 1989.

306 "I have to begin . . . uncovering everything.": Ed Little at Moreno sentencing, April 13, 1989.

306-07 "When I started . . . have no anger.": Moreno at his sentencing.

307 "Deciding an appropriate . . . truly repentant.": Federal Judge Charles Stewart at Moreno sentencing.

INDEX

Jamar, Jeff, 278
J & L (*later* Welbilt Electronic Die), 13
Javits, Jacob, 31, 32
Jeffboat Co., 128
Jenkins, James, 122, 149, 176, 210, 235,
246, 248, 250; and Army engine
contract for W., 65–71, 72–73, 89,
269, 285; as consultant to W., 161–62,
174; and EDA loan subordination,
99–100, 106; name raised in W. trial,
295–96, 297, 298–99
Jofre Associates, 130, 238
Johnson, Lyndon B., 10
Jones, Adm. John Paul, 128, 172
Jones, Lee, 233
Jordan, Gary, 203, 204
Justice Department, 145, 153, 156, 267–70,
299; Criminal Div. probe of Meese-W.
and Wallach ties, 261, 273, 276, 278,
280–83; Data Center lease, 176, 288;
demoralized by Meese problem,
288–90; and Mideast pipeline project,
213, 287; instructions to Giuliani re
info on Meese and White House, 273;
last word on Meese, 301; Nofziger
investigation of, 246, 261, 267; top
staff resignations, 289–90; W. probe
information channeled to, 261, 267–69,
273, 275–76, 280, 286

Kalikow, Peter, 134
Kampelman, Max, 148
Kaplan, Julius, 210
Kasanoff, Nicholas, 241
Kasten, Robert, 66
Kaufman, Alan, 296
Kaufman, Steve, 251–52, 256
Keenan, Thomas, 34–35, 39–40, 51, 58–59,
65, 89
Kehoe, John, 252–53, 255–56, 259–60
Kelley, Capt. Tim, 174
Kemp, Jack, 62, 183
Kennedy, Edward, 147
Koch, Ed, 54, 135, 139, 141–42, 143,
182–83, 226, 233
Korten, Patrick, 268, 293, 299
Kotelly, John, 252

Labor Party (Israel), 212, 213
Lang, John, 270
LaRossa, James, 295–96, 298
Latin American Manufacturers Association
(LAMA), 32–33, 51, 56, 57, 63, 69,
118, 191, 196
Lawrence, Ralph, 134–35, 138
Laxalt, Paul, 123
Leadership Conference on Civil Rights,
192
League of United Latin American Citizens,
185
Leavitt, Walter, 11
Lee, Frank, and Lee Engineering, 123
Leesonia Enterprises, 184

Lehman, John F., Jr., 119, 121–22, 124,
127, 131, 296
Levin, Carl, 250, 305, 306
Levine, Randy, 290
Lewin, Nathan, 283
Lewis, Ceil, 82, 120, 138, 239
Lipset, Harold, 38–40, 42, 46, 47
Little, Ed, 22, 284, 297–99, 303–4, 306
lobbying, illegal, 285, 305; *see also* Nofziger,
Lyn; Wallach, E. Robert
Lockhart, Lenny, 189–90, 191, 198–99, 201
Lockhart, Leonard, Sr., 190, 198–99
London, Rusty Kent, 155, 165–66, 168,
208–9, 210–11, 212, 214–16, 221–24,
275–76, 296; indictment of, 286;
"promotional compensation" to,
215–16, 222–23; trial of, 303
Lonstein, Garrie, 14
Lonstein, Irving, 13–15
Loscalzo, Anthony, 190–91, 198, 199,
201–2, 203
Luce, Gordon, 147

McCoy, Kevin, 234, 244, 250
McFarlane, Robert, 161, 210, 213
McGovern, George, 59
McGovern, Kevin, 296
McGuirk, Harry, 199
McKay, James, 127, 274, 275, 276, 306;
investigation of Meese, 281–83,
286–88, 293; Meese not indicted by,
292, 293, 301; Meese report, 293, 299,
300–1; and Nofziger case, 282, 285,
305
McKean, John R., Jr., 104–5, 145, 147–48,
149, 300
Main Hurdman, 4, 84–88, 207, 234, 250,
255–59
Margiotta, Joseph, 31–32
Mariel, Serafin, 75–76
Marine Engineers Beneficial Association,
122, 285
Mariotta, Jennie, 8, 14, 81, 179–80
Mariotta, John, 2, 7–8, 46, 52, 108–9, 137,
159, 164, 207–9, 217–19, 223,
228–30, 249–50; and Army engine
contract, 32, 34–36, 56–58; background
of, 7–8, 11–14; Biaggi and, 21, 90–91;
Biaggi stock gift promise of, 36–37, 81,
94–98; as Chairman of Board and Chief
Executive Officer, 111, 209, 217;
dismissal of, 218–19, 228; 8(a) minority
firm scam of, 10–11, 17, 81, 111,
113–17, 208, 217, 228–29, 231;
employee relations of, 8–9, 46, 218–19;
extolled by Denlinger, 66; extolled by
Rather on CBS, 73; extolled by Sanchez
to Nofziger, 58; extolled by Wallach to
Meese, 47–48, 176–77; and financial
crises at W., 73–80, 82–89; Garcia and,
179–80, 187; "God and Country"
speech of, 35, 62, 170, 179; and House
Small Business Committee probe of W.,

Marilyn Walser Thompson was born in Salisbury, North Carolina, and began her journalism career with the *Columbia Record* in South Carolina. She also worked as an investigative reporter at the *Philadelphia Daily News* and the New York *Daily News.* She lives in Washington, D.C., and is a reporter for the *Washington Post.*